RUSSIAN
phrasebook

James Jenkin

Russian phrasebook
   2nd edition

Published by
   Lonely Planet Publications
   Head Office: PO Box 617, Hawthorn, Vic 3122, Australia
   Branches: 155 Filbert St, Suite 251, Oakland, CA94607, USA
                     10 Barley Mow Passage, Chiswick, London W4 4PH, UK
                     71 bis rue du Cardinal Lemoine, 75005 Paris, France

Printed by
   Colorcraft Ltd., Hong Kong

Photograph by
   St Basil's Cathedral, Red Square, Moscow by Harald Sund (The Image Bank)

Published
   March 1995

About this Book
This book was produced from an original manuscript by James Jenkin, with
assistance from Kesha Gelbak and Grant Taylor. Sally Steward edited the book.
Maliza Kruh and Ann Jeffree were responsible for design and Valerie Tellini
designed the cover. The author would particularly like to thank Natalie Vodovozova
for her comments.

National Library of Australia Cataloguing in Publication Data

Jenkin, James
   Russian Phrasebook.

   2nd ed.
   ISBN 0 86442 307 1.
   1. Russian language - Conversation and phrase books - English.
   I. Title. (Series : Lonely Planet language survival kit.)

491.783421

Contents

Introduction

Russian is the first language of more than 220 million people throughout the world, and is the official language of the Russian Federation. It is also spoken to some extent by the 130 million people in former republics of the USSR. Russian is, in fact, amongst the four most widely spoken languages in the world, together with Chinese, English and Spanish. Despite demographic variations in the language, the standard Moscow variety is understood by virtually all Russian speakers.

Although its alphabet may look unusual, Russian is, in fact, related to English. Both belong to the Indo-European family of languages. Russian, along with Polish, Czech, and others, belongs to the Slavonic branch, one of the three largest subgroups of Indo-European, the other two being Romance (which includes Italian and French) and Germanic (which includes English).

The fact that Russian and English are distant relations means that you will often find similarities between basic words in the two languages, such as 'three', *tri*, три; 'daughter', *doch'*, дочь; and 'brother', *brat*, брат. Sometimes the relationship is more subtle as in 'house, apartment block', *dom*, дом, which is related to the English word 'domestic', and the '*-grad*' in 'Volgograd' which is actually related to the English 'garden'.

The Russian alphabet was devised quite late, probably around the 9th century, and many letters were taken from Greek. Legend has it that the alphabet was invented by a missionary St Cyril – thus its name Cyrillic. The alphabet might seem intimidating, but actually a number of letters look and sound similar to letters in English (А, Б (b), Д (d), Е, К, М, О, Т). What is most tricky is not to mispronounce the few that look like English but sound totally different; for example, В is pronounced like a 'v'! Happily, most letters have only one or two possible pronunciations, and this is almost always predictable from the context. It is quite easy to acquire a rough working knowledge of the alphabet, which is handy for reading maps and street signs, and may make you feel a bit more at home. Nevertheless, all Russian words in this book are given with a transliterated equivalent, using a system designed to be accurate, yet easy and quick to read.

Russia does not have a tradition of superficial warmth in public. You may be startled by offhandedness, or even rudeness, in shops and offices. However, if you are able to break the ice, Russians can change dramatically, showing immense warmth, generosity and openness about personal matters. It is not generally rude to ask how someone's relationship is getting along, or what they think of a political issue, or how their finances are! Since there has been only limited contact between Russia and the West, people can be surprised and pleased if you make an effort to speak their language.

While Russian may be very useful in other parts of the former USSR, some sensitivity is required, as in certain areas Russian and Russians are not particularly popular. You could try getting something on the local language, such as Lonely Planet's *Baltic States phrasebook*.

Don't be shy and you will soon be communicating in Russian! *Fsyevo kharosheva!*

Pronunciation

The Alphabet

Below is the Russian alphabet, followed by the phonetic symbols which this book uses to transliterate Russian letters, along with examples of English words containing similar sounds.

А а	'a' as in father
Б б	'b' as in but
В в	'v' as in van
Г г	'g' as in god
Д д	'd' as in dog
Е е	'ye' as in yet
Ё ё	'yo' as in yonder
Ж ж	'zh' as the 's' in measure
З з	'z' as in zoo
И и	as the English 'i' but stretch your lips, a bit like the 'ee' in see
Й й	'y' as in boy
К к	'k' as in kind
Л л	'l' as in lamp
М м	'm' as in mad
Н н	'n' as in not
О о	'o' as in more (when stressed) 'a' as in about (when unstressed)
П п	'p' as in pig

7

PRONUNCIATION

Р р	'r' as in rub (but rolled if you can!)	
С с	's' as in sing	
Т т	't' as in ten	
У у	'u' as in pull (**not** as in 'but'!)	
Ф ф	'f' as in fan	
Х х	'kh' as the 'ch' in Bach	
Ц ц	'ts' as in bits	
Ч ч	'c' as in chin	
Ш ш	'sh' as in shop	
Щ щ	'sh' as in sheet	
Ъ	a 'hard sign' – means a slight gap between letters (very rare)	
Ы	'i' as in 'ill'	
Ь	' – a 'soft sign' – means the consonant before it is 'softened' ie pronounced as if there is a very short 'y' sound after it.	
Э э	'e' as in end	
Ю ю	'yu' as in useful	
Я	'ya' as in yard	

Stress

Russian words are strongly stressed on one syllable. Unfortunately, you can't predict which one! So throughout this book stressed syllables are printed in bold. Note that some Russian words sound similar to English words except for the stress. For example, 'taxi' in Russian is pronounced *taksi*, 'tourist' is *turist*.

Intonation

To turn a statement into a question in Russian, you don't have to change the word order at all, but simply change the intonation – how your voice goes up and down when you say the sentence. As a rule, in a statement, your voice stays quite level and then falls on the stressed syllable of the last word (and stays as low). In a question, your voice also stays quite level and then rises very sharply on the stressed syllable of the last word (and then comes back down a bit):

They sell beer. (statement)

pradayut piva   Продают пиво.

Do they sell beer? (question)

pradayut piva?   Продают пиво?

Transliteration

A Note for Users of Guidebooks

This phrasebook and Lonely Planet guidebooks such as *Russia, Ukraine & Belarus – a travel survival kit* and *Baltic States & Kaliningrad – a travel survival kit* use basically the same transliteration system for Russian, except for the following specific differences. Transliterations in the guidebooks are designed to correspond closely to official transliterations (such as on maps), while this book concentrates on accuracy of pronunciation. For example, the city Новосибирск is written 'Novosibirsk' in a travel survival kit, which is how it will be written on signs and maps, but this book transliterates it as *navasibirsk*, which reflects exactly how it is pronounced.

The specific differences are:

Russian letter	guidebooks	phrasebook
e	e	ye
o (unstressed)	o	a
щ	shch	sh
ы	y	i
ь	not written	'
-ие	ie	iye
-ий, -ый	y	iy

In addition, the phrasebook shows changes created by certain combinations of sounds (eg в is normally pronounced *v* but before an unvoiced consonant such as к it sounds like *f*: therefore в Калининграде, 'in Kaliningrad', is written *f kaliningradye*).

Grammar

Word Order

Normally you can use English word order in Russian and you will be understood. However, you may notice that Russians will sometimes put the most important or interesting information last in a sentence, as if they were building up to a punch line:

There's milk for sale in the food shop!

v gastranomye pradayotsa malako!

В гастрономе продаётся молоко!
(lit: In the food shop is for sale milk!)

Verbs

Most simply, verbs can be described as 'doing words' – such as 'I **work** in a shop', 'She **loves** vodka'. In English and Russian, you can put endings on a verb to show when this action takes place: present, past or future, eg 'I work**ed** in a shop' is called the 'past tense'.

Present

Russian verbs in the present tense add endings depending on whether I, you, a third person, we, or they are doing whatever it is.

to work *rabotat'* работать

This is called the 'dictionary form' – if you look up a verb in the dictionary, like 'work', this is the form you'll find. However, it is also generally a useless form – to use it, you have to drop the ending -ТЬ *(-t')* and put endings on as we discussed earlier.

I work	*ya rabotayu*	я работаю
you work	*vi rabotayetye*	вы работаете
she/he works	*ana/on rabotayet*	она/он работает
we work	*mi rabotayem*	мы работаем
they work	*ani rabotayut*	они работают

to speak *gavarit'* говорить

When you find a dictionary form ending in -ИТЬ *(-it')*, drop the -И *(-i)*, as well as the -ТЬ *(-t')*, and add the endings -Ю *(-yu)*, -ИТЕ *(-itye)*, -ИТ *(-it)*, -ИМ *(-im)* and -ЯТ *(-yat)*.

I speak	*ya gavaryu*	я говорю
you speak	*vi gavaritye*	вы говорите
she/he speaks	*ana/on gavarit*	она/он говорит
we speak	*mi gavarim*	мы говорим
they speak	*ani gavaryat*	они говорят

Some verbs do not follow these patterns exactly but if you use these endings you will be understood.

There is an alternative word for 'you'; ТЫ *(ti)*, with its own verb ending –ЕШЬ *(-yesh')*; or for the second pattern –ИШЬ *(-ish')*. This is informal and generally only used between good friends or with children and family – therefore all the phrases in this book use the formal *vi*. However, young adults sometimes use *ti* amongst themselves, even with strangers, but it requires some feel before you know whether *ti* will be appropriate. Therefore it is advisable to use the formal *vi* until you are invited to use *ti*. Even Russians sometimes worry about which 'you' to use!

Note that Russian leaves out the verb 'to be' in the present tense ('am', 'is', 'are'). Whereas we would say in English 'That is our bus', Russians just say 'That our bus', *eta nash aftobus*, Это наш автобус.

GRAMMAR

Past Tense

English can put '-ed' on the end of a verb to show something happened in the past. Russian has an equivalent: -ла *(-la)*. Just drop the ending -ть *(-t')* from the dictionary form first.

to see
   vidyet'   видеть
I saw Leningrad.
   ya vidyela   Я видела
   lyeningrat   Ленинград.

to ask
   sprasit'   спросить
Natasha asked where
the museum is.
   natasha sprasila,   Наташа спросила,
   gdye muzyey   где музей.

The past tense doesn't have a set of endings like the present tense, but you have to drop the -a *(-a)* from the -ла *(-la)* if you are a male.

I (m) saw Leningrad.
   ya vidyel   Я видел
   lyeningrat   Ленинград.
Boris asked where the museum
is.
   baris sprasil, gdye   Борис спросил,
   muzyey   где музей.

After 'we', any other plural, and the formal 'you', вы *(vi)* you have to change -ла *(-la)*, to -ли *(-li)*.

We saw Leningrad.
   mi vidyeli   Мы видели
   lyeningrat   Ленинград.

The tourists asked where the museum is.
turisti sprasili, gdye muzyey

Туристы спросили, где музей.

To Be

Remember that although Russian doesn't use 'to be' in the present tense, it has a regular past tense – but note the -ла (*-la*) is stressed, but the plural -ли (*-li*) is not.

to be
bit'

быть

Natasha was there. Natasha has been there.
natasha bila tam

Наташа была там.

We were there. We have been there.
mi bili tam

Мы были там.

To Have

Russian doesn't usually use a verb meaning 'to have' – you have to learn the following expressions, which roughly mean 'With me exists ...'

I have ...
u myenya yest' ...

У меня есть ...

Do you have ...?
u vas yest' ...?

У вас есть ...?

We have ...
u nas yest' ...

У нас есть ...

GRAMMAR

If you don't have something, the following expression is very useful:

I don't have one/We don't have
any/There aren't any/ etc.
   nyetu   Нету.

Future

English sometimes uses the future tense, 'will' + verb, but very often uses the present tense to refer to future arrangements, eg 'I'm working tomorrow'. The future is obvious from the context, especially the word 'tomorrow'. Russian is similar: it often uses the present tense to refer to the future:

I'm working tomorrow.
   ya rabotayu zaftra   Я работаю завтра.

Modals

This is a term for when you want to modify a verb by saying, for instance, you can, or want to, or should do something, eg 'I want to buy badges'.

In Russian, the verb following a modal is always just in the dictionary form:

buy (dictionary form)
   pakupat'   покупать
I buy
   ya pakupayu   я покупаю

But:

I want to buy
  ya khachu pakupat'
  (**not** *pakupayu*)

Я хочу покупать

Can

In English, 'can' usually expresses ability.

I can ...
  ya magu ...

Я могу ...

I can't ...
  ya nye magu ...

Я не могу ...

Can you ...?
  vi mozhetye ...?

Вы можете ...?

In colloquial English, 'can' sometimes replaces 'may' to express being allowed to do something.

Can I (take photos?)
  mozhna mnye
  (fatagrafiravat')?

Можно мне (фото-графировать)?

You're not allowed to ...
  vam nyel'zya ...

Вам нельзя ...

These two words *mozhna*, МОЖНО, and *nyel'zya*, НЕЛЬЗЯ, can be used on their own, as in the following typical conversation :

May I?
  mozhna?

Можно?

No you may not.
  nyel'zya

Нельзя.

GRAMMAR

Want

I want to (know)
 ya khachu (znat')   Я хочу (знать)
I would like to ... (more
polite)
 ya khatyela bi ...   Я хотела бы ...(f)
 ya khatyel bi ...   Я хотел бы...(m)
Would you like to ...
 vi khatyeli bi ...?   Вы хотели бы ...?
I don't want to ...
 ya nye khachu ...   Я не хочу ...

Must, Have To

I have to (go)
 mnye nuzhna (itti)   Мне нужно (идти)
Do you have to ...?
 vam nuzhna ...?   Вам нужно ...?

Negatives

To say you are not doing something, Russian simply puts не *(nye)* before the verb. This is simpler than English, which sometimes has to put in other words as well (like 'do'), as you can see in the following examples.

She works here.
 ana rabotayet zdyes'   Она работает здесь.
She doesn't work here.
 ana nye rabotayet zdyes'   Она не работает здесь.

I like wine.
  ya lyublyu vino   Я люблю вино.
I don't like wine.
  ya nye lyublyu vino   Я не люблю вино.

Articles
Russian does not have articles ('the' and 'a'). Remembering that Russian does not use the verb 'to be' in the present tense either, the English sentence 'I am a tourist' will simply become 'I tourist' *ya turist*, Я турист.

Nouns
Plurals
The most common plural ending is -ы *(-i)*, and will always be understood. Note that nouns ending in -a *(-a)* replace the -a *(-a)* with the -ы *(-i)*.

That is a shop.
  eta magazin   Это магазин.
Those are shops.
  eta magazini   Это магазины.

But:

That is a flat.
  eta kvartira   Это квартира.
Those are flats.
  eta kvartiri   Это квартиры.

GRAMMAR

Note that the word Это... *(eta ...)*, stays the same whether you are pointing out one thing or several things; it can mean 'This is ...', 'That is ...', 'These are ...' or 'Those are ...'

Location

Note that after 'in/at', в *(v)*, and 'on/by (train etc)', на *(na)*, you have to put -е *(-ye)* ,on the end of the word afterwards (or if there is already a vowel on the end you have to replace it):

restaurant
  · *ryestaran*   ресторан
I was at the restaurant.
  ya bila v ryestaranye   Я была в ресторане.

But:

car
  mashina   машина
She is in the car.
  ana v mashinye   Она в машине.

Accusative Case

Many verbs involve doing something to something. 'I am painting my house' means the house is having something done to it – it is being painted. 'My sister bought a record' means the record had something done to it – it got bought. A noun having something done to it is said to be in the 'accusative case'. In Russian, if a noun ends in -a *(-a)*, in the accusative case you have to change this to -у *(-u)*.

newspaper
  gazyeta

газета

I bought a newspaper.
  ya kupila gazyetu

Я купила газету.

Moscow
  maskva

Москва

We saw Moscow.
  mi vidyeli maskvu

Мы видели Москву.

This rule does *not* apply after the 'have' expressions described earlier:

car
  mashina

машина

I have a car.
  u myenya yest' mashina

У меня есть машина.
(not *mashinu* машину)

Adjectives & Adverbs
Adjectives
When you look up an adjective (a word which describes a noun, like 'wonderful', 'expensive', 'interesting') in the dictionary, it will usually end in -ый *(-iy)*, or occasionally in -ий *(-iy)*, or -ой *(-oy)*. Just remember that when it describes a noun ending in -а *(-a)*, you must change the adjective ending to -ая *(-aya)*.

That is a wonderful view.
  eta pryekrasniy vit   Это прекрасный вид.
The room is expensive.
  nomyer daragoy   Номер дорогой.
He is interesting.
  on intyeryesniy   Он интересный.

But:

That is a wonderful street.
  *eta pryekrasnaya
  ulitsa*   Это прекрасная
                                  улица.
The book is expensive.
  kniga daragaya   Книга дорогая.
She is interesting.
  ana intyeryesnaya   Она интересная.

Possessive Adjectives

Words like 'my', 'your' etc, sometimes also have an alternative form if they go with a word ending in -a *(-a)*:

my	*moy/maya*	мой/моя
your	*vash/vasha*	ваш/ваша
your (informal)	*tvoy/tvaya*	твой/твоя
her	*yeyo*	её
his	*yevo*	его
our	*nash/nasha*	наш/наша
their	*ikh*	их

Adverbs

Something Russians use often on adjectives is the simple ending

-o (pronounced -*a* when unstressed, which is in most cases). This is the adverb ending, like English '-ly'. An adverb doesn't describe a person or thing, but describes how someone does something. Note the adverb usually comes second in Russian.

He is a wonderful guide.
(adjective – describes the guide)
   on pryekrasniy gid   Он прекрасный гид.
He speaks English wonderfully.
(adverb – describes how he
speaks)
   on pryekrasna gavarit   Он прекрасно говорит
   pa angliyski   по-английски.

GRAMMAR

The ending -o has further uses – you can use it just to refer to a state of affairs without having to name any particular object:

Wonderful! That's wonderful!
   pryekrasna!   Прекрасно!
How expensive!
   doraga!   Дорого!
This is really interesting!
   intyeryesna!   Интересно!
It's cold.
   kholadna   Холодно.
Good.
   kharasho   Хорошо.

These one-word sentences are perfectly acceptable and very common in Russian.

Questions

Like English, Russian has a number of small question words with which you can start a sentence.

what	*shto*	что
who	*kto*	кто
why	*pachyemu*	почему
when	*kagda*	когда
where	*gdye*	где
where (to)	*kuda*	куда

Use this last one when you're talking about going somewhere:

Where are you going?
kuda vi idyotye?   Куда вы идёте?

Note that after question words you don't change the sentence around (as you do in English), you just leave it as it was.

You are working.
vi rabotayetye.   Вы работаете.
Where are you working?
gdye vi rabotayetye?   Где вы работаете?

In addition, as we read in the section on 'Intonation' in the Pronunciation chapter, Russian does not change the word order for a question without a question word either, but has a sharp rise on the last word.

If you don't feel confident about using intonation, you can put да? *(da?)*, (literally 'yes?') on the end of a statement, equivalent to English expressions such as 'aren't you?', 'isn't it?' etc:

That's the Kremlin, isn't it?
eta kryeml', da?   Это Кремль, да?

Some Useful Words

and	*i*	и
at	*v*	в
because	*pata**mu** shto*	потому что
because of	*iz za*	из-за
but	*no*	но
by (train etc)	*na*	на
for	*dlya*	для
here	*zdyes'*	здесь
in	*v*	в
on	*na*	на
near	*okala*	около
there	*tam*	там

GRAMMAR

Greetings & Civilities

Greetings

Russian has an all-purpose greeting like English 'hello' – *zdrast*viytye!, Здравствуйте! It can be used at any time of day, and both between friends and when being formally introduced. Russians tend to shake hands when they greet each other. Other more specific (and less common) greetings include:

Good morning.
> *dobraye utra*   Доброе утро.

Good afternoon.
> *dobriy dyen'*   Добрый день.

Good evening.
> *dobriy vyechyer*   Добрый вечер.

Asking 'How are you?' sounds a bit un-Russian – as a rule, *zdrast*viytye, Здравствуйте, covers 'Hello/How are you?/ How do you do?' However, if you are on friendly terms with someone, you can get them to talk about what's been happening with something like:

How are things?
> *kag dyela?*   Как дела?

How's life?
> *kag zhizn'?*   Как жизнь?

What's new?
> *shto novava?*   Что нового?

26

Possible answers include:

Fine, thank you.
spasiba *spasiba, kharasho* OK Спасибо, хорошо. *either way*
Not bad. *fine*
  nichyevo Ничего.
There's nothing new.
  nichyevo novava nyet Ничего нового нет.
And with you?
  a u vas? А у вас?

Attracting Someone's Attention

The Russian equivalent of 'Excuse me, please' is *izvinitye, pazhalsta*, Извините, пожалуйста. However, if you are attracting someone's attention in order to ask a question, the usual expression is 'Tell me, please ...', *skazhitye, pazhalsta*, Скажите, пожалуйста.

To enter somewhere like an office it is polite to ask 'May I?', *mozhna?*, Можно?, or 'I'm not disturbing you?', *ya vam nye myeshayu?*, Я вам не мешаю?.

Goodbyes

Goodbye.
  dasvidanya До свидания.
  shasliva (more informal Счастливо.
  but common)
See you tomorrow.
  dazaftra До завтра.

It was very nice (to meet you).
*bila ochyen' priyatna
(paznakomit'sa s vami)*

Было очень приятно
(познакомиться с
вами).

I hope we see each other soon.
*nadyeyus', shta skora
uvidimsa*

Надеюсь, что
скоро увидимся.

Sorry, but I have to get going.
*izvinitye, pazhalsta,
mnye para iti*

Извините, пожалуйста,
мне пора идти.

Say hello to your husband/
your wife.
*pyeryedaytye privyet
vashemu muzhu/
vashey zhenye*

Передайте привет
вашему мужу/
вашей жене.

Good night.
spakoynay nochi!

Спокойной ночи!

Civilities

Please.
  pazhalsta Пожалуйста.
Thank you (very much).
  spasiba (bal'shoye) Спасибо (большое).
Thank you very much for all
your trouble.
  spasiba za fsye Спасибо за все
  vashi khlopati ваши хлопоты.

If someone thanks you, you should say *pazhalsta*, пожалуйста,
in return. We saw above that this means 'please', but – very
importantly – it's also used for 'Don't mention it/That's all right'.
Russians also use *pazhalsta*, пожалуйста, when they hand
you something. In this context you might also hear (literally) 'to
your health', *na zdarovye*, на здоровье.

Apologies

Sorry.
  prastitye, pazhalsta Простите, пожалуйста.
Sorry? (What did you say?)
  prastitye? Простите?
  (shto vi skazali?) (Что вы сказали?)
Excuse me.
  izvinitye, pazhalsta Извините, пожалуйста.
Excuse me. (When trying to
get past)
  prapustitye, pazhalsta Пропустите,
  пожалуйста.

GREETINGS

I didn't mean to.
   ya eta sluchayna   Я это случайно.
That's all right/It doesn't
matter.
   nichyevo   Ничего!
Don't worry.
   nye byespakoytyes'!   Не беспокойтесь!

Small Talk

Help!
Language Difficulties

An expression well worth memorising:

Could you please write that
down?
    zapishitye eta,   Запишите это,
    pazhalsta!   пожалуйста!

You may find this useful whenever you need to know any little bit
of precise information – like a price, a time or an address. Other
expressions that may help you if you don't understand are:

What does that mean?
    shto eta znachit?   Что это значит?
Sorry, what did you say?
    prastitye, shto vi   Простите, что вы
    skazali?   сказали?
Could you please speak more
slowly?
    gavaritye pamyedlyenyeye, Говорите помедленее,
    pazhalsta   пожалуйста.
Just a minute!
(eg while you look something
up)
    minutachku!   Минуточку!

31

pastooritsia, pazhalsta
repeat

I understand.
  ya panimayu   Я понимаю.
I see.
  panyatna   Понятно.
I don't understand.
  ya nye panimayu   Я не понимаю.
Can you show me?
  pakazhitye,   Покажите,
  pazhalsta   пожалуйста.
I'll show you.
  ya vam pakazhu   Я вам покажу.

Ya nyepanyal
I didn't
understand

If you are having real problems you can always try:

Do you speak ...?	*vi gavaritye ...?*	Вы говорите ...?
Does anyone speak ...?	*kto nibud' gavarit ...?*	Кто-нибудь говорит ...?
Chinese	*pa kitayski*	по-китайски
English	*pa angliyski*	по-английски
French	*pa frantsuski*	по-французски

SMALL TALK

German	*pa nyemyetski*	по-немецки
Japanese	*pa yaponski*	по-японски
Spanish	*pa ispanski*	по-испански

Top Useful Phrases

The following are all-purpose expressions that you might need on the spur of the moment.

May I?/Do you mind?/Is it all right?
    mozhna?   Можно?

Yes.
    da   Да.

No.
    nyet   Нет.

Hello!/How do you do?
    zdrastviytye!   Здравствуйте!

Good bye!
    dasvidanya!   До свидания!

Thank you.
    spasiba   Спасибо.

Please/Don't mention it.
(after 'Thank you')
    pazhalsta   Пожалуйста.

Excuse me/Sorry!
    prastitye, pazhalsta!   Простите, пожалуйста!

It doesn't matter/That's all right.
    nichyevo!   Ничего!

SMALL TALK

I am (a tourist/Susan).
   *ya (**turist/Suzan**)*   Я (турист/Сузан).
What's that?
   shto eta?   Что это?
Where is (the toilet)?
   gdye (tualyet)?   Где (туалет)?
How much?
   skol'ka?   Сколько?

Don't be shy about talking to people! Russians will be very open concerning anything from politics to how much they earn.

Meeting People

What is your name?
   *kak vas za**vut**?*   Как вас зовут?
My name is ...
   *my**e**nya zavut*   Меня зовут...
I am ...
   ya ...   Я ...

To be very friendly and informal, you can use your first name, as in English.

My name is Anna.
   *my**e**nya zavut Ana*   Меня зовут Анна.

Or to be more formal you can use the Russian word for Mrs/Ms/ Miss, *gaspazha*, госпожа, or Mr, *gaspadin*, господин, with your surname to refer to yourself and other non-Russians.

SMALL TALK

I am Mrs Clarke.
   ya gaspazha Klark   Я госпожа Кларк.

However, Russians do not use these words for themselves. Instead they use their first name with their patronymic, a second name taken from their father's first name (so try to remember both names when you are introduced!).

My name is Irina Pavlovna.
(Irina, daughter of Pavel)
   myenya zavut Irina   Меня зовут Ирина
   Pavlavna   Павловна.

Hello, Boris Ivanich. (Boris, son of Ivan)
   zdrastviytye,   Здравствуйте,
   Baris Ivanich   Борис Иванович!

If you're not sure what to call someone, you can always ask: 'What should I call you?' *kak mnye vas nazvat'?* Как мне вас назвать?

This is ...	*eta* ...	Это ...
my colleague	*maya kalyega*	моя коллега (f)
	moy kalyega	мой коллега (m)
my (female, girl-) friend	*maya padruga*	моя подруга
my (male, boy-) friend	*moy druk*	мой друг
my husband	*moy mush*	мой муж
my wife	*maya zhena*	моя жена

If you have been introduced, shake hands and say 'It's very nice.' – it's understood you mean 'to meet you' – *ochyen' priyatna,* очень приятно. Russians of both sexes shake hands a lot, even when they know each other.

Nationalities

Where are you from?

atkuda vi?   Откуда вы?

I'm from ...	*ya iz ...*	Я из ...
Africa	*afriki*	Африки
Australia	*afstralii*	Австралии
Asia	*azii*	Азии
Canada	*kanadi*	Канады
China	*kitaya*	Китая
Denmark	*dani*	Дании
England	*anglii*	Англии
Europe	*yevropi*	Европы
Finland	*finlandii*	Финляндии
France	*frantsii*	Франции
Germany	*gyermanii*	Германии
Holland	*golandii*	Голландии
India	*indii*	Индии
Ireland	*irlandii*	Ирландии
Israel	*izrailya*	Израиля
Italy	*italii*	Италии
Japan	*yaponii*	Японии
Middle East	*sryednyeva vastoka*	Среднего востока
New Zealand	*novay zyelandii*	Новой Зеландии
Norway	*narvyegii*	Норвегии
Scotland	*shatlandii*	Шотландии
Singapore	*singapura*	Сингапура
South America	*yuzhnay amyeriki*	Южной Америки
Spain	*ispanii*	Испании
Sweden	*shvyetsii*	Швеции
Switzerland	*shvyetsarii*	Швецарии
USA	*amyeriki*	Америки

In the Russian Federation you are assured of meeting people of varied and interesting backgrounds. Russians were only one of over 100 nationalities in the former Soviet Union. You could ask:

What nationality are you?
kto vi pa natsional'nasti? — Кто вы по национальности?

What city are you from?
vi is kakova gorada? — Вы из какого города?

Where is that?
gdye eta? — Где это?

Show me.
pakazhitye — Покажите.

What's life like there?
kak tam zhivut? — Как там живут?

Age

How old are you?
skol'ka vam lyet? — Сколько вам лет?

I am ... years old.   *mnye ... lyet*   Мне ... лет.
18   *vasyemnatsat'*   восемнадцать
25   *dvatsat' pyat'*   двадцать пять

Occupations

What do you work as?
kyem vi rabotayetye? — Кем вы работаете?

I'm a/an ...	ya ...	Я ...
artist	*khudozhnitsa*	художница (f)
	khudozhnik	художник (m)
business person	*kamyersant*	коммерсант
doctor	*vrach*	врач
driver (bus, taxi, truck)	*vadityel'*	водитель
engineer (a broader term than in English)	*inzhenyer*	инженер
factory worker, manual labourer	*rabochaya*	рабочая (f)
	rabochiy	рабочий (m)
journalist	*zhurnalist*	журналист
lawyer	*advakat*	адвокат
mechanic	*myekhanik*	механик
musician	*muzikant*	музыкант
nurse	*myetsyestra*	медсестра
office worker	*sluzhashaya*	служащая (f)
	sluzhashiy	служащий (m)
scientist	*uchyonaya*	учёная (f)
	uchyoniy	учёный (m)
secretary	*syekryetarsha*	секретарша (f)
	syekryetar'	секретарь (m)
student	*studyentka*	студентка (f)
	studyent	студент (m)
teacher	*uchityel'nitsa*	учительница (f)
	uchityel'	учитель (m)
waiter ...	*afitsiant*	официант
waiter ...	*afitsiantka*	официантка
writer	*pisatyel'nitsa*	писательница (f)
	pisatyel'	писатель (m)

SMALL TALK

Where do you work?
gdye vi rabotayetye?   Где вы работаете?

I work ...	*ya pabotayu ...*	Я работаю ...
for the army	*varmii*	в армии
for a bank	*v bankye*	в банке
for a company	*ffirmye*	в фирме
in a factory	*na zavodye*	на заводе
for the government	*v gasudarstvyenam uchryezhdyenii*	в государственном учреждении
at home	*doma*	дома
in a hospital	*v bal'nitse*	в больнице
in a library	*v bibliatyekye*	в библиотеке
in a school	*fshkolye*	в школе
in a university	*v univyersityetye*	в университете

I've come here ...	*ya priyekhala syuda ...*	Я приехала-сюда ... (f)
	ya priyekhal syuda ...	Я приехал-сюда... (m)
on business	*padyelam*	по делам
on holiday	*votpusk*	в отпуск
to learn Russian	*uchit'sa ruskamu yaziku*	учиться русскому языку
to study	*uchit'sa*	учиться
to work	*rabotat'*	работать

Religion

What is your religion?

| | *kakaya vasha ryeligiya?* | Какая ваша религия? |

I am ...	*ya ...*	Я ...
Buddhist	*budistka*	будистка (f)
	budist	будист (m)
Catholic	*katolichka*	католичка (f)
	katolik	католик (m)
Christian	*khristianka*	христианка(f)
	khristianin	христианин (m)
Hindu	*induska*	индуска (f)
	indus	индус (m)
Jewish	*yevryeyka*	еврейка (f)
	yevryey	еврей (m)
Muslim	*musul'manka*	мусульманка (f)
	musul'manin	мусульманин(m)
Orthodox	*pravaslavnaya*	православная (f)
	pravaslavniy	православный (m)

not religious	*nyevyeruyushaya*	неверующая (f)
	nyevyeruyushiy	неверующий (m)

Family

Are you married?
   (to a woman) *vi zamuzhem?*

Вы замужем?

   (to a man) *vi zhenat?*

Вы женат?

I am single.
   ya nye zamuzhem
   ya nye zhenat

Я не замужем. (f)
Я не женат. (m)

How many children do you have?
   skol'ka u vas dyetyey?

Сколько у вас детей?

I don't have any children.
   dyetyey u myenya nyet

Детей у меня нет.

I have a daughter/son.
   u myenya yest' doch'/sin

У меня есть дочь/сын.

How many brothers/sisters do
you have?
   skol'ka u vas
   brat'yef/syestyor?

Сколько у вас
братьев/сестёр?

Is your husband/wife here?
   vash mush/vasha
   zhena zdyes'?

Ваш муж/ваша
жена здесь?

Do you have a boyfriend/
girlfriend?
   u vas yest' druk/
   padruga?

У вас есть друг/
подруга?

Some Useful Words

aunt	*tyotya*	тётя
brother	*brat*	брат

children	*dyeti*	дети
daughter	*doch'*	дочь
family	*syem'ya*	семья
father	*papa*	папа
	atyets (formal)	отец
grandfather	*dyedushka*	дедушка
grandmother	*babushka*	бабушка
husband	*mush*	муж
mother	*mama*	мама
	mat' (formal)	мать
sister	*syestra*	сестра
son	*sin*	сын
uncle	*dyadya*	дядя
wife	*zhena*	жена

Expressing Feelings

I am ...

angry	*ya syerditaya*	Я сердитая. (f)
	ya syerditiy	Я сердитый. (m)
cold	*mnye kholadna*	Мне холодно.
grateful	*ya blagadarna*	Я благодарна. (f)
	ya blagadaryen	Я благодарен. (m)

SMALL TALK

happy	*mnye vyesyela*	Мне весело.
hot	*mnye zharka*	Мне жарко.
hungry	*ya khachu yest'*	Я хочу есть.
in a hurry	*ya spyeshu*	Я спешу.
right	*ya prava.* (f)	Я права. (f)
	ya praf	Я прав. (m)
sleepy	*ya khachu spat'*	Я хочу спать.
sorry	*mnye ochyen'*	Мне очень
(condolence)	*zhal'*	жаль.
thirsty	*ya khachu pit'*	Я хочу пить.
tired	*ya ustala.* (f)	Я устала. (f)
	ya ustal	Я устал. (m)
uncomfortable	*mnye nyeudobna*	Мне неудобно.

Opinions

It is a time of big changes in Russia, and you will have opportunities to argue about everything!

| Do you like ...? | | |
| *vam nravitsa ...?* | Вам нравится ...? | |

I (really) like ...	*mnye (ochyen')*	Мне (очень)
	nravitsa ...	нравится ...
I don't (really)	*mnye nye (ochyen')*	Мне не (очень)
like ...	*nravitsa ...*	нравится ...
that building	*eta zdaniye*	это здание
your city	*vash gorad*	ваш город
your country	*vasha rodina*	ваша родина
this film	*etat fil'm*	этот фильм
Lenin	*lyenin*	Ленин
her	*ana* *	она

SMALL TALK

him	*on* *	он
this music	*eta muzika*	эта музыка
the service	*apsluzhivaniye*	обслуживание
this / that	*eta* *	это

Look up anything in the vocabulary that you like or dislike, and slot it in! Note that the words marked above with an asterisk should come at the start of the sentence, not the end.

Yes!
   da!   Да!
I agree!
   saglasna!   Согласна! (f)
   saglasyen!   Согласен! (m)
No!
   nyet!   Нет!
I'm afraid I don't agree.
   ya bayus', shto   Я боюсь, что я
   ya nye saglasna   не согласна (f)/
   saglasyen   согласен (m).
Do you agree?
   vi saglasni?   Вы согласны?

Interests

What do you do in your spare time?
   kak vi pravoditye   Как вы проводите
   svayo svabodnaya   своё свободное
   vryemya?   время?

I like ...	ya lyublyu ...	Я люблю ...
Do you like ...?	vi lyubitye ...?	Вы любите ...?
films	kino	кино
football	futbol	футбол
music	muziku	музыку
reading	chitat'	читать
seeing ...	vidyet' ...	видеть ...
(going) shopping	khadit' pa magazinam	ходить по магазинам
travelling	putyeshestvovat'	путешествовать
watching TV	smatryet' tyelyevizar	смотреть телевизор

I play ...	ya igrayu ...	Я играю ...
Do you play ...	vi igrayetye ...?	Вы играете ...?
cards	karti	в карты
chess	f shakhmati	в шахматы
football	f futbol	в футбол
guitar	na gitarye	на гитаре
in an orchestra	varkyestrye	в оркестре
piano	na pianina	на пианино
in a team	f kamandye	в команде

SMALL TALK

Let's go (to a disco)!
  paydyomtye
  (na diskatyeku)!

Пойдёмте
(на дискотеку)!

Let's play (cards)!
  davaytye igrat'
  (f karti)!

Давайте играть
(в карты)!

Let's give it a try!
paprobuyem!

Let's!
davaytye!

Попробуем!

Давайте!

Getting Around

Finding Your Way

How do I get to ...?
kak mnye papast' v ...? Как мне попасть в ...?

Where is the ...?	*gdye ...?*	Где ...?
bus station	*aftobusnaya*	автобусная
	stantsiya	станция
train station	*vagzal*	вокзал
airport	*aeraport*	аэропорт
subway station	*stantsiya myetro*	станция метро
ticket office	**ka**ssa	касса

Buying Tickets

As with accommodation, travel arrangements are normally booked through *Intourist*, the official tourist agency, but this is changing. Travel within Russia can be remarkably cheap. Note that at metro stations you can buy a monthly ticket for public transport, *yediniy bilyet*, единый билет.

TICKET OFFICE/TICKETS	КАССА/БИЛЕТЫ
INFORMATION	СПРАВОЧНОЕ БЮРО/ СПРАВКИ/ ИНФОРМАЦИЯ

Excuse me, where is the ticket
office/information desk?
skazhitye, pazhalsta, Скажите, пожалуйста,
gdye kassa/ где касса/
spravachnaye byuro? справочное бюро?

How much is ...? *skol'ka stoit ...?* Сколько стоит ...?
I'd like ... *daytye, pazhalsta ...* Дайте,
пожалуйста, ...

one ticket	*adin bilyet*	один билет
(toIrkutsk)	*(v irkutsk)*	(в Иркутск)
two tickets	*dva bilyeta*	два билета
a reservation	*platskartu*	плацкарту
single (one way)	*vadin kanyets*	в один конец
return (round trip)	*tuda i abratna*	туда и обратно
economy	*turistskiy klass*	туристский
(aeroplane)		класс
economy (train)	*zhostkiy*	жёсткий

АЭРОПОРТ

Air

Even to book an internal flight foreigners must show their passport and pay at a special rate. If you're with Intourist you'll sit in a separate departure lounge and may be put on the plane first. If you're travelling independently, beware! Planes are sometimes overbooked and so there is a mad rush to get seats.

REGISTRATION	РЕГИСТРАЦИЯ
DEPARTURES	ОТЛЕТ/ВЫЛЕТ
LUGGAGE PICK-UP	ВЫДАЧА БАГАЖА
TO CITY	(ВЫХОД) В ГОРОД

Is there a flight to (Omsk)?
  *yest' li ryeys v
  (omsk)?*
Есть ли рейс в
(Омск)?

When is the next flight
to (Leningrad)?
  *kagda slyeduyushiy
  samalyot v
  (ulan-ude)?*
Когда следующий
самолёт в
(Улан-Удэ)?

What is the flight number?
  *kakoy nomyer
  ryeysa?*
Какой номер рейса?

Where do we check in?
  gdye ryegistratsiya?
Где регистрация?

When do we have to check in?
  *kagda nuzhna bit'
  v erapartu?*
Когда нужно быть
в аэропорту?

One hour/Two hours before
the flight.

za chas/za dva chasa da vilyeta	За час/За два часа до вылета.

Where do you check in/pick up luggage?

gdye zdat'/paluchit' bagash?	Где сдать/ получить багаж?

Could I please have (a) ...?	*prinyesitye, pazhalsta ...*	Принесите, пожалуйста, ...
cup of coffee	*chashku kofi*	чашку кофе
cup of tea	*chashku chayu*	чашку чаю
glass of water	*stakan vadi*	стакан воды

I feel sick.

myenya tashnit	Меня тошнит.

Train

Note that dining cars are rare and it is wise to bring your own food
on longer trips. Sharing food can become quite a social event.

TIMETABLE	РАСПИСАНИЕ
TO TRAINS	К ПОЕЗДАМ
TO PLATFORMS	К ПЕРРОНАМ
ARRIVALS	ПРИБЫТИЕ
DEPARTURES	ОТПРАВЛЕНИЕ

Which train goes to (Zagorsk)?
kakoy poyezd idyot v (zagorsk)?

Какой поезд идёт в (Загорск)?

Does this train go to (Novosibirsk)?
etat poyezd idyot v (navasibirsk)?

Этот поезд идёт в (Новосибирск)?

Do I need to change?
nuzhna dyelat' pyeryesatku?

Нужно делать пересадку?

When does the train leave?
kagda otpravlyayetsa poyezd?

Когда отправляется поезд?

What is this station called?
kak nazivayetsa eta stantsiya?

Как называется эта станция?

What is the next station?
kakaya slyeduyushaya stantsiya?

Какая следующая станция?

Metro

The older metro stations are amazing, and trains run from 6 am until 1 am, at some times of the day every fifty seconds. To get into the metro you buy a token which you insert in the turnstile, and you can stay on the system as long as you like.

THIS WAY TO (CIRCULAR LINE)	ПЕРЕХОД НА (КОЛЬЦЕВУЮ ЛИНИЮ)
WAY OUT	ВЫХОД В ГОРОД

A token please.
  zheton, pazhalsta   Жетон, пожалуйста.
Which line takes me to ...?
  kakaya liniya idyot v ...?   Какая линия идёт в ...?

Bus, Tram & Trolleybus

You generally have to buy a strip of tickets, and when you enter the vehicle you punch one ticket in a machine on the wall. If it's crowded, you can ask someone else to punch it for you.

Please, punch my ticket!
  kampastiruytye,   Компостируйте,
  pazhalsta!   пожалуйста!

Signs

BUS	A
TROLLEYBUS/TRAM	T/Ш

Which ... goes to (the Hotel Bukharest)?	*kakoy ... idyot do (gastinitsi bukharyest)?*	Какой ... идёт до (гостиницы Бухарест)?
bus	*aftobus*	автобус
minibus (usually red)	*marshrutnaye taksi*	маршрутное такси
tram	*tramvay*	трамвай
trolleybus	*ralyeybus*	троллейбус

Please let me know when I
have to get off.
   pazhalsta,
   pryedupryeditye myenya,
   kagda mnye
   nuzhna vikhadit'

Пожалуйста,
предупредите меня,
когда мне
нужно выходить.

What is the next stop?
   kakaya slyed
   uyushaya astanofka?

Какая следующая
остановка?

To squeeze past people to get off:

Excuse me while I get past!
   prapustitye,
   pazhalsta!

Пропустите,
пожалуйста!

Are you getting off here?
vi vikhoditye? Вы выходите?

Taxi

Most government taxis are yellow with a chequered line along the side. However, they are few and far between. Instead, private cars will stop for you and take you to your destination for an agreed fee. Hold out your arm to all the cars that pass.

TAXIS	ТАКСИ

Are you free?
svabodni? Свободны?

Could you take me to ...?	*do ... nye davyezyotye?*	До ... не довезёте?
this address	*etava adryesa*	этого адреса
(Sheremetevo) Airport	*eraporta sheryemyet'yeva*	аэропорта (Шереметьево)
central bank	*sentral'nava banka*	центрального банка
Australian Embassy	*afstraliyskava pasol'stva*	австралийского посольства
British Embassy	*britanskava pasol'stva*	британского посольства

US Embassy	*amyerikanskava pasol'stva*	американского посольства
(Rossia) Hotel	*gastinitsi (rassiya)*	гостиницы (Россия)
market	*rinka*	рынка
post office	*glafpachtamta*	главпочтамта
shops	*magazinav*	магазинов
(Dinamo) Stadium	*stadiona (dinama)*	стадиона (Динамо)
(Park Kultury) Station	*stantsi (park kul'turi)*	станции (Парк культуры)
(Pushkin) St	*ulitsi (**pushkina**)*	улицы (Пушкина)

Please slow down.
   *za**my**edlitye khod, pa**zhal**sta*

Замедлите ход, пожалуйста!

Please stop here.
   *astanavityes' zdyes', pa**zhal**sta*

Остановитесь здесь, пожалуйста!

Please wait for a minute.
   *pada**zh**ditye, pa**zhal**sta, **mi**nutachku*

Подождите, пожалуйста, минуточку!

How much (do I owe you)?
   *skol'ka (s my**enya**)?*

Сколько (с меня)?

GETTING AROUND

On Foot

Russian drivers are scary and by law you must cross a major road at a crossing/subway, *pyeryekhot*, ПЕРЕХОД, or a zebra crossing. Note, however, that a zebra crossing just indicates where you are allowed to cross, but you must give way to drivers!

Excuse me, where is ...?	*skazhitye, pazhalsta, gdye ...?*	Скажите, пожалуйста, где ...?
the nearest bank	*blizhayshiy bank*	ближайший банк
a bar	*bar*	бар
a bus stop	*astanofka aftobusa*	остановка автобуса

a church	*tserkav'*	церковь
the nearest department store	*blizhayshiy univyermag*	ближайший универмаг
the (Ukraina) Hotel	*gastinitsa (ukraina)*	гостиница (Украина)

an information booth	*spravachnaye byuro*	справочное бюро
a mosque	*myechyet'*	мечеть
the main post office	*glafpachtamt*	главпочтамт
a restaurant	*ryestaran*	ресторан
a snack bar	*zakusachnaya*	закусочная
a metro station	*stantsiya myetro*	станция метро
a swimming pool	*baseyn*	бассейн
a synagogue	*sinagoga*	синагога
a taxi rank	*stayanka taksi*	стоянка такси

Directions & Instructions

Is it nearby?
  bliska?   Близко?

Is it far?
  dalyeko?   Далеко?

Can I walk there?
  mozhna iti tuda   Можно идти туда
  pyeshkom?   пешком?

Can you show me on the map?
  pakazhitye mnye na   Покажите мне на
  kartye, pazhalsta   карте, пожалуйста.

How many minutes?
  skol'ka minut?   Сколько минут?

Go straight ahead.
  iditye pryama   Идите прямо.

Turn left ...
  pavyernitye nalyeva ...   Поверните налево ...

GETTING AROUND

Turn right ...
   pavyernitye naprava ...   Поверните направо ...
... at the corner
   ... *zaugal*   ... за угол
... at the traffic lights
   ... *u svyetafora*   ... у светофора

What ... is this?	*kak nazivayetsa ...?*	Как называется ...?
street	*eta ulitsa*	эта улица
suburb	*etat rayon*	этот район

What street number is this?
   kakoy etat nomyer?   Какой этот номер?

Some Useful Words

address	*adryes*	адрес
arrival	*pribitiye*	прибытие
behind	*za*	за
bicycle	*vyelasipyet*	велосипед
departure	*atyezt*	отъезд
early	*rana*	рано
economy (ticket)	*turistskiy klas*	туристский
– plane		класс
economy (ticket)	*v zhostkam*	в жёстком вагоне
– train	*vagonye*	
1st class (ticket)	*pyerviy klas*	первый класс
– plane		
1st class (ticket)	*v myakhkam*	в мягком
– train	*vagonye*	вагоне
next to	*ryadam s*	рядом с

seat	*myesta*	место
sleeper	*spal'naye myesta*	спальное место
stop	*astanofka*	остановка
ticket	*bilyet*	билет
timetable	*raspisaniye*	расписание

Accommodation

As you probably know, it has always been quite difficult travelling with any sort of flexible itinerary: all accommodation has generally been organised by a travel agent and Intourist, which was also expensive! However, Intourist has lost its monopoly. You don't need to book hotel rooms and private accommodation is easy to find. Many people rent out a room in their apartment.

Finding Accommodation

Where is a ... (around here)?	*gdye (zdyes')* ...?	Где (здесь) ...?
hotel	*gastinitsa*	гостиница
room	*komnata*	комната
tourist bureau	*byuro turizma*	бюро туризма
youth hostel	*maladyozhnaya turbaza*	молодёжная турбаза

Can I stay at a ...?	*mozhna astanavit'sa v* ...?	Можно остановиться в ...?
different hotel	*drugoy gastinitse*	другой гостинице
private flat	*chasnay kvartirye*	частной квартире

I'd like a hotel ...	*ya ishu gastinitsu ...*	Я ищу гостиницу ...
as cheap as possible	*kak mozhna dyeshevlye*	как можно дешевле
near the centre of town	*bliska at tsentra gorada*	близко от центра города
that's not too expensive	*nye slishkam daraguyu*	не слишком дорогую

How much does it cost (per day/week)?
  skol'ka stoit (f sutki/ v nyedyelyu)?   Сколько стоит (в сутки/в неделю)?
What is included?
  shto fklyuchyeno?   Что включено?
Are there any cheaper rooms?
  yest' nomyera padyeshevlye?   Есть номера подешевле?
Is there a reduction for children?
  yest' skitka dlya dyetyey?   Есть скидка для детей?

*I would like
→ ya khotela
bi (beah)*

I'd ~~like~~ to reserve a room. →
  ya khachu zakazat' nt nomyer   Я хочу заказать номер.

Khoochu

Please write down ... *zapishitye, pazhalsta, ...*   Запишите, пожалуйста, ...
  the address *adryes*   адрес
  the price *tsenu*   цену

Checking In

When you first arrive at a hotel you need to fill out a registration form (in English!) and leave your passport at the desk. There is almost always someone who can speak English, certainly at the Intourist desk in larger hotels.

Here is my passport.
> *vot moy paspart*   Вот мой паспорт.

I have a reservation.
> *dlya myenya uzhe*   Для меня уже
> *zabraniravali nomyer*   забронировали номер.

I need a room	*mnye nuzhen*	Мне нужен
for ...	*nomyer dlya ...*	номер для ...
myself	*syebya*	себя
two people	*dvaikh*	двоих
one night	*tol'ka sutki*	только сутки
two nights	*dvoye sutak*	двое суток

In the room, is there ...?
   *yest' v **nom**yerye ...?*   Есть в номере ...?
Where is the room?
   *gdye **nom**yer?*   Где номер?
Can I see the room?
   *mozhna pasma**try**et'*   Можно посмотреть
   *etat **nom**yer?*   этот номер?
Fine, I'll take it.
   *kha**ra**sho, sni**mu***   Хорошо, сниму.
Is there another room?
   *yest' dru**goy nom**yer?*   Есть другой номер?
Thanks anyway, but it's not
suitable.
   *spa**si**ba, no eta nye*   Спасибо, но это
   *paday**dyot***   не подойдёт.

Where is ...?	*gdye ...?*	Где ...?
hot water	*gar**ya**chaya **va**da*	горячая вода
a shower	*dush*	душ
a telephone	*tyelye**fon***	телефон
a TV	*tyelye**vi**zar*	телевизор
a toilet	*tua**lyet***	туалет

Is there somewhere to wash
clothes?
   *mozhna gdye**ni**bud'*   Можно где-нибудь
   *pasti**rat' adyezh**du?*   постирать одежду?
When will there be hot water?
   *kag**da bu**dyet*   Когда будет
   *gar**ya**chaya **va**da?*   горячая вода?

66 Checking Out

Can I leave my valuables in your safe?
mozhna astavit' svai tsenasti u vas f syeyfye?
Можно оставить свои ценности у вас в сейфе?

Can I please have ...?	*daytye, pazhalsta, ...*	Дайте, пожалуйста, ...
the bill	*shot*	счёт
the (spare) key	*(zapasnoy) klyuch*	(запасной) ключ
my passport	*moy pas*part	мой паспорт

Checking Out

I'm checking out ...	*ya uyezhayu ...*	Я уезжаю ...
now	*syeychas*	сейчас
midday	*f poldyen'*	в полдень
tomorrow	*zaftra*	завтра

Can you please call me a taxi?
vizavitye, pazhalsta, taksi
Вызовите, пожалуйста, такси.

Requests & Complaints

BELL (for service)	ЗВОНОК

Excuse me, something's the matter.
izvinitye, pazhalsta, shto-ta nye f paryatkye

Извините, пожалуйста, что-то не в порядке.

I have a request.
u myenya yest' proz'ba

У меня есть просьба.

I can't open/close the (door/window).
ya nye magu atkrivat'/ zakrivat' (dvyer'/akno)

Я не могу открывать/ закрывать (дверь/окно).

The toilet won't flush.
slivnoy bachok isportilsa

Сливной бачок испортился.

It's too (hot/cold/noisy).
slishkam (zharka/ kholadna/shumna)

Слишком (жарко/ холодно/шумно).

68 Some Useful Words

It smells.
   plokha pakhnyet

Плохо пахнет.

There are insects/mice.
   yest' nasyekomiye/
   – mishi

Есть насекомые/
мыши.

The ... doesn't work.
   ... nye rabotayet

... не работает.

Do you have (a) ...?
   u vas yest' ...?

У вас есть ...?

Some Useful Words

air-conditioning	*kanditsianyer*	кондиционер
basin	*tas*	таз
blanket	*adyeyala*	одеяло
cot	*dyetskaya kravatka*	детская кроватка
cupboard	*shkaf*	шкаф
curtain	*zanavyeska*	занавеска
dirty	*gryazniy*	грязный
electricity	*elyektrichyestva*	электричество

excluded	*isklyuchyeno*	исключено
heating	*ataplyeniye*	отопление
hot water	*garyachaya vada*	горячая вода
included	*fklyuchyeno*	включено
lift (elevator)	*lift*	лифт
light	*svyet*	свет
lock	*zamok*	замок
mattress	*matrats*	матрац
pillow	*padushka*	подушка
pillowcase	*navalachka*	наволочка
plug	*propka*	пробка
sheet	*prastinya*	простыня
shower	*dushem*	душ
soap	*mila*	мыло
tap (faucet)	*kran*	кран
TV	*tyelyevizar*	телевизор
toilet	*Stualyet om*	туалет
toilet paper	*tualyetnaya bumaga*	туалетная бумага

svanoy ubath

| towel | *palatyentse* | полотенце |
| window | *akno* | окно |

Laundry

Is there a laundry nearby?
gdye zdyes' Где здесь
prachechnaya? прачечная?

Can you please ... this?
pazhalsta, vi nye Пожалуйста,
mozhetye ... eta? вы не можете ... это?

Where can I ... this?	*gdye mozhna ... eta?*	Где можно ... это?
clean	*pachistit'*	почистить
iron	*vigladit'*	выгладить
mend	*pachinit'*	починить
wash	*pastirat'*	постирать

I need it ...	*nuzhna ...*	Нужно ...
today	*syevodnya*	сегодня
tomorrow	*zaftra*	завтра
as soon as possible	*kak mozhna skaryeye*	как можно скорее

This isn't mine.
eta nye mayo Это не моё.

Around Town

Addresses

Russian addresses are written the reverse way round to the way English-speakers are accustomed. The city and postcode come first, followed by the street, then the number, then the person's name:

г.Иркутск 664000
ул. Некрасова
д.33, корп.2, кв.15
ИВАНОВУ И.И.

In the first line, the letter г. stands for the Russian word for 'city'. Looking up the alphabet you'll be able to figure out what the next word is: Irkutsk.

The next line starts with ул. which is short for 'street', улица, *ulitsa*. Other possible words used in street names include:

boulevard	*bul'var*	бул. (бульвар)
lane	*pyeryeulak*	пер. (переулок)
square	*ploshat'*	пл. (площадь)
avenue	*praspyekt*	пр. (проспект)

The third line looks confusing, but it's not really! The letter д. stands for *dom* ДОМ which dictionaries normally tell you means 'house', but in fact usually refers to either an apartment block or

71

a whole housing complex. The word корп. – *korpus*, корпус, means one building within a complex. Then кв. – *kvartira*, квартира, is the actual apartment.

You may have difficulties finding addresses; often streets are not named, and maps can be hard to get. You can ask for information at a *spravachnaye byuro*, СПРАВОЧНОЕ БЮРО. It might be helpful to ask which metro station a certain street is near, and once you get off the metro ask passers-by for directions (See the Getting Around chapter, page 59). Or catch a taxi!

At the Post Office

POST OFFICE	*pochta*	ПОЧТА
MAIN POST OFFICE	*glavpachtamt*	ГЛАВПОЧТАМТ
BOOK POST	*bandyeroli*	БАНДЕРОЛИ

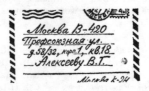

Note that you can only send parcels overseas from main post-offices. Sending books is easy – just take them unwrapped to the book post counter, and they will wrap them and send them for you.

However, all other things you have to wrap yourself and you will need to fill out customs forms – make sure you know the weight and value of each item. Mail to and from overseas can be very slow.

Please give me ...	*daytye, pazhalsta,* ...	Дайте, пожалуйста, ...
an airmail letter	*aviapis'mo*	авиаписьмо
a stamp (for this)	*marku*	марку
	(dlya etava)	(для этого)
a postcard	*atkritku*	открытку

I'd like to send this/these ...	*ya khachu paslat' eta* ...	Я хочу послать это ...
by airmail	*aviapochtay*	авиапочтой
express	*snarochnim*	с нарочным
by registered mail	*zakaznim*	заказным

I'd like to send a telegram.
ya khachu paslat' tyelyegramu   Я хочу послать телеграмму

How much will that be?
skol'ka stoit?   Сколько стоит?

I'm expecting ...	*ya zhdu* ...	Я жду ...
a letter	*pis'mo*	письмо
a parcel	*pasilku*	посылку

Here is my passport.
vot moy paspart   Вот мой паспорт.

Telephone

Local and international calls are relatively cheap. You can book international calls at your hotel, but it is quite straightforward to go to a telegraph office, *tyelyegraf,* ТЕЛЕГРАФ, with the number and place written down; they will ring the number for you and call you to a booth.

I'd like to book a call to ...
(for ... minutes).

ya khachu zakazat'	Я хочу заказать
tyelyefoniy razgavor	телефонный разговор
s ... (na ... minut)	с ... (на ... минут).

How much will it cost?

skol'ka eta	Сколько это
budyet stoit'?	будет стоить?

We were cut off.

nas razyedinili	Нас разъединили.

I got the wrong number.

vi myenya sayedinili	Вы меня соединили
nyepravil'na	неправильно.

At the Bank

CURRENCY EXCHANGE	ОБМЕН ВАЛЮТЫ
BANK	БАНК

The era of separate rouble and hard currency shops is coming to an end, but many private businesses prefer you to pay in hard currency. People you meet may offer to exchange money at good rates, but you can easily be shortchanged, and you must have official receipts to change roubles back into hard currency.

AROUND TOWN

Where can I change money?
  *gdye **mozhna** abmye**nyat'** dyeng'i?* Где можно обменять деньги?

I'd like to change ... *ya kha**chu** abmye**nyat'** ...* Я хочу обменять ...
  this into roubles *eta na rubli* это на рубли
  a travellers' cheque *da**rozh**niy chyek* дорожный чек
  $100 *(sto) **do**larav* (сто) долларов
  £100 *(sto) **fun**tav* (сто) фунто 100
  deutschmarks *(sto) **ma**rak* (сто) марок

What is the exchange rate?
  *ka**koy** kurs?* Какой курс?
What is your commission?
  *skol'ka vi byer**yo**tye za ab**myen**?* Сколько вы берёте за обмен?
Please write it down.
  *zapi**shi**tye eta, pa**zhal**sta* Запишите это, пожалуйста.
Do you accept this credit card/ foreign currency?
  *vi prini**ma**yetye etu krye**dit**nuyu kar**tach**ku/ val**yu**tu?* Вы принимаете эту кредитную карточку/ валюту?

Can I have money transferred
to here?

mozhna paluchit'
zdyes' dyen'gi
pa pyeryevodu?

Можно получить
здесь деньги
по переводу?

How long will it take?

skol'ka nuzhna
vryemyeni?

Сколько нужно
времени?

Have you received my money
yet?

vi paluchili mai
dyen'gi?

Вы получили мои
деньги?

Sightseeing

I'd like to see (a/the) ...	*ya khachu ... pasmatryet'*	Я хочу посмотреть ...
cemetery	*kladbishye*	кладбище
church	*tserkaf'*	церковь
(Tretyakov) Gallery	*(tryet'yakofskuyu) galyeryeyu*	(Третьковскую) Галерею
Hermitage	*ermitash*	Эрмитаж
Kremlin	*kreml'*	Кремль
Lenin's Mausoleum	*mavzalyey lyenina*	Мавзолей Ленина

memorial	*pamyatnik*	памятник
mosque	*myechyet'*	мечеть
museum	*muzyey* (moon)	музей
palace	*dvaryets*	дворец
Red Square	*krasnuyu ploshat'*	Красную площадь
synagogue	*sinagogu*	синагогу
university	*univyersityet*	университет

What do you recommend seeing?

shto vi savyetuyetye pasmatryet'?   Что вы советуете посмотреть?

I'm interested in ...	*ya intyeryesuyus'*	Я интересуюсь
architecture	*arkhityekturay*	архитектурой
art	*iskustvam*	искусством
churches	*tserkvami*	церквами
handicrafts	*ryemyoslami*	ремёслами
history	*istoriyey*	историей
icons	*ikonami*	иконами
literature	*lityeraturay*	литературой
sculpture	*skul'pturay*	скульптурой

Is there a discount for students/children?

yest' skitka dlya studyentav/dyetyey?   Есть скидка для студентов/детей?

AROUND TOWN

Do you have ... ?	u vas yest' ...?	У вас есть ...?
a catalogue (in English)	katalok (na angliyskam yazikye)	каталог (на английском языке)
postcards	atkritki	открытки
slides	slaydi	слайды
souvenirs	suvyeniri	сувениры

Some Useful Words

ancient	dryevniy	древний
archaeological	arkhyealagicheskiy	археологический
market	rinak	рынок
monument	pamyatnik	памятник
old city	dryevniy gorat	древний город
ruins	razvalini	развалины

NO CAMERAS!	fotografiravat' vaspryeshayetsa!	ФОТОГРАФИРОВАТЬ ВОСПРЕЩАЕТСЯ!

Signs

A big part of culture shock is when things look similar to what you're used to – as in any big city – but all the writing is in another alphabet! You'll find more specific signs in other sections (like names of shops under 'Shopping') but here is a list of common signs you'll find everywhere.

CASHIER	*kassa*	КАССА
CAUTION	*astarozhna*	ОСТОРОЖНО
CAUTION	*byeryegis'*	БЕРЕГИСЬ
CLOSED	*zakrita*	ЗАКРЫТО
ENTRANCE	*fkhod*	ВХОД
ENTRY	*fkhod*	ВХОД
PROHIBITED	*vaspryeshyon*	ВОСПРЕЩЕН
EXIT	*vikhad*	ВЫХОД
GENTS	*mushskoy*	М/МУЖСКОЙ
	tualyet	ТУАЛЕТ
INFORMATION	*sprafki*	СПРАВКИ
INFORMATION	*spravachnaye*	СПРАВОЧНОЕ
DESK	*byuro*	БЮРО
INTOURIST	*inturist*	ИНТУРИСТ
LADIES	*zhenskiy tualyet*	Ж/ЖЕНСКИЙ
		ТУАЛЕТ
LIFT (ELEVATOR)	*lift*	ЛИФТ
LOST PROPERTY	*byuro nakhodak*	БЮРО
OFFICE		НАХОДОК
METRO/	*myetro*	М/МЕТРО
UNDERGROUND		
NO ENTRY	*fkhoda nyet*	ВХОДА НЕТ
NO EXIT	*vikhada nyet*	ВЫХОДА НЕТ
NO SEATS (SOLD OUT)	*myest nyet*	МЕСТ НЕТ
NO SMOKING	*nye kurit'*	НЕ КУРИТЬ
OUT OF ORDER	*nye rabotayet*	НЕ РАБОТАЕТ

PROHIBITED	zapryeshayetsa	ЗАПРЕЩАЕТСЯ
PULL	syebye/tyanitye	К СЕБЕ/ ТЯНИТЕ
PUSH	at syebya/ talkaytye	ОТ СЕБЯ/ ТОЛКАЙТЕ
REFRESHMENTS	bufyet	БУФЕТ
RESERVED/ ENGAGED	zanyata	ЗАНЯТО
SALE	raspradazha	РАСПРОДАЖА
TAXI	taksi	Т/ТАКСИ
TELEPHONE	tyelyefon	ТЕЛЕФОН
TOILETS	tualyet	ТУАЛЕТ
TRAFFIC POLICE		ГАИ (abbreviation)
UNDER REPAIR	ryemont	РЕМОНТ
VACANT	svabodna	СВОБОДНО
WAY TO ...	pyeryekhod v/na ...	ПЕРЕХОД В/НА

Entertainment

Soviet entertainment had a reputation of being dull, but now there is a kind of cultural catharsis, with an extremely lively theatre, cinema and art scene. Newly opened nightspots offer all types of entertainment. Some new restaurants have an intimate atmosphere, but generally Russians go to restaurants in groups, where a whole evening of food, drink and dancing is provided.

Prostitution, strip shows and pornography are booming, not least due to cashed-up Western men taking advantage of Russian hardship.

CINEMA	Knho *(handwritten)*	КИНО
RESTAURANT	bahĩ *(handwritten)*	РЕСТОРАН
BAR		БАР
DISCO		ДИСКОТЕКА

AROUND TOWN

I want to go ...	*ya khachu payti ...*	Я хочу пойти ...
to a bar	*v bar*	в бар
to the cinema	*f kino*	в кино
to a concert	*na kantsert*	на концерт
dancing	*patantsevat'*	потанцевать
to a disco	*na diskatyeku*	на дискотеку
to a nightclub	*v nachnoy klub*	в ночной клуб
to see a show	*pasmatryet' spyektakl'*	посмотреть спектакль
to a skating rink	*na katok*	на каток
to the theatre	*f tyeatr*	в театр
for a walk	*pagulyat'*	погулять
to the zoo	*zaapark*	в зоопарк

Where is the ticket office?
gdye kassa? shop *(handwritten)* Где касса?

How much is a ticket?
skol'ka stoit bilyet? Сколько стоит билет?

What's on?
shto idyot? Что идёт?

One ticket/Two tickets please.
adin bilyet/dva bilyeta, pazhalsta Один билет/два билета, пожалуйста.

In the Country

Weather

It's ...

(too) cold	*(slishkam) kholadna*	(Слишком) холодно
cool	*prakhladna*	Прохладно.
hot	*zharka*	Жарко.
humid	*dushna*	Душно.
raining	*idyot dozhd'*	Идёт дождь.
snowing	*idyot snyeg*	Идёт снег.
warm	*tyeplo*	Тепло.
windy	*vyetryena*	Ветрено.

Some Useful Phrases

What's the weather like today?

kakaya syevodnya pagoda?

Какая сегодня погода?

Will it be cold/warm?
**budyet kholadna/
tyeplo?**

Будет холодно/
тепло?

Will it rain?
budyet dozht'?

Будет дождь?

Will it snow?
budyet snyek?

Будет снег?

Some Useful Words

ice	*lyot*	лёд
slippery	*skol'skiy*	скользкий
slush	*slyakat'*	слякоть
snow	*snyek*	снег

Seasons

spring	*vyesna*	весна
summer	*lyeta*	лето
autumn	*osyen'*	осень
winter	*zima*	зима

IN THE COUNTRY

Sights

I'd (f) like to see ...	ya ochyen' khatyela bi pasmatryet'	Я очень хотела бы посмотреть ...
I'd (m) like to see ...	ya ochyen' khatyel bi pasmatryet'	Я очень хотел бы посмотреть ...
We'd really like to see ...	mi ochyen' khatyeli bi pasmatryet'	Мы очень хотели бы посмотреть ...
a beach	plyash	пляж
a collective farm	kalkhos	колхоз
a factory	fabriku	фабрику
a forest	lyes	лес
the harbour	gavan'	гавань
the lake	ozyera	озеро
mountains	gori	горы
the river	ryeku	реку
the sea	morye	море

How long will it take to get there?

| skol'ka nuzhna vryemyeni papast' tuda? | Сколько нужно времени попасть туда? |

Can we walk?

| mozhna itti pyeshkom? | Можно идти пешком? |

Animals, Birds & Insects

Are there ... around here?	fstryechayesh' zdyes' ...?	Встречаешь здесь ...?
Do you have ...?	u vas nyet ...?	У вас нет ...?
bears	myedvyedyei	медведей
birds	ptits	птиц
cats	koshek	кошек

chickens	*kur*	кур
cows	*karof*	коров
dogs	*sabak*	собак
fish	*rip*	рыб
flies	*mukh*	мух
horses	*lashadyey*	лошадей
mosquitoes	*maskitaf*	москитов
pigs	*svinyey*	свиней
rats	*kris*	крыс
sheep	*avyets*	овец
spiders	*paukof*	пауков
wild animals	*zvyeryeh*	зверей
wolves	*valkof*	волков

Camping

Where is a/the camping ground?
gdye kemping? — Где кемпинг?

Can we put up a tent here?
mozhna pastavit' palatku zdyes'? — Можно поставить палатку здесь?

Where is the administration?
gdye administratsiya? — Где администрация?

Can we hire a boat/a tent?
mozhna vzyat' naprakat' lotku/palatku? — Можно взять напрокат лодку/палатку?

Some Useful Words

camping ground	*kemping*	кемпинг

farm	*fyerma*	ферма
field	*polye*	поле
food	*yeda*	еда
matches	*spichki*	спички
saucepan	*kastryulya*	кастрюля
shower	*dush*	душ
tent	*palatka*	палатка
toilet	*tualyet*	туалет
tree	*dyeryeva*	дерево
(drinking) water	*(pit'yevaya) vada*	питьевая вода

IN THE COUNTRY

Food

Russians have a different tradition of eating out – they tend to see it as a whole evening's entertainment, with multiple courses, music and dancing. Service can be slow but this is partly because there is no rush to finish. Western restaurants can seem very restrained in comparison.

Russians toast before each round (usually then downing vodka followed by a bite of something). 'To your health!' is *za vashe zdarov'ye!*, За ваше здоровье! It is also polite to say before eating 'Bon appetit!', *priyatnava apyetita!*, Притного апе-тита!

Restaurants

It is generally difficult to get into a decent restaurant without booking, but it is also difficult to book, especially by telephone. The best strategy seems to be going to the restaurant the day before or that morning, and speaking personally to the manager, *administratar*, администратор.

Where can I get a quick
snack?
>   *gdye mozhna*
>   *bistra pyeryekusit'?*

Где можно быстро
перекусить?

Is there a good restaurant
around here?
>   *yest' zdyes' kharoshiy*
>   *ryestaran?*

Есть здесь хороший
ресторан?

nam nushen stoilic *nacluoye=*
We need *table for 2 person*
nepadwoinik

SOK = juice
soak

Kvas = beverage from Rye

Where is a ...?
gdye yest' ...?　　　　Где есть ...?

bar
　bar　　　　БАР
cafe (generally you have
to order a meal)
　kafeh　　　　КАФЕ
cafeteria (very basic, no
alcohol)
　stalovaya　　　　СТОЛОВАЯ
coffee shop
　kafeh-kandityerskaya　　　　КАФЕ-
　　　　　　　　КОНДИТЕРСКАЯ
ice-cream cafe
　kafeh-marozhenaye　　　　КАФЕ-МОРОЖЕНОЕ
restaurant (most up-
market)
　ryestaran　　　　РЕСТОРАН
snack bar
　bufyet/　　　　БУФЕТ/
　zakusachnaya　　　　ЗАКУСОЧНАЯ

zakuski - appetizer = cold plates salad

Napitki = beverage
morse = cranberry

(handwritten annotations:)
prinisitya bringme.

beer - pivo (peera)

butilkoo = bottle

| BOOKED OUT | myest nyet | МЕСТ НЕТ |
| RESERVED | stol zakazan | СТОЛ |

My surname is (Simmons).
maya familiya – (simans)
Моя фамилия – (Симмонс).

I'm by myself.
ya adna/adin
Я одна (f)/один (m).

I need a table	*mnye nuzhen*	Мне нужен
for ... people.	*stolik na ...*	столик на ...
two	*dvaikh*	двоих
three	*traikh*	троих

breakfast	*zaftrak*	завтрак
lunch	*abyet*	обед
dinner (evening meal)	*uzhin*	ужин

FOOD

Tonight at (nine o'clock).
syevodnya vyecheram v (dyevyat' chyasof)
Сегодня вечером в девять часов.

I have booked.
ya uzhe zakazala/ zakazal stolik
Я уже заказала (f)/ заказал (m) столик.

Should we wait?
nam padazhdat'?
Нам подождать?

Ordering & Paying

Can I have a menu please?
*daytye, pazhalsta,
myenyu*

Дайте, пожалуйста,
меню.

Do you have a fixed menu?
*u vas komplyeksniy
abyet?*

У вас комплексный
обед?

How much is it/this?
skol'ka eta stoit?

Сколько это стоит?

Is (this) available?
(eta) yest'?

(Это) есть?

What is this?
shto eta?

Что это?

~~I'd like~~ I will take
ya vaz'mu ...

Я возьму ...

We'd like ...
mi vaz'myom ...

Мы возьмём ...

I'd like
ya hotela bi

FOOD

yshø adnö =else, add

Please bring ...	*prinyesitye, ...*	Принесите,
	pazhalsta,	пожалуйста, ...
an ashtray	*pyepyel'nitsu*	пепельницу
another bottle	*yesho adnu*	ещё одну
	butilku	бутылку
a fork	*vilku*	вилку
a (wine) glass	*ryumku*	рюмку
a glass of water	*stakan vodi*	стакан воды
a knife	*nosh*	нож
a napkin	*salfyetku*	салфетку
a spoon	*loshku*	ложку

Delicious! *ochyen' fkusna* Очень вкусно!

This dish is cold/inedible.
blyuda khalodnaye/
nyesyedobnaye Блюдо холодное/
несъедобное.
We've been waiting ages.
mi uzhe davno zhdyom Мы уже давно ждём.
Nothing else, thank you.
spasiba, bol'she
nichyevo Спасибо, больше
ничего.

Could we have the bill please?
daytye, pazhalsta, shot Дайте, пожалуйста,
счёт.

FOOD

Do you take credit cards/
foreign currency?
*vi prinimayetye
kryeditniye kartachki/
inastranuyu valyutu?*

Вы принимаете
кредитные карточки/
иностранную валюту?

Hors d'Oeuvres

caviar (red/black)	*ikra (krasnaya/ chyornaya)*	икра (красная/ чёрная)
diced vegetable salad	*vinyegryet*	винегрет
eggs	*yaytsa*	яйца
pickled	*marinovaniye*	маринованные
with onions	*slukam*	с луком
with sour cream	*sa smyetanay/ f smyetanye*	со сметаной/ в сметане
in vinegar	*suksusam*	с уксусом
gherkins	*agurtsi*	огурцы
herrings	*syelyotka*	селёдка
mushrooms	*gribi*	грибы
pate	*pashtyet*	паштет
salad	*salat*	салат
sprats (like sardines)	*shproti*	шпроты

FOOD

Soup

beetroot (normally with meat)	*borsh*	борщ
broth	*bul'yon*	бульон
cold	*akroshka*	окрошка
cucumber & kidney	*rassol'nik*	рассольник
fish	*ukha*	уха
thick cabbage	*shyi*	щи
heavily seasoned (normally with meat)	*salyanka*	солянка
creamed	*sup pyurey*	суп-пюре
with noodles	*vyermishelyeviy*	вермишелевый
with meat	*myasnoy*	мясной
with fish	*ribniy*	рыбный
with meatballs	*s frikadyel'kami*	с фрикадельками
with an egg	*syaytsom*	с яйцом

Meat & Fish Dishes

Good quality meat is not easy to get. However, Russian cooking tends to centre around meat.

beef	*gavyadina*	говядина
beef stroganoff	*byefstroganaf*	бефстроганов
chicken	*kuritsa*	курица
chicken Kiev	*katlyeti pakiyefski*	котлеты по-киевски
cod	*tryeska*	треска
fillet	*filyeh*	филе
fish	*riba*	рыба

FOOD

garlic sausage	*kupati*	купаты
goulash	*gulyash*	гуляш
kebab	*kyebap*	кебаб
lamb	*baranina*	баранина
meatballs	*bitochki*	биточки
pork	*svinina*	свинина
rabbit	*krolik*	кролик
rissoles	*katlyeti*	котлеты
salmon	*syomga*	сёмга
sausages	*sasiski*	сосиски
schnitzel	*shnitsel'*	шницель
shaslik	*shashlik*	шашлык
steak	*bifshteks*	бифштекс
stew	*ragu*	рагу
tongue	*yazik*	язык
veal	*tyelyatina*	телятина

Fruit & Vegetables
In Russia it takes some patience being a vegetarian, or even just wanting a change from meat. Vegetables are generally seen as an accompaniment, and apart from a limited number of staples such as potatoes, they can be hard to get, or just very expensive such as at the private markets. Preserved vegetables, such as pickles, are very common.

I'm a vegetarian.
  ya vyegyetarianka
  ya vyegyetarianyets

Я вегетарианка. (f)
Я вегетарианец. (m)

I'm on a strict diet.
  ya sablyudayu
  stroguyu diyetu

Я соблюдаю строгую
диету.

I don't eat meat.
  ya nye yem myasnova

Я не ем мясного.

I don't eat dairy products.
  ya nye yem malochnava

Я не ем молочного.

Fruit

apples	*yablaki*	яблоки
berries	*yagadi*	ягоды
grapes	*vinagrat*	виноград
lemon	*limon*	лимон
oranges	*apyel'sini*	апельсины
watermelon	*arbus*	арбуз

Vegetables

beetroot	*svyokla*	свёкла
broad beans	*babi*	бобы
cabbage	*kapusta*	капуста
carrots	*markof'*	морковь
chips	*zharyenaya kartoshka*	жареная картошка
gherkins	*agurtsi*	огурцы
mashed potato	*kartofyel'naye pyureh*	картофельное пюре
mushrooms	*gribi*	грибы

FOOD

onions	*luk*	лук
peas	*garokh*	горох
potatoes	*kartofyel'*	картофель
tomatoes	*pamidori*	помидоры

Dairy Products

butter	*masla*	масло
cheese	*sir*	сыр
cottage cheese	*tvarok*	творог
cream	*slifki*	сливки
ice cream	*marozhenaye*	мороженое
sour cream	*smyetana*	сметана

Other Food & Condiments

baked cheesecake (delicious!)	*zapyekanka tvorazhnaya*	запеканка творожная
biscuits	*pyechyen'ye*	печенье
bread (white/black)	*khlyeb (byeliy/chyorniy)*	хлеб (белый/чёрный)
cabbage rolls	*galuptsi*	голубцы
cake	*tort*	торт
cake (small)	*prozhnaye*	пирожное
cereal (groats)	*kasha*	каша
dumplings (large meat or cabbage)	*pirashki*	пирожки
dumplings (small boiled meat)	*pyel'myeni*	пельмени
egg	*yaytso*	яйцо
fried egg	*yaichnitsa*	яичница

FOOD

jam	*varyen'ye*	варенье
mustard	*garchitsa*	горчица
omelette	*amlyet*	омлет
open sandwich	*butyerbrot*	бутерброд
pancakes (small)	*blinchiki*	блинчики
pancakes (buckwheat)	*blini*	блины
pasta	*makaroni*	макароны
pepper	*pyeryets*	перец
pilaf (rice dish, usually with meat)	*plof*	плов
pudding (baked)	*zapyekanka*	запеканка
rice	*ris*	рис
rolls	*bulachki*	булочки
salt	*sol'*	соль
sauce	*sous*	соус
stewed fruit (sometimes a drink)	*kampot*	компот
sugar	*sakhar*	сахар
waffles	*vafli*	вафли

FOOD

Methods of Cooking

baked	*zapyechoniy*	запечённый
boiled	*varyoniy*	варёный
fried	*zharyeniy*	жареный

grilled	*zharyeniy na* **rash***pyerye*/'*gril*'	жареный на рашпере/ 'гриль'
stuffed	*farshirovaniy*	фар шированный
in tomato sauce	*f* **ta***matye*	в томате
with apples	*sya***bla***kami*	с яблоками
with cabbage	*ska***pus***tay*	с капустой
with meat	*smya***sam*	с мясом
with onions	*slu***kam*	с луком

Drinks

While supply of alcoholic beverages is erratic, wines and spirits, especially those imported from neighbouring countries such as Georgia, can be of good quality. 'Cognac' is becoming as popular as vodka. Fruit juices are even harder to get than alcohol – be prepared to get a vodka and orange that is a glass of vodka with a bit of orange juice poured on top.

Could you please chill this?

| *akhla***di***tye eta,* *pa***zhal***sta* | Охладите это, пожалуйста. |

coffee	*kofi*	кофе
fruit juice	*sok*	сок
hot chocolate	*kakao*	какао
kvass (cold drink made from bread and yeast)	*kvas*	квас
milk	*ma***la***ko*	молоко
milkshake	*ma***loch***niy* *kak***teyl'*	молочный коктейль

mineral water	*minyeral'naya vada*	минеральная вода
Russian lemonade	*limanat*	лимонад
soda water	*gazirovannaya vada*	газированная вода
starchy drink	*kisyel'*	кисель
water	*vada*	вода
tea	*chay*	чай
thick sour milk	*kyefir*	кефир
Turkish coffee	*kofi pavastochnamu*	кофе повосточному

Extras

with ice	*sal'dom*	со льдом
with lemon	*slimonam*	с лимоном
with milk	*smalakom*	с молоком
with sugar	*s sakharam*	с сахаром

Alcoholic Drinks

beer	*piva*	пиво
champagne	*shampanskaye*	шампанское
cocktail	*kakteyl'*	коктейль
cognac	*kan'yak*	коньяк
liqueur	*likyor*	ликёр
vodka	*votka*	водка
whisky	*viski*	виски
wine	*vino*	вино
white	*byelaye*	белое
red	*krasnaye*	красное
dry	*sukhoye*	сладкое
sweet	*slatkaye*	сладкое

FOOD

Shopping

Supply in shops may be quite unpredictable, and at times forms of rationing have been introduced even in Moscow and St Petersburg. However, staples such as bread and milk are generally available. Since *perestroika* private shops have sprung up, ranging from kiosks selling odd collections of luxury items to Western-style supermarkets. However, these are comparatively expensive and cater primarily to Westerners and Russia's *nouveaux riches*.

Some eccentricities of shopping in Russia include the fact that shop assistants still commonly use an abacus instead of a cash register; your change may be rounded off automatically; and making a purchase sometimes requires the three queue system, whereby you choose an item at the counter, collect a ticket for it, take the ticket to a cashier where you pay and have your ticket stamped, and then go back to the counter to collect the item.

Shops are normally open six days a week; the day they are closed is often not Sunday, but a weekday, which is written on the front. There may be an hour-long lunch break. Food shops generally stay open seven days a week until 9 pm.

BUSINESS HOURS FROM ... TO ...	*atkrita/magazin rabotayet s ... do ...*	ОТКРЫТО/ МАГАЗИН РАБОТАЕТ С ... ДО ...
CLOSED FOR LUNCH FROM ... TO	*pyeryeriv na abyed ...s ... do ...*	ПЕРЕРЫВ НА *ОБЕД* С ... ДО ...
CLOSED TUESDAYS	*vikhadnoy dyen': ftornik*	ВЫХОДНОЙ ДЕНЬ: ВТОРНИК
SELF-SERVICE	*sama- apsluzhivaniye*	САМООБ- СЛУЖИВАНИЕ

Finding Shops

An alternative in inverted commas indicates what might actually be written above the shop, eg 'Books' as opposed to Bookshop.

bookshop	*knizhniy magazin*	КНИЖНЫЙ МАГАЗИН 'КНИГИ'
bookshop (second-hand)	*bukhinist*	БУКИНИСТ
bottle shop	*viniy magazin*	ВИННЫЙ МАГ- АЗИН - 'ВИНО'
bread shop	*bulashnaya*	БУЛОЧНАЯ
camera shop	*fotamagazin*	ФОТОМАГАЗИН
clothing shop	*magazin adyezhdi*	МАГАЗИН ОДЕЖДЫ
children's clothing shop	*dyetskaya adyezhda*	ДЕТСКАЯ ОДЕЖДА
men's clothing shop	*mushskaya adyezhda*	МУЖСКАЯ ОДЕЖДА
women's clothing shop	*zhenskaya adyezhda*	ЖЕНСКАЯ ОДЕЖДА
department store	*univyermak*	УНИВЕРМАГ
dry-cleaner's	*khimchistka*	ХИМЧИСТКА
electrical shop	*elyektratavari*	ЭЛЕКТРОТОВАРЫ
florist	*tsvyetochniy magazin*	ЦВЕТОЧНЫЙ МАГАЗИН 'ЦВЕТЫ'
food shop	*gastranom*	ГАСТРОНОМ
haberdashery	*galantyeryeya*	ГАЛАНТЕРЕЯ
hairdresser	*parikmakher-skaya*	ПАРИКМАХЕР-СКАЯ

money = alinge

hardware	*khazyaystvyeniy magazin*	ХОЗЯЙСТВЕННЫЙ МАГАЗИН 'ИНСТРУМЕНТЫ'
jeweller's	*yuvyelirniy magazin*	ЮВЕЛИРНЫЙ МАГАЗИН
laundry	*prachyechnaya*	ПРАЧЕЧНАЯ
market	*rinak*	РЫНОК
second-hand (usually clothing) shop	*kamissioniy magazin*	КОМИССИОННЫЙ МАГАЗИН
newspaper stand	*gazyetniy kiosk*	ГАЗЕТНЫЙ КИОСК 'СОЮЗПЕЧАТЬ'
pharmacy	*aptyeka*	АПТЕКА
shoe shop	*magazin obuvi*	МАГАЗИН ОБУВИ 'ОБУВЬ'
shop(s)	*magazin(i)*	МАГАЗИН(Ы)
souvenir shop	*magazin suvyeniraf*	МАГАЗИН СУВЕНИРОВ 'СУВЕНИРЫ'
sports shop	*sport tavari*	СПОРТТОВАРЫ
State record label	*myelodiya*	'МЕЛОДИЯ'
stationer's	*kantselyarskiye tavari*	КАНЦЕЛЯРСКИЕ ТОВАРЫ
supermarket	*univyersam*	УНИВЕРСАМ
tobacconist	*tabachniy magazin*	ТАБАЧНЫЙ МАГАЗИН 'ТАБАК'
toy shop	*magazin igrushek*	МАГАЗИН ИГРУШЕК

Making a Purchase.

Service has improved since Soviet times, but still be prepared for surliness and fights between customers and staff!

I'd like to buy ...	*ya khachu kupit'* ...	Я хочу купить ...
Could you	*pakazhitye,*	Покажите,
please show me ...	*pazhalsta,* ...	пожалуйста, ...
one of those	**vot tak***oy*	вот такой
that	*eta*	это
half a kg	*polkilo*	полкило

I'm just looking.
    ya tol'ka smatryu   Я только смотрю.
How much does it cost?
    skol'ka eta stoit?   Сколько это стоит?
Do you have a different one?
    u vas yest' drugoy?   У вас есть другой?

I want something ...	*ya ishu koye-shto* ...	Я ищу кое-что ...
a bit cheaper	*padyeshyevlye*	подешевле
of better quality	**luch***sheva*	лучшего
	kachestva	качества

SHOPPING

a different colour	*drugova tsvyeta*	другого цвета
bigger	*pabol'she*	побольше
smaller	*pamyen'she*	поменьше

Does it have a guarantee?
   garantiya yest'?

Гарантия есть?

I'll take it.
   vaz'mu

Возьму.

That's all, thanks.
   spasiba, eta fsyo

Спасибо, это всё.

Thanks, but it's not quite what I'm after.
   spasiba, no eta nye safsyem to, shto ya khachu

Спасибо, но это не совсем то, что я хочу.

How much altogether?
   skol'ka fsyevo?

Сколько всего?

Do you take credit cards?
   vi prinimayetye kryeditniye kartachki/ inastranuyu valyutu?

Вы принимаете кредитные карточки/ иностранную валюту?

Can you please wrap it?
zavyernitye, pazhalsta

Заверните,
пожалуйста.

Do you have a bag?
u vas yest' pakyet?

У вас есть пакет?

Some Useful Words

adaptor (for this)	*pyeryekhodnuyu razyetku (dlya etava)*	переходную розетку (для этого)
amber	*yantar'*	янтарь
bag	*myeshok*	мешок
battery (for this)	*bataryeyku (dlya etava)*	батерейку (для этого)
bottle	*butilka*	бутылка
camera	*fotaparat*	фотоаппарат
candles	*svyechi*	свечи
coffee	*kofi*	кофе
handbag	*sumku*	сумку
map	*kartu*	карту
matches	*spichki*	спички
plug (for this)	*vilku (dlya etava)*	вилку (для этого)

SHOPPING

postcard	*atkritku*	открытку
(short-wave) radio	*(karatkavol-*	(коротковол-
	navniy)	новный)
	radiopriyomnik	радиоприёмник
receipt	*kvitantsiya*	квитанция
Russian peasant doll	*matryoshku*	матрёшку
slides	*slaydi*	слайды
souvenir	*suvyenir*	сувенир
thread	*nitachku*	ниточку
watch	*chasi*	часы
watch strap	*ryemyeshok*	ремешок
	dlya chasov	для часов

Film & Photography

I'd like ...	*mnye nada ...*	Мне надо ...
(for this camera).	*(dlya etava*	(для этого
	fotaparata)	фотоаппарата).
a battery	*bataryeyku*	батарейку
B&W film	*chyorna-byeluyu*	чёрно-белую
	plyonku	плёнку
colour film	*tsvyetnuyu*	цветную
	plyonku	плёнку
slide film	*plyonku dlya*	плёнкудля-
	slaydaf	слайдов
a video tape	*vidyeokasyetu*	видеокассету

Can you please develop (and
print) this?

pazhalsta, prayavitye   Пожалуйста, проявите
(i atpyechataytye) eta   (и отпечатайте) это.

When will they be ready?

kagda snimki budut gatovi?

Когда снимки будут готовы?

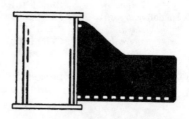

Clothing & Jewellery

I'd like to buy (a) ..	*ya khachu kupit'* ...	Я хочу купить ...
belt	*poyas*	пояс
blouse	*blusku*	блузку
dress	*plat'ye*	платье
earrings	*syer'gi*	серьги
gloves	*pyerchatki*	перчатки
handkerchief	*nasavoy platok*	носовой платок
hat	*shlyapu*	шляпу
jacket	*kurtku*	куртку
jeans	*dzhinsi*	джинсы
jumper	*dzhempyer*	джемпер
necklace	*azheryel'ye*	ожерелье
pyjamas	*pizhamu*	пижаму
raincoat	*dazhdyevik*	дождевик

SHOPPING

pantyhose - Colgotky

ring	*kal'tso*	кольцо
scarf	*sharf*	шарф
shirt	*rubashku*	рубашку
shoes	*tufli*	туфли
skirt	*yupku*	юбку
socks	*naski*	носки
stockings	*chulki*	чулки
suit	*kastyum*	костюм
swimsuit	*kupal'niy*	купальный
	kastyum	костюм
tie	*galstuk*	галстук
trousers	*bryuki*	брюки
T-shirt	*mayku*	майку

It's (not) for me.
  eta (nye) dlya myenya

Это (не) для меня.

I don't know Russian sizes.
  ya nye znayu ruskikh razmyeraf

Я не знаю русских размеров.

Can you please measure me?
  pazhalsta, snimitye smyenya myerku

Пожалуйста, снимите с меня мерку.

Can I try it on?
  mozhna primyerit'?

Можно примерить?

Where's the changing room?
  gdye primyerachnaya?

Где примерочная?

Do you have a mirror?
  u vas yest' zyerkala?

У вас есть зеркало?

That's fine, I'll take it.
  eta kak ras, ya eta vaz'mu

Это как раз, я это возьму.

Do you have anything ...?	u vas yest' **shto-nibut'**...?	У вас есть что-нибудь ...?
a bit bigger (especially here)	**pabol'she** (*asobyenna zdyes'*)	побольше (особенно здесь)
a bit smaller	**pamyen'she**	поменьше
a bit longer	**padlinyeye**	подлиннее
a bit shorter	**pakarochye**	покороче
a bit warmer	**patyeplyeye**	потеплее
a different colour	**drugova tsvyeta**	другого цвета
with spots	**v garoshek**	в горошек
with stripes	**f palosku**	в полоску

made out of ...	*iz* ...	из ...
amber	*yantarya*	янтаря
cotton	**bumazhnay tkani**	бумажной ткани
fake fur	*iskustvennava myekha*	искусственного меха
gold	**zolata**	золота
leather	**kozhi**	кожи
silver	**syeryebra**	серебра
wool	**shersti**	шерсти

Colours

English	Transliteration	Russian
black	*chyorniy*	чёрный
blue (light)	*galuboy*	голубой
blue (dark)	*siniy*	синий
brown	*karichnyeviy*	коричневый
dark	*tyomna* (niy)	тёмно
green	*zyelyoniy*	зелёный
light	*svyetla*	светло
orange	*aranzheviy*	оранжевый
pink	*rozaviy*	розовый
purple	*fialyetaviy*	фиолетовый
red	*krasniy*	красный
white	*byeliy*	белый
yellow	*zholtiy*	жёлтый

Hairdresser

Can I make an appointment
for (Tuesday)?
   *mozhna zapisat'sa
   na (ftornik)?*
(Just) a haircut, please.
   *(tol'ka) pastrigitye,
   pazhalsta*
Just a trim/neaten it up.
   *pazhalsta,
   padravnyaytye
   mnye volasi*

Можно записаться
на (вторник)?

(Только) постригите,
пожалуйста.

Пожалуйста,
подравняйте мне
волосы.

Books & Stationery

Newspapers and magazines are generally sold at newspaper
stands along the footpath.

Do you have ...?	*u vas yest' ...?*	У вас есть ...?
a book about Russian art	*kniga a ruskam iskustvye*	книга о русском искусстве
children's books	*dyetskiye knigi*	детские книги
a textbook to learn Russian	*uchyebnik pa ruskamu yaziku*	учебник по русскому языку
a nice book with photographs (ofthis city/ of this region)	*kharoshiy fotoal'bom (etava gorada/ etava rayona)*	хороший фотоальбом (этого горада/ этого района)
a Russian cookbook	*kniga a ruskay kukhnye*	книга о русской кухне

SHOPPING

a guidebook	*putyevadityel'*	путеводитель
a map of the town	*plan gorada*	план города
a road map	*karta darok*	карта дорог
a book about Russia	*kniga a rassii*	книга о России
posters	*plakati*	плакаты
(books) in English	*(knigi) na angliyskam y azikye*	(книги) на английском зыке
a (pocket) dictionary	*(karmaniy) slavar'*	(карманный) словарь
(foreign) newspapers/ magazines	*(inastraniye) gazyeti/ zhurnali*	(иностранные) газеты/ журналы

Moscow News	*maskofskiye novasti*	Московские новости

(a very popular weekly paper, also published in English)

I need ...	*mnye **nada** ...*	Мне надо ...
airmail paper	*bumagu dlya aviapochti*	бумагу для авиапочты
a biro	***ruchku***	ручку
envelopes	*kanvyerti*	конверты
a notebook	***blaknot***	блокнот
a pencil	*karandash*	карандаш
sellotape	***lyentu***	ленту
string	*byechyofku*	бечёвку
wrapping paper	*abyortachnuyu bumagu*	обёрточную бумагу
writing paper	*pachtovuyu*	почтовую

Health

You can always receive quick but basic medical attention by contacting the desk or Intourist in your hotel. Government medical care is free, but medication will cost some money and is sometimes very hard to get. Tampons and condoms are rare. If possible, avoid tap water; mineral water is sold everywhere.

Could you please call a doctor?

vizavitye vracha, pazhalsta?

Вызовите врача, пожалуйста.

Where is a/the ...?	*gdye ...?*	Где ...?
chemist (pharmacy)	*aptyeka*	аптека
dentist	*zubnoy vrach*	зубной врач
doctor	*vrach*	врач
hospital	*bal'nitsa*	больница

БОЛЬНИЦА

Complaints

I have ...	*u tyenya ...*	У меня...
She has ...	*u nyeyo ...*	У неё ...
He has...	*u nyevo ...*	У него ...

115

an allergy	*allyergiya*	аллергия
asthma	*astma*	астма
backache	*bol' f spinye*	боль в спине
a burn	*azhok*	ожог
a chill	*prastuda*	простуда
a cold	*nasmark*	насморк
constipation	*zapor*	запор
a cough	*kashyel'*	кашель
cramps	*spazmi*	спазмы
diabetes	*diabyet*	диабет
diarrhoea	*panos*	понос
an earache	*balit ukha*	болит ухо
epilepsy	*epilyepsiya*	эпилепсия
a fever	*tyempyeratura*	температура
food poisoning	*atravlyeniye*	отравление
frost bite	*atmarazheniye*	отморожение
glandular fever	*zhelyezistaya likharatka*	железистая лихорадка
a headache	*balit galava*	болит голова
hepatitis	*gyepatit*	гепатит
high blood pressure	*gipyertaniya*	гипертония
indigestion	*nyesvaryeniye zhelutka*	несварение желудка
an infection	*infyektsiya*	инфекция
influenza	*grip*	грипп
insomnia	*byesonitsa*	бессонница
an itch	*zut*	зуд
lice	*fshi*	вши
low blood pressure	*panizhenaye davlyeniye*	пониженное давление

a pain here	*balit tut*	болит тут
a rash	*sip'*	сыпь
a sore throat	*balit gorla*	болит горло
a sprain	*rastyazheniye*	растяжение
a stomachache	*balit zheludak*	болит желудок
a temperature	*tyempyeratura*	температура
toothache	*balit zup*	болит зуб
venereal disease	*vyenyerichyeskaya balyezn'*	венерическая болезнь
worms	*glisti*	глисты

I feel nauseous.
  myenya tashnit Меня тошнит.

I keep vomiting.
  myenya rvyot Меня рвёт.

I feel dizzy.
  u myenya kruzhitsa galava У меня кружится голова.

It started when I ...	*nachalos', kagda ya ...*	Началось, когда ...
ate (fish)	*syela/syel (ribu)*	съела (f)/съел (m) (рыбу).
drank (water)	*vipila/vipil (vodu)*	выпила (f)/выпил (m) (воду).

I'm allergic to ...	*u myenya alyergiya k ...*	У меня аллергия к ...
antibiotics	*antibiotikam*	антибиотикам
penicilin	*pyenitsilinu*	пенициллину

I have been vaccinated.
  mnye zdyelali privifku

Мне сделали
прививку.

I have my own syringe.
  *u myenya svoy
  sopstveniy shprits*

У меня свой
собственный шприц.

What is the matter?
  shto samnoy?

Что со мной?

Is it serious?
  eta syer'yozna?

Это серьёзно?

Parts of the Body

arm	*ruka*	рука
back	*spina*	спина
blood	*krof'*	кровь
breast	*grud'*	грудь
chest	*grud'*	грудь
ear(s)	*ukha (ushi)*	ухо (уши)
eye	*glas (glaza)*	глаз (глаза)
finger	*palyets*	палец
foot	*naga*	нога

hand	*ruka*	рука
head	*galava*	голова
heart	*syertse*	сердце
knee	*kalyena*	колено
kidney(s)	*pochka (pochki)*	почка (почки)
leg	*naga*	нога
liver	*pyechyen'*	печень
mouth	*rot*	рот
nose	*nos*	нос
shoulder	*plyecho*	плечо
teeth	*zup*	зуб
throat	*gorla*	горло
tongue	*yazik*	язык

Pharmaceuticals

Do you have ...?	*u vas yest' ...?*	У вас есть ...?
aspirin	*aspirin*	аспирин
baby powder	*pudra dlya rye byonka*	пудра для ребёнка
Band-aids	*plastir'*	пластырь

a bandage	*bint*	бинт
something for a cold	*shtonibud' atnasmarka*	что-нибудь от насморка
comb	*gryebyonka*	гребёнка
condoms	*pryezyervativi*	презервативы
contraceptives	*prativaza-chatachniye sryetstva*	противоза-чаточные средства
cough mixture	*mikstura atkashlya*	микстура от кашля
deodorant	*dyezodorant*	дезодорант
disinfectant	*dyezinfitsi-ruyushyeye sryetstva*	дезинфици-рующее средство
hairbrush	*shyotka dlya volas*	щётка для волос
insect repellent	*sryetstva at nasyekomikh*	средство от насекомых
something for a headache	*shto-nibut' ad galovnay boli*	что-нибудь от головной боли
lozenges	*tablyetki dlya gorla*	таблетки для горла
moisturiser	*kryem dlya litsa*	крем для лица
nail clippers	*shyipchiki*	щипчики
nappies	*pyelyonki*	пелёнки
needle	*igolku*	иголку
razor (disposable razors)	*britvu (britvi dlya adnavo raza)*	бритву (бритвы для одного раза)
razor-blades	*lyezviya*	лезвия
sanitary napkins	*gigiyenichyeskiye salfyetki*	гигиенические салфетки

shampoo	*shampun'*	шампунь
shaving cream	*kryem dlya brit'ya*	крем для бритья
soap	*mila*	мыло
talcum powder	*tal'k*	тальк
tampons	*tamponi*	тампоны
tissues	*bumazhniye platki*	бумажные платки
toilet paper	*tualyetnuyu bumagu*	туалетную бумагу
toothbrush	*zubnuyu shyotku*	зубную щётку
toothpaste	*zubnuyu pastu*	зубную пасту

Can you fix these glasses?
vi mozhetye pachinit' mai achki?

Вы можете починить мои очки?

When will they be ready?
kagda ani budut gatovi?

Когда они будут готовы?

Please make up this prescription.
prigatof'tye, pazhalsta, etat ryetsept

Приготовьте, пожалуйста, этот рецепт.

When will it be ready?
kagda lyekarstva budyet gatova?

Когда лекарство будет готово?

How many times a day?
skol'ka raz v dyen'?

Сколько раз в день?

Some Useful Words

accident	*nyeshasniy sluchay*	несчастный случай
addiction	*narkamaniya*	наркомания
AIDS	*spit*	СПИД
antibiotics	*antibiotiki*	антибиотики
antiseptic	*antisyeptik*	антисептик
bite	*ukus*	укус
bleeding	*kravatyechyeniye*	кровотечение
blood pressure	*davlyeniye*	давление
blood test	*analis krovi*	анализ крови
injection	*inyektsiya*	инъекция
medication	*lyekarstva*	лекарство
menstruation	*myenstruatsiya*	менструация
(disposable) syringe	*shprits (dlya adnavo raza)*	шприц (для одного раза)
ointment	*mas'*	мазь
pregnant	*byeryemyenaya*	беременная
prescription	*ryetsept*	рецепт
pills	*pilyuli*	пилюли
vitamins	*vitamini*	витамины
wound	*rana*	рана

HEALTH

Times, Dates & Holidays

Remember the all-purpose expression with times, dates and numbers:

Can you please write that down?

zapishitye eta, pazhalsta

Запишите это, пожалуйста.

Telling the Time

Except for telling the time 'on the hour' (one o'clock, two o'clock, etc), the easiest and most precise way to tell the time in Russian is to say the hour, and then the minutes, as in English; eg 'eight forty-two'. You will also notice when reading timetables that Russians often use the twenty-four hour clock; therefore 'fourteen twenty' means 'twenty past two in the afternoon'.

What time is it?

katoriy chas?

Который час?

Could you please show me
your watch?
  pakazhitye, pazhalsta,   Покажите, пожалуйста,
  vashi chasi   ваши часы.

1 o'clock	*chas*	Час
2 o'clock	*dva chasa*	Два часа
3 o'clock	*tri chasa*	Три часа
4 o'clock	*chyetiri chasa*	Четыре часа
5 o'clock	*pyat' chasov*	Пять часов
6 o'clock	*shest' chasov*	Шесть часов
7 o'clock	*syem' chasov*	Семь часов
8 o'clock	*vosyem' chasov*	Восемь часов
9 o'clock	*dyevyat' chasov*	Девять часов
10 o'clock	*dyesyat' chasov*	Десять часов
11 o'clock	*adinatsat' chasov*	Одиннадцать часов
12 o'clock	*dvyenatsat' chasov*	Двенадцать часов

am	*utra*	утра
pm	*dnya* (in the afternoon)	дня
	vyechyera (in the evening)	вечера

You don't need to put in any word for 'it is' (a certain time):

It's 2.10 pm. (literally
'Fourteen ten')
  chyetirnatsat'   Четырнадцать
  dyesyat'   десять.

Note that if the minutes are under ten you need to insert the word for 'zero', *nol'*, НОЛЬ:

It's 2.08 pm (literally
'fourteen zero eight')
chyetirnatsat'   Четырнадцать
nol' vosyem'   ноль восемь.

in the ...		
morning	*utram*	утром
afternoon	*dnyom*	днём
evening	*vyechyeram*	вечером
night	*noch'yu*	ночью

at	*v*	в

When ...?	*kagda...?*	Когда ...?
does it open	*atkrivayetsa*	открывается
does it shut	*zakrivayetsa*	закрывается
does it start	*nachinayetsa*	начинается
does it finish	*kanchayetsa*	кончается

Days

On what day?
f kakoy dyen'?   В какой день?
On what days (is the bank
shut)?
f kakiye dni   В какие дни (банк
(bank zakrit)?   закрыт)?

TIMES, DATES & HOLIDAYS

On ...	v ...	в ...
Monday	*panyedyel'nik*	понедельник
Tuesday	*ftornik*	вторник
Wednesday	*sryedu*	среду
Thursday	*chyetvyerk*	четверг
Friday	*pyatnitsu*	пятницу
Saturday	*subotu*	субботу
Sunday	*vaskryesyen'e*	воскресенье

Months

January	*yanvar'*	январь
February	*fyevral'*	февраль
March	*mart*	март
April	*apryel'*	апрель
May	*may*	май
June	*iyun'*	июнь
July	*iyul'*	июль
August	*avgust*	август
September	*syentyabr'*	сентябрь
October	*aktyabr'*	октябрь
November	*nayabr'*	ноябрь
December	*dyekabr'*	декабрь

What is the date today?
   kakoye syevodnya   Какое сегодня
   chislo?   число?

On what date (are you
leaving)?
   kakova chisla   Какого числа (вы
   (vi uyezhayetye)?   уезжаете)?

When writing the date, Russians tend to put the month in Roman
numerals: 17 April 1994 will be 17/IV/94.

Present

today	*syevodnya*	сегодня
this ...		
year	*vetam gadu*	в этом году
month	*vetam myesyatsye*	в этом месяце
week	*na etoy nyedyelye*	на этой неделе

Past

yesterday	*fchyera*	вчера
the day before yesterday	*pazafchyera*	позавчера
last ...		
year	*f proshlam gadu*	в прошлом году
month	*f proshlam myesyatsye*	в прошлом месяце
week	*na proshloy nyedyelye*	на прошлой неделе

Future

tomorrow	*zaftra*	завтра
the day after tomorrow	*paslyezaftra*	послезавтра
next ...		
year	*v budushyem gadu*	в будущем году
month	*v budushyem myesyatsye*	в будущем месяце
week	*na budushyey nyedyelye*	на будущей неделе

Some Useful Words

(a year) ago	*(god) tamu nazat*	(год) тому назад
always	*fsyegda*	всегда
at the moment	*tyepyer'*	теперь
century	*vyek*	век
during	*vavryemya*	во время
early	*rana*	рано
every day	*kazhdiy dyen'*	каждый день

for (time you intend being somewhere)	*na*	на
for the time being	*paka*	пока
forever	*nafsyegda*	навсегда
just then (ie only minutes ago)	*tol'ka shto*	только что
late	*pozna*	поздно
later on	*patom*	потом
never	*nikagda*	никогда
not any more	*bol'she nyet*	больше нет
not yet	*yeshyo nyet*	ещё нет
now	*syeychas*	сейчас
since	*s*	с
sometimes	*inagda*	иногда
sundown	*zakat*	закат
sunrise	*rasvyet*	рассвет
soon	*skora*	скоро
still	*fsyo yeshyo*	всё ещё
straight away	*syeychas*	сейчас
used to	*ran'she*	раньше

National Holidays

A handy expression for any special occasion:

Happy holiday!
    spraznikam!   С праздником!

At present there are days off for the following occasions:

New Year's Day (1 January) People have elaborate parties on New Year's Eve, and at midnight everyone toasts champagne and wishes 'Happy New Year!', *'snovim godam!',* S novym godom! Greetings telegrams are more popular than cards. Children look forward to presents from Grandfather Frost, who is similar to Santa Claus.

Army Day (23 February) This day is significant for Russian men since most serve in the army. The day is also marked by demonstrations by conservatives who want a return to the days of the USSR.

International Women's Day (8 March) Also called 'Mothers' Day'. On this day men give flowers to women. Life is generally miserable for Russian women; as well as occupying the most menial jobs, women are also expected to do all the household chores, thus suffering most of the terrible frustrations we hear about like queues and lack of facilities.

Easter (March/April) Easter is a much more important occasion than Christmas. Believers tend to observe Lent strictly, and then, after a beautiful midnight Easter service, gather at each other's homes to celebrate.

ᛏᛏᛏᛏᛏᛏᛏᛏᛏᛏᛏ

Victory Day (9 May) This day commemorates the victory over the Nazis. Twenty million people in the former USSR were killed during the war, and it is still an important memory. Even if you are cynical about the Government's motives in reminding people, it could be very offensive to say so.

Anniversary of the Great October Socialist Revolution (7 November; 8 November is also a holiday) This is still celebrated despite the break-up of the USSR. It takes place in November, for before the Revolution, Russia used a different (Julian) calendar. The Tsar was actually overthrown earlier in 1917, and the Bolsheviks then seized power from the provisional government.

Numbers & Amounts

Numbers

How many?
*skol'**ka**?* Сколько?

1	*adin*	один
2	*dva*	два
3	*tri*	три
4	*chyetiri*	четыре
5	*pyat'*	пять
6	*shest'*	шесть
7	*syem'*	семь
8	*vosyem'*	восемь
9	*dyevyat'*	девять
10	*dyesyat'*	десять
11	*adinatsat'*	одиннадцать
12	*dvyenatsat'*	двенадцать
13	*trinatsat'*	тринадцать
14	*chyetirnatsat'*	четырнадцать
15	*pyatnatsat'*	пятнадцать
16	*shesnatsat'*	шестнадцать
17	*syemnatsat'*	семнадцать
18	*vasyemnatsat'*	восемнадцать
19	*dyevyatnatsat'*	девятнадцать
20	*dvatsat'*	двадцать
21	*dvatsat' adin*	двадцать один
30	*tritsat'*	тридцать

40	*sorak*	сорок
50	*pidyesyat'*	пятьдесят
60	*shest 'dyesyat'*	шестьдесять
70	*syem'dyesyat'*	семьдесят
80	*vosyem'dyesyat'*	восемьдесят
90	*dyevyanosta*	девяносто
100	*sto*	сто
134	*sto tritsat' pyat'*	стотридцать пять
200	*dvyesti*	двести
300	*trista*	триста
400	*chetiryesta*	четыреста
500	*pyat'sot*	пятьсот
600	*shest'sot*	шестьсот
700	*syem'sot*	семьсот
800	*vasyem'sot*	восемьсот
900	*dyevyat'sot*	девятьсот
1000	*tisyacha*	тысяча

one million
  milion миллион
two million
  dva miliona два миллиона
zero
  nol' ноль

If you're asking for a specific amount in a shop – such as 'ten, please' – Russians put a word that means something like 'items' after the numeral – 'ten items, please'. The word is *shtuki*, ШТУКИ, after 2 (in this context *dvye*, две), 3 and 4; and *shtuk*, ШТУК, after 5 and above.

Three, please.
  *tri **shtuki**, pazhalsta*

Три штуки,
  пожалуйста.

Eight, please.
  *vosyem' shtuk,
  pazhalsta*

Восемь штук,
  пожалуйста.

Fractions

$^1/_4$	*chyetvyert'*	четверть
$^1/_3$	*tryet'*	треть
$^1/_2$	*palavina*	половина
$^3/_4$	*tri chyetvyerti*	три четверти
$^2/_3$	*dvye tryeti*	две трети

Ordinal Numbers

1st	*pyerviy*	первый
2nd	*ftaroy*	второй
3rd	*tryetiy*	третий
4th	*chyetvyortiy*	четвёртый
5th	*pyatiy*	пятый
6th	*shestoy*	шестой
7th	*syed'moy*	седьмой
8th	*vas'moy*	восьмой
9th	*dyevyatiy*	девятый
10th	*dyesyatiy*	десятый
20th	*dvatsatiy*	двадцатый
21st	*dvatsat' pyerviy*	двадцать первый

Amounts

How much?/ How many?

skol'ka?		Сколько?
Could you	*daytye*	Дайте,
please	*pazhalsta,* ...	пожалуйста, ...
give me ...		
I need ...	*mnye na**da** ...*	Мне надо ...
a bottle	*butilku*	бутылку
half a kg	*polkilo*	полкило
100 grams	*sto gram*	сто грамм
a jar	*ban**ku***	банку
a kg	*lo*	кило
a packet	*pakyet*	пакет
a slice	*kusok*	кусок
a tin	*ban**ku***	банку

Some Useful Words

enough	*dastatachna*	достаточно
less	*myenshe*	меньше
(just) a little	*(tol'ka)*	(только)
	nyemnoshka	немножко
many, much, a lot	*mnoga*	много

NUMBERS

NUMBERS

too many, too much	*slishkam mnoga*	СЛИШКОМ МНОГО
more	*bol'she*	больше
some	*nyemnoga*	немного

Vocabulary

Essential words you will need are included within this book, in the specific chapters. Here are the key words you may need quick reference to, plus extra words that you may find useful as you get to know the language and the people of Russia.

A

able (to be able/can)	*magu*	могу
I can (not) ...	*ya (nye) magu ...*	Я (не) могу ...
Can I (take photos?)	*mozhna mnye (fatagrafiravat')?*	Можно мне (фотографировать)?
acupuncture	*akupunktura*	акупунктура
addict	*narkaman*	наркоман
all	*fsye*	все
all of us	*mi fsye*	мы все
alternative	*al'tyernativa*	альтернатива
amusement park	*atraktsioni*	аттракционы
annoyance	*dasada*	досада
armaments	*varuzheniye*	вооружение
army	*armiya*	армия
art	*iskustva*	искусство
atheist	*atyeist*	атеист
(It's) awful	*kashmar*	кошмар

VOCABULARY

B

| babysitter | *prikhadya-shaya nyanya* | приходящая няня |

137

ballet	*balyet*	балет
Baltic States (the)	*pribaltika*	Прибалтика
believe (v)	*vyerit'*	верить
believer	*vyeruyushaya*	верующая (f)
	vyeruyushiy	верующий (m)
better	*luchshe*	лучше
Bible	*bibliya*	Библия
birthday	*dyen' razhdyeniya*	день рождения
boring	*skuchniy*	скучный
botanical garden	*batanichyeskiy sat*	ботанический-сад

C

calculator	*mikro-kal'kulyatar*	микро-калькулятор
careful	*vnimatyel'niy*	внимательный
cassette	*kasyeta*	кассета
central	*tsentral'niy*	центральный
Central Asia	*sryednyaya aziya*	Средняя Азия
Cheers!	*za vashe zdarov'ye!*	За ваше здоровье!
chess	*shakhmati*	шахматы
child (for a)	*dlya ryebyonka*	для ребёнка
cigarette (Western style)	*sigaryeta*	сигарета
cigarette (Russian style)	*papirosa*	папироса
citizen	*grazhdanka*	гражданка (f)
	grazhdanin	гражданин (m)

communist	*kamunistka*	коммунистка (f)
	kamunist	коммунист (m)
compact disc	*kompakt disk*	компакт-диск
computer	*kamp'yutyer*	компьютер
concert	*kantsert*	концерт
Congratulations!	*pazdravlyayu!*	Поздравляю!
contact lens	*kantaktnaya linza*	контактна линза
contact lenses	*(kantaktniye linzi)*	(контактные линзы)
contraceptives	*prativaza-chatachniye sryedstva*	противоза-чаточные средства
cooperative	*kaapyerativ*	кооператив
country (nation)	*strana*	страна
country (in the)	*zagaradam*	за городом
coupon	*talon*	талон
crazy	*sumashetshiy*	сумасшедший
creche	*yasli*	ясли
credit card	*kryeditnaya kartachka*	кредитная карточка

D

democracy	*dyemakratiya*	демократия
dictionary	*slavar'*	словарь
dictionary (English-Russian)	*angla-ruskiy slavar'*	англо-русский словарь
dictionary (Russian-English)	*ruska-angliyskiy slavar'*	русско-английский словарь

disco	*diskatyeka*	дискотека
discrimination	*diskriminatsiya*	дискриминация
dream (n)	*son*	сон
drugs (illegal)	*narkotiki*	наркотики
drunk	*p'yaniy*	пьяный

E

economy	*khazyaystva*	хозяйство
emigrate (v)	*emigriravat'*	эмигрировать
the environment	*akruzhayushaya sryeda*	окружающая среда
exchange rate	*valyutniy kurs*	валютный курс
exhibition	*vistafka*	выставка

F

factory	*fabrika*	фабрика
fault (It's not my)	*ya nye vinavata*	Я не виновата. (f)
	ya nye vinavat	Я не виноват. (m)
film	*fil'm*	фильм
fragile	*khrupkiy*	хрупкий
funny	*smyeshnoy*	смешной

G

garden	*sat*	сад
glass of water	*stakan vadi*	стакан воды
glass of wine	*ryumka vina*	рюмка вина

VOCABULARY

glasses	*achki*	очки
government	*pravityel'stva*	правительство
guidebook	*putyevadityel'*	путеводитель
guided tour	*ekskursiya*	экскурсия
gynaecologist	*ginyekolag*	гинеколог

H

hello	*zdrastvitye*	здравствуйте
hitchhike	*yekhat' aftastopam*	ехать автосто-пом
home (at)	*doma*	дома
how	kag	Как
How are things?	*kag dyela?*	Как дела?
How's life?	*kag zhizn'?*	Как жизнь?
How much?	*skol'ka?*	Сколько?
hypnotism	*gipnatizm*	гипнотизм

I

identification	*dakumyenti*	документы
if	*yesli*	если
inflation	*inflyatsiya*	инфляция
(It's) impossible	*nyevazmozhna*	Невозможно
interesting	*intyeryesniy*	интересный
interpreter	*pyeryevotchik*	переводчик
invitation	*priglasheniye*	приглашение

VOCABULARY

K

king	*karol'*	король
Koran	*karan*	Коран

L

lens	*abyektif*	объектив
lost-property office	*byuro nakhodak*	бюро находок
love (to be in)	*lyubit'*	любить

M

make-up	*kasmyetika*	косметика .
manager	*administratar*	администратор
May I?	*mozhna?*	Можно?
modern	*savryemyeniy*	современный
music	*muzika*	музыка
music (classical)	*klasichyeskaya muzika*	классическая музыка
music (dance)	*tantseval'naya muzika*	танцевальная музыка
music (popular)	*papulyarnaya muzika*	популярная музыка
music (rock)	*rokmuzika*	рок-музыка

N

no	*nyet*	нет
nothing	*nichyevo*	ничего

nuclear	*yadyerniy*	ядерный
nuclear waste	*atkhodi atamnay*	отходы атомной
	pramishlyenasti	промышлен-
		ности

O

off (food)	*tukhliy*	тухлый
offensive	*abidniy*	обидный
Okay!	*kharasho!*	Хорошо!
old-fashioned	*staramodniy*	старомодный
opera	*opyera*	опера .
operation	*apyeratsiya*	операция

P

party	*vyechyerinka*	вечеринка
(get-together)		
Party	*partiya*	партия
(Communist)	*(kamunisti-*	(Коммунисти-
	chyeskaya)	ческая)
peace	*mir*	мир
pension (on a/the)	*na pyensi*	на пенсии
performer/	*artistka*	артистка (f)
celebrity	*artist*	артист (m)
permission	*razryesheniye*	разрешение
personal	*lichniy*	личный
petrol	*byenzin*	бензин
petrol station	*byenzakalonka*	бензоколонка
play	*p'yesa*	пьеса

(performance)

play (cards)	*igrat'* (*f karti*)	играть (в карты)
pollution	*zagryaznyeniye*	загрязнение
president	*pryezidyent*	президент
prime minister	*pryem'yer-ministr*	премьер-министр
private	*chastniy*	частный

Q

| queen | *karalyeva* | королева |

R

rationed	*patalonam*	по талонам
revolution	*ryevalyutsiya*	революция
rip-off	*abdiralafka*	обдираловка
romantic	*ramantichyeskiy*	романтический
rubbish	*musar*	мусор

S

salary	*zarplata*	зарплата
Siberia	*sibir'*	Сибирь
skates	*kan'ki*	коньки
skis	*lizhi*	лыжи
state (belongs to government)	*gasudarstvyeniy*	государственный
stereo system	*styeryeo-sistyema*	стерео-система

T

tipsy	*pat khmyel'kom*	под хмельком
Torah	*tora*	Тора
trade union	*prafsayus*	профсоюз

U

uncomfortable	*nyeudobniy*	неудобный
unemployed	*byezrabotniy*	безработный
unfair! (That's)	*eta nyespravyedliva!*	Это несправед-ливо!
unfortunately	*k sazhalyeniyu*	к сожалению
urgent	*srochniy*	срочныйW
war	*vayna*	война
war (civil)	*grazhdanskaya vayna*	гражданская война
West (in the)	*na zapadye*	на Западе
what	*shto*	что
What's new?	*shto novava?*	Что нового?
What's that?	*shto eta?*	Что это?
when	*kagda*	когда
When does the train leave?	*kagda otpravlyayetsa poyezd?*	Когда отправляется поезд?
where	*gdye*	где
Where is the toilet?	*gdye tualyet?*	Где туалет?
where (to)	*kuda*	куда
Where are you going?	*kuda vi idyotye?*	Куда вы идёте?

who	*kto*	кто
why	*pachyemu*	почему
wonderful	*pryekrasniy*	прекрасный

Y

| yes | *da* | да |

Z

| zoo | *zaapark* | зоопарк |

Emergencies

Help!
na pomash!
На помощь!

Watch out!
astarozhna!
Осторожно!

Go away!
iditye atsyuda!
Идите отсюда!

Get lost!
pashol!
Пошёл!

Stop it (or I'll scream)!
pyeryestan'
(a ta zakrichu)!
Перестань (а то закричу)!

Police!
militsiya!
Милиция!

Stop thief!
dyerzhitye vora!
Держите вора!

Call a doctor!
pazavitye vracha!
Позовите врача!

There's been an accident.
praizashol nyeshasniy sluchay
Произошёл несчастный случай.

Call an ambulance.
vizavitye skoruyu pomash'
Вызовите скорую помощь.

I am ill.
ya bal'na
ya bolyen
Я больна (f)/
Я болен (m).

147

I am lost.
   ya patyeryalas'   Я потерялась (f)/
   ya patyeryalsa   Я потерялся (m).

I've been raped.
   myenya iznasilavali   Меня износиловали.

I've been robbed.
   myenya agrabili   Меня ограбили.

I've lost my ...   *ya patyeryala/*   Я потеряла (f)/
               ya patyeryal ...   Я потерял (m)...

bag	*sumku*	сумку
money	*dyen'gi*	деньги
travellers' cheques	*darozhniye chyeki*	дорожные чеки
passport	*paspart*	паспорт

Could I use the telephone?
   mozhna   Можно
   vaspol'zavat'sa   воспользоваться
   vashim tyelyefonam?   вашим телефоном?

I have medical insurance.
   u myenya yest'   У меня есть
   myeditsinskaye   медицинское
   strakhavaniye   страхование.

Index

w(v)inyesca zité mne *me*
gave _ _ _ _ ?

can you tell me where
is . . . ?

u menya zakazan
nomer,
I have a reservation

stchet - bill

soup - supntucore
ftoroye - entree

sladkoye - dessert *or*
dessert

chto ve budete piet ?pye
what would you like to drink

butilku piva pazahulsta

mala pomalo little by little

nim noge - not much

di'engi – money

raspeshites zdes' paz(ahulsta) halsta
    sign here please

napishetya tse'no
        pazahulsta
    write ~~that~~ ~~down~~ n, please
        price
how much ''
    skoilko stovet

Language Survival Kits

Complete your travel experience with a Lonely Planet phrasebook. Developed for the independent traveller, the phrasebooks enable you to communicate confidently in any practical situation – and get to know the local people and their culture.

Skipping lengthy details on where to get your drycleaning ironed, information in the phrasebooks covers bargaining, customs and protocol, how to address people and introduce yourself, explanations of local ways of telling the time, dealing with bureaucracy and bargaining, plus plenty of ways to share your interests and learn from locals.

Australian
Introduction to Australian English, Aboriginal and Torres Strait languages.
Arabic (Egyptian)
Arabic (Moroccan)
Brazilian
Burmese
Cantonese
Central Europe
Covers Czech, French, German, Hungarian, Italian and Slovak.
Eastern Europe
Covers Bulgarian, Czech, Hungarian, Polish, Romanian and Slovak.
Fijian
Hindi/Urdu
Indonesian
Japanese
Korean
Mandarin
Mediterranean Europe
Covers Albanian, Greek, Italian, Macedonian, Maltese, Serbian & Croatian and Slovene.

Nepali
Pidgin
Pilipino
Quechua
Russian
Scandinavian Europe
Covers Danish, Finnish, Icelandic, Norwegian and Swedish.
Spanish (Latin American)
Sri Lanka
Swahili
Thai
Thai Hill Tribes
Tibet
Turkish
Vietnamese
Western Europe
Useful words and phrases in Basque, Catalan, Dutch, French, German, Irish, Portugese and Spanish (Castilian).

Lonely Planet Audio Packs

The best way to learn a language is to hear it spoken in context. Set within a dramatic narrative, with local music and local speakers, is a wide range of words and phrases for the independent traveller – to help you talk to people you meet, make your way around more easily, and enjoy your stay.

Each pack includes a phrasebook and CD or cassette, and comes in an attractive, useful cloth bag. These bags are made by local community groups, using traditional methods.

Forthcoming Language Survival Kits
Greek, the USA (American English and dialects, Native American languages and Hawaiian), Baltic States (Estonian, Latvian and Lithuanian), Lao, Mongolian, Bengali, Sinhalese, Hebrew, Ukrainian

Forthcoming Audio Packs
Indonesian, Japanese, Thai, Vietnamese, Mandarin, Cantonese

LONELY PLANET PUBLICATIONS
Australia: PO Box 617, Hawthorn, Victoria 3122
USA: 155 Filbert Street, Suite 251, Oakland CA 94607-2538
UK: 10 Barley Mow Passage, Chiswick, London W4 4PH
France: 71 bis, rue du Cardinal Lemoine – 75005 Paris

PLANET TALK

Lonely Planet's FREE quarterly newsletter

We love hearing from you and think you'd like to hear from us.

When...is the right time to see reindeer in Finland?
Where...can you hear the best palm-wine music in Ghana?
How...do you get from Asunción to Areguá by steam train?
What...should you leave behind to avoid hassles with customs in Iran?

*For the answer to these and
many other questions read
PLANET TALK.*

Every issue is packed with up-to-date travel news and advice including:

- *a letter from Lonely Planet founders Tony and Maureen Wheeler*
- *travel diary from a Lonely Planet author - find out what it's really like out on the road*
- *feature article on an important and topical travel issue*
- *a selection of recent letters from our readers*
- *the latest travel news from all over the world*
- *details on Lonely Planet's new and forthcoming releases*

To join our mailing list contact any Lonely Planet office.

LONELY PLANET PUBLICATIONS
Australia: PO Box 617, Hawthorn, Victoria 3122 (tel: 03-819 1877)
USA: 155 Filbert Street, Suite 251, Oakland, CA 94607 (tel: 510-893 8555)
UK: 10 Barley Mow Passage, Chiswick, London W4 4PH (tel: 0181-742 3161)
FRANCE: 71 bis, rue du Cardinal Lemoine – 75005 Paris (tel: 1-46 34 00 58)

Also available Lonely Planet T-Shirts. 100% heavy weight cotton (S, M, L, XL)

"A walk in the p   e by isn't against th

"Good. What if I w   , or reach out to pick some dust from your shoulder?"

"Ah, then you'll be whispered about forevermore as that woman who just couldn't keep her hands off the dashing and debonair Captain Fitzgerald."

"Dashing and debonair?"

"Just a couple of the words I've heard describe me."

"Hmm," Emma said, leaning back and regarding him as if weighing up whether the words were true. "I suppose these mystery admirers aren't completely wrong."

"It would be hard to argue with so many."

Emma stepped closer again, her side brushing against his arm as they walked. Guy was surprised at how content he felt with Emma here with him. After the previous night at the ball, he'd been worried their friendship would be marred by the attraction he felt for her rearing its head. Though he couldn't lie to himself and say he didn't still feel the irresistible pull when she was near, they had slipped back into an easy companionship.

He wondered how she would feel when he told her the real reason he had left Egypt, the real reason he had been summoned home. Part of him knew he needed to tell her, keeping it secret much longer would be a betrayal of the openness they normally shared, but he couldn't bring himself to cast a shadow over their reunion.

Author Note

I can't imagine not writing. For so long it has been what I've turned to when something else in life has been difficult or stressful. It allows me to relax, to escape to another world. I love creating two characters and then taking them on the journey to fall in love. I dream about the worlds I create, and even if they were just for me, writing would always be a big part of my life.

Whether you have read all of my books or this is your first, I feel privileged to have had the opportunity to write them all. I still remember the feeling when I got "the call" to tell me Harlequin wanted to publish my first book, and now every time I hold a new book in my hands, that feeling comes rushing back. Thank you for picking up Guy and Emma's love story, my twentieth book. Here's to many more happy-ever-afters.

LAURA
MARTIN

———

The Captain's
Impossible Match

HARLEQUIN®
HISTORICAL™

Recycling programs
for this product may
not exist in your area.

ISBN-13: 978-1-335-40752-8

The Captain's Impossible Match

Copyright © 2021 by Laura Martin

Harlequin Enterprises ULC
22 Adelaide St. West, 41st Floor
Toronto, Ontario M5H 4E3, Canada
www.Harlequin.com

Printed in U.S.A.

Laura Martin writes historical romances with an adventurous undercurrent. When not writing, she spends her time working as a doctor in Cambridgeshire, UK, where she lives with her husband. In her spare moments Laura loves to lose herself in a book and has been known to read from cover to cover in a single day when the story is particularly gripping. She also loves to travel—especially to visit historical sites and far-flung shores.

Books by Laura Martin

Harlequin Historical

The Pirate Hunter
Secrets Behind Locked Doors
Under a Desert Moon
A Ring for the Pregnant Debutante
An Unlikely Debutante
An Earl to Save Her Reputation
The Viscount's Runaway Wife
The Brooding Earl's Proposition
Her Best Friend, the Duke
One Snowy Night with Lord Hauxton
The Captain's Impossible Match

The Ashburton Reunion

Flirting with His Forbidden Lady
Falling for His Practical Wife

Scandalous Australian Bachelors

Courting the Forbidden Debutante
Reunited with His Long-Lost Cinderella
Her Rags-to-Riches Christmas

Visit the Author Profile page
at Harlequin.com for more titles.

To Luke,
I love you and I'm looking forward
to getting back to some of our
adventures this year.

Chapter One

'Isn't this the most magnificent sight you've ever seen?' Emma gushed as she spun around, taking everything in.

'Oh, yes. Forget the sight of an oasis in the desert or a long-lost Egyptian temple, an English ballroom is so much more impressive.'

Emma laughed. 'You have to admit, Cece, it is marvellous.'

Looking around with one eyebrow ever so slightly raised, Cecilia gave a non-committal shrug. 'It's just a ball, like hundreds of others.'

'Ah, hundreds of others for you. This is my first real English ball and I am enchanted.'

For a moment the two women stood arm in arm, admiring the candlelight glittering off the glass of the chandelier above their heads, enjoying the swell of the music and the swish of fabric as the couples danced in the middle of the ballroom. There was a buzz of excitement in the air, the sense that this was the start of something wonderful.

'Are all balls like this or is it special because it is the first of the Season?'

'You speak as though I am an expert. I haven't socialised in England for over ten years, Emma. Everything has changed.'

For an instant Emma saw the glimmer of sadness in Cecilia's eyes and gave her arm a quick squeeze.

'I'm glad you made the trip with me,' Emma said. It was comforting to have her friend at her side as she navigated a new world. At twenty-two she was older than most of the debutantes, the young women who were giving her curious looks across the ballroom. She didn't know what the latest fashions were, or how best to wear her hair, but with Cecilia as her companion, together they would find their way in this exciting new world.

Their hostess, Lady Thorne, walked over gracefully, a full skirt trailing behind her. 'Lady Emma, I'm so glad to see you this evening. I hope you don't mind my saying, but for a moment I thought it was your mother standing there.' She took Emma by the hand and studied her, nodding in satisfaction. 'You look exactly like Clara at her debut, the same beautiful brown eyes, the same smile of wonder on your lips.'

'Thank you for inviting me, Lady Thorne. I can't tell you how nervous I was. It was such a relief that the first ball I was invited to was yours.'

'It is nerve-racking, isn't it? Although you have nothing to be afraid of, my dear. Already I can tell you will be a success.'

'May I introduce my dear friend, Mrs Cecilia Willow?'

'A pleasure, Mrs Willow.' The two older women

murmured pleasantries to each other before Lady Thorne took her leave to circulate among the other guests at the party.

Emma could feel eyes on her, furtive glances from the younger debutantes, curious stares from their mothers, even some of the gentlemen seemed to be intrigued by her.

'You must remember, my dear, you are new and that means you are interesting,' Cecilia said as Emma gazed around the ballroom.

'You're saying I'm not normally interesting?' she teased.

'Of course not, cheeky minx, but these people see a pretty young woman in fine clothes and they want to know who you are and where you have been hiding the last few years.'

'Perhaps I should go and introduce myself to some of them,' she said, taking a step forward. Cecilia laid a cautionary hand on her arm.

'Patience, my dear. They will come to you. Wait to be introduced, it is the way of things.'

Emma scrunched up her nose. Patience wasn't her strongest characteristic. She was impulsive, enthusiastic, but not patient.

'Can you introduce me to people?'

'It's been years, Emma, and I was always on the fringes of this sort of high society. I married Mr Willow very young and we mainly lived in the country. I recognise a few of the older women from the time I spent in London after Mr Willow passed away, but for the life of me I can't remember their names.'

'Well, if I can't go talk to people and I can't dance

until someone asks me, can I at least keep myself oc-
cupied at the refreshment table?'

'A young lady does not stuff her face at balls.'

'Who said anything about stuffing my face?'

'You forget how well I know you, Emma.'

'The pastries do look incredible...'

Cecilia sighed, but a smile was tugging at the corner of her lips. 'Just do it gracefully.'

Emma squeezed her friend's arm, then wove her
way through the crowds, picking up a glass of lemon-
ade before perusing the pastries.

'I should have known I'd find you here,' a deep, familiar voice came from behind her.

Emma dropped the pastry she had selected and
turned round, unable to keep the huge grin from her
face.

'Guy!' she shouted, knowing immediately she was
being too loud, too excited but unable to help herself.
After she had spent so many months travelling with
just Cecilia for company, it felt wonderful to see another friendly face. She flung herself at him, wrapping her arms around his neck and pulling him into
an embrace.

She felt him stiffen in her arms. Normally he would
have picked her up and spun her round, but instead
he placed a careful hand on her waist and pushed her
gently away from him.

'What's wrong?'

'Nothing, Emma,' he muttered. 'We can't be like
that here. Look, everyone is watching us.'

She let her eyes move across the ballroom to find
the groups of guests staring in their direction.

'Why are they watching us?'

'Oh, Emma.'

'What?'

'For a woman of the world you can be naïve.'

She frowned. 'Don't call me naïve, just because they have all these rules and customs that are unfathomable to the uninitiated. Really, why can't I greet my closest friend in the manner I choose?'

'It's not done. Do it again and there will be a scandal.'

'And then you'd be forced to marry me? To save my reputation?'

'I've never known you need saving from anything, Em.'

They were standing a respectable four feet apart now and Emma wanted to reach out and draw her friend towards her. She hadn't realised quite how unsettled and nervous she had been feeling. It seemed silly to be scared of making her first steps into society—in reality, it was only talking and dancing, both things she excelled at—but here she was scared all the same. Guy was familiar, comforting, in a world where everything else was new.

'Can I at least take your arm?'

'As long as you promise not to pounce on me.'

'It was hardly a pounce.'

'It felt like a pounce. Looked like a pounce, too. And, by the disapproving looks Lady Reddington is giving us, I'd say she thinks it was a pounce.'

Emma glanced over her shoulder and frowned. 'No one is even looking any more,'

Guy smiled.

'Is there even a Lady Reddington here?'

'Who knows? I find it impossible to keep track of

all the titles and names. I've been introduced to so many people in recent months I think I stopped listening to names after the first fifty or so.'

Taking Guy's arm, Emma felt herself relax properly for the first time since she'd arrived in London a week ago. Guy had been visiting his family in the country and as such hadn't been able to call on her this past week, while Emma had longed for his company. The city was foreign to her, completely unfamiliar. She had left England with her father when she was four and never once visited since. The few memories she had of England were of their country estate, vast grounds and gardens to play in. She was sure she had been to London before, but it didn't feature in any of her memories.

'Is it really eighteen months since I last saw you?'

Guy nodded, the smile slipping from his face for a second. 'Yes, I left Luxor in April last year. I took the overland route through Europe and arrived here ten months ago.' He stopped for a moment and looked at her. 'I was very sorry to hear about your father, Emma. He was a good man and I will miss him very much.'

She swallowed back the tears that still threatened to fall whenever she allowed herself to acknowledge that she would never see her father again, never see his eyes light up as he spoke about his travels, never sit with him as he told her stories of her mother. Her father had been far from perfect, but she had loved him more than any other man.

'How are you coping?'

'Cecilia keeps me strong and I think a new city to explore will keep my mind busy.'

'Yes, although sorrow has a way of burrowing in deep. Remember to let it out sometimes.'

'I will.'

Guy paused as the musicians struck up the first notes of a new piece of music and the couples started to assemble on the dance floor.

'Would you care to dance?'

'I thought you would never ask.'

He led her over to the dance floor and Emma felt her heart begin to pound in her chest as they joined the other couples. She had learned the dances as a young girl, twirled across the veranda overlooking the Nile in Cecilia's arms thousands of times, but never before had she danced with a real partner in a real ballroom. It felt right somehow that the partner should be Guy.

'It's a waltz.'

'The king of dances.'

'Why do you think that?'

He smiled a seductive smile at her and then ruined it by raising an eyebrow in a comedic manner. 'It is one of the only dances where you get to hold your partner close for the whole dance. No stopping or hopping or changing places. Just you and your partner in one another's arms.'

The music swelled and Guy swept her round on the first turn and, as they spun together, Emma felt her heart soar. *This* was what she had travelled all this way for. For years she'd pored over her mother's diaries from when she was a debutante, getting lost in the descriptions of the balls and the suitors. She had dreamed of promenading through Hyde Park, of waltzing through ballrooms and discussing the little intrigues of society in muted tones with a close friend.

All the experiences her mother had detailed in her diary she wanted for herself.

'You're smiling.'

'Is there something wrong with smiling?'

'No. I'd forgotten how much I liked your smile, that's all.'

Emma squeezed Guy's hand and felt some of the nerves begin to settle. She wasn't alone in this endeavour to conquer London society and enjoy a Season. She had Cecilia, always constant, and now she had Guy.

The dance had finished far too quickly, as did the next in the set, and as that one ended she threw her arms around Guy's neck and embraced him. It was nothing, a gesture of friendship, one she had performed hundreds of times back in Egypt, but as she felt Guy's body freeze under her touch she immediately knew she had overstepped again.

Quickly Guy pulled away and, with a blank expression, escorted her over to where Cecilia was standing at the edge of the ballroom.

'I need to go,' he said, his bearing more upright than ever. 'Stay here and act normal. Perhaps we will get away with this.'

'Guy...' Emma whispered, biting her lip.

She watched him, hoping he would give her one of his customary winks, even just the hint of a smile, anything to show that he was doing this for the audience that was surely watching, but there was nothing, only Guy's retreating form.

'Was it that bad?' she murmured to Cecilia.

'You threw your arms around a man's neck in front

of everyone, Emma. Most women don't even get that close to their husbands.'

She groaned quietly and closed her eyes. 'For a moment I forgot where I was.'

Cecilia patted her on the hand and gave a stiff smile. 'Come, let's see if we can find you some nice, boring men to ask you to dance who you won't feel the need to embrace. Hopefully something more scandalous will happen before the evening is out and everyone will forget about you.'

Stealthily Guy slipped out of the ballroom and inhaled the cool autumn air. It was stifling inside and his head was pounding. He needed just a few minutes without having to be on his guard the whole time, without smiling and making inane small talk with women he had absolutely no interest in or men who wanted to hear all about his military career.

He walked quickly past the couples in the shadows, head bent, not wanting to see anything he shouldn't, and went down the stone steps into the little garden. He was drawn to a trickling sound and meandered through the flower beds until he came to a little fountain channelling water into a sunken pond.

It had been a shock to see Emma again, even though he knew she would be here. If he was honest, the only reason *he* was here tonight was to see her. Eighteen months since he'd last set eyes upon her. Eighteen months of convincing himself he felt purely friendship for the woman he'd known for so long. There had been so many miles between them, so much time, that he'd almost believed his own lies, then one look, one touch, and he was back to thinking of her in a way he really shouldn't.

'Guy.'

He spun, so surprised he almost tripped over the stone surround of the pond, but his quick reflexes meant he was able to right himself before taking a tumble into the dark water.

'You can't be out here, Emma.'

'I couldn't bear to think you were annoyed with me.'

'I'm not annoyed with you.'

'But you left so quickly.'

He couldn't help but smile. He'd seen Emma barter with the wiliest market-trader in Cairo and calmly back away from an approaching crocodile. In many ways she was more worldly-wise than the other young women crowded in the ballroom, but society in Egypt had been a very different affair. Emma and her father had often entertained, but it had been informal, a collection of people who had made Luxor their home, not shackled by the normal constraints of society. Here she was floundering.

'Do you want to be forced to marry me, Emma?'

The horrified look on her face should have hurt, but Guy found himself laughing.

'That is what could happen if we are over-familiar with each other in company. Everyone will gossip and the only way to save your reputation will be to marry quickly.'

'All I did was hug you,' she grumbled, coming over and sitting on the wall around the sunken pond. He hesitated and then sat with her. If they were caught alone outside together there would be no saving things, but she clearly needed a little buoying up.

'The rules are ridiculous,' he said slowly. 'But they are there to protect you. You haven't completely rejected the idea of marrying one day? Of having a husband and a family?'

She gave a little shrug.

'Reputation is what matters more than anything for a young lady wanting to marry. You should guard yours carefully...' He paused, then pushed on, knowing he wouldn't forgive himself if he didn't issue a warning and then something happened. 'Some gentlemen are unscrupulous, Emma. They would take advantage of you. Entice you outside for a walk in the dark and then force a proximity that you didn't want.'

For a moment Emma remained silent, then he felt her shuffle closer.

'I'm glad you're here, Guy. I've missed you.'

'I've missed you, too.'

'Tell me about your travels through Europe.'

He settled back on to the stone wall and allowed himself to relax a little. He hadn't wanted to leave Egypt, hadn't wanted to return to England, but duty called. The trip, however, had done a little to compensate for the move.

'I thought I had seen some of Europe during the war, but snatched glances of ports from the deck of a ship, or muddy marches through the countryside, didn't prepare me for how much I would love it.'

'Did you sail to Greece?'

'Yes, stopping off on a few idyllic islands. Then from Athens I went north and hopped on a boat to Italy.'

'I begged Cecilia to go that way, to see the Acropolis in Athens and the ruins of Rome, but she said overland was no way for two women to travel unaccompanied.'

Guy could imagine the face Emma was pulling in the darkness.

'I spent a few days in Venice. I rented an apartment in an old palazzo and I almost didn't leave. Then it was Switzerland and Germany and the Netherlands. You should have seen the mountains, Em, the ranges stretch out for as far as the eye can see, mountain after mountain covered in ice and snow, the tops in the clouds.'

'Maybe one day,' she said and then sighed. 'But first I am determined to conquer London.'

'I have no doubts that you will.'

She was about to speak when he held up a hand in front of her lips and motioned for her to be quiet. In the darkness he had forgotten how risky this innocent little conversation was and now cursed himself for not insisting she return to the ballroom immediately when she followed him out.

The sound of footsteps was accompanied by the rustling of material and a lady's low laugh piercing through the air.

'We need to get you back,' Guy whispered and Emma nodded silently. Quietly they slipped from the wall and started to hurry through the garden, stopping suddenly as they almost ran into another couple.

'Fitzgerald,' the man said, peering round him at Emma.

'Gilby.'

'Perhaps we can keep this to ourselves,' Gilby said, a faint look of panic on his face.

Guy inclined his head and then hurried Emma away.

'Will they say anything?' Emma asked, concern on her face. At least she was fast learning the dangers of scandal.

'No. Gilby is married and that was not his wife. They have as much reason as we do to want to keep quiet.'

They reached the steps to the veranda and Guy paused, taking Emma's hand and giving it a squeeze. 'Walk calmly on to the veranda and go back into the ballroom, find Cecilia and stick with her. I will slip in discreetly in a few minutes.'

'Will I see you again tonight?'

'Best not, Emma, but perhaps we can see each other tomorrow.'

She leaned in ever so slightly and he had to resist the urge to embrace her, then she was gone, walking calmly up the steps as he had instructed her to.

Chapter Two

Emma tried not to lean out of the carriage window and stare in wonder at the buildings and people as they travelled through the streets. She had been in London for a week and still she couldn't get used to how different it was from anywhere else she had been. Their house in Luxor had been large and sprawling, but set over one single level, as were many of the dwellings in Egypt. Some had an upper floor, but none were like these tall stone or brick buildings that dominated the capital.

Pulling her shawl around her shoulders, she settled back in her seat, allowing herself a small sigh of satisfaction. It had been wonderful to see Guy again. She'd missed him when he had left Egypt and had waited eagerly for the letters he had written detailing his journey through Europe. Then her father had died and grief had almost consumed her. Emma knew she would mourn her father for a long time, perhaps for her whole life, but seeing Guy had lifted her spirits more than she could have hoped. He made London feel as though it could be her home.

'I have a little shopping I need to do. Do you want me to accompany you or shall I meet you afterwards?' Cecilia asked as the carriage slowed outside the British Museum.

'Do your shopping. Guy has arranged for a curator to show us the collections so it isn't as though I will be unchaperoned.' Emma managed to stop herself from rolling her eyes at the idea she couldn't be trusted to walk around a museum with a friend because he was male. At home she had often gone for a stroll with Guy or taken tea overlooking the Nile, but it seemed here in England that wasn't the way things were done.

Guy was waiting outside Montagu House, leaning against the railings, and Emma felt herself smile as she caught sight of him. He stepped forward as the carriage slowed and opened the door to help first her and then Cecilia down.

He smiled as he saw them both huddled up in their shawls. 'Not used to the English weather yet?'

'It's freezing.' It was late October, most of the leaves had dropped from the trees and the days were getting shorter, but Emma was well aware that it could only get colder as they headed for winter. She would need to invest in some warm winter clothes this year as her body adjusted to a cooler climate.

'I was thinking what a glorious balmy day it is.'

Emma gave him a withering look, but he just smiled infuriatingly back at her.

'I shall leave you to enjoy the museum. Emma tells me you do not need a chaperon.'

'No, one of the curators, Mr Paxton, has agreed to show us around. I know him well and his wife will be present, too. I think they are keen to try to bring Emma on board as a patron of the museum.'

'Very well. I shall meet you back here in half an hour, will that be enough time?'

'Perhaps an hour? The collection is quite impressive.'

Cecilia hurried off and Guy fell in beside Emma.

'Is this what you do in London?'

'How do you mean?'

'Well, I know how you spent your days in Egypt, poring over shipping schedules and your import and export logs, and rushing off to sites of possible historical interest when one of your informants brought you information. I wondered how you spend your time in England?'

'And you think it is mid-afternoon trips to museums and dancing in ballrooms?'

Emma shrugged. It had been one of the only times she and Guy had argued, when he'd announced he was leaving Egypt and returning to England. Emma hadn't been able to understand it. He was happy in Egypt, he ran a successful company, spent his free time chasing down ancient Egyptian artefacts and always had a smile on his face. When he'd informed her he was leaving he hadn't seemed happy about it. He'd cited *duty* as his reason for returning home, but had been peculiarly tight-lipped about what he actually meant by that.

'My father,' he said slowly now. 'His health is failing and his mind wanders. I am trying to take on as much of the responsibility for the family as I can to ease the burden.'

Suddenly Emma felt selfish. She had been thinking of how much Guy leaving Egypt had affected her, but of course his family would need him. He was the eldest son, probably soon to be the head of the family. He had responsibilities she couldn't even imagine.

They reached the grand entrance to Montagu House and Guy knocked on the door, some of the tension easing from his shoulders as a small man opened it and peered up at them from behind some round spectacles.

'Captain Fitzgerald, come in, come in. We've been eagerly awaiting your arrival.'

'May I introduce Lady Emma Westcombe? Emma, this is Mr Paxton, the curator of the Egyptian collection.'

Mr Paxton ushered them inside and then took Emma warmly by the hand.

'My wife and I have been so looking forward to meeting you, Lady Emma. Captain Fitzgerald has told us so much about you and our shared love of all things ancient Egyptian.'

'I've heard wonderful things about your collection, Mr Paxton. The idea of a public museum to showcase some of the treasures from around the world is marvellous.'

'We're very proud of what we do here. Although most of our visitors are by appointment only, I hope one day we will be able to open our collections to the wider public.'

He motioned for them to follow him through the grand entrance hall to a room off to one side. Emma felt herself relax as they started to wander past glass cabinets filled with treasures from around the world.

'As you can see, we have an extensive Egyptian collection—much of it arrived in 1803 after the Battle of the Nile. We are very privileged to have received them,' Mr Paxton said.

His voice was low and melodious and Emma wondered how many people had fallen asleep in the talks he must give as curator.

Guy was walking next to her, one hand lightly grazing her lower back, guiding her among the cabinets.

They paused in front of the free-standing Rosetta Stone, one of the items Emma had been most excited about seeing.

'It's beautiful,' she said, her hand starting to reach out to the huge grey-black stone. She knew better than to touch it, but there was something captivating about it, something that made her want to run her fingers over the inscriptions, to see if she could understand the mysterious hieroglyphics. Ever since she was a young girl she had stared up at the hieroglyphics on the temples or on the fragments of pottery or papyrus men brought to show her father and wished she would be the one to decipher the mysterious language. Here was the key and it made her heart beat faster in her chest to stand so close to it.

'Please excuse me for a moment,' Mr Paxton said as his wife came in, murmuring a muted message into his ear. 'There is a matter I must see to. I will be only a few minutes.'

Emma watched the Paxtons hurry away before turning to Guy. 'I never imagined it would be like this. I thought there might be a couple of dozen objects, battered by transit with dubious provenance, but this is incredible.' She looked around in amazement at the large number of artefacts, all beautifully displayed and labelled. There were treasures from temples and tombs, mummified remains, jewellery and statues, and in the middle of them all the Rosetta Stone.

'I knew you would like it.' Emma looked at her friend, taking in the glimmer of excitement in his eyes, and knew he felt the same wonder as she did. They both shared a love of the country they had so recently left and the rich history hiding under the layers of sand waiting to be discovered.

'Have a look at this,' Guy said, leading her over to a glass cabinet to one side of the room. As she peered inside he directed her focus to a collection of objects placed haphazardly to one side. 'These are all awaiting classification and labelling—there are hundreds more in storage downstairs.'

Emma spun and almost collided with Guy, his arms reaching out to steady her, a grounding force. She looked up at him, her eyes meeting his, and she felt something stir inside her. She must have looked into his eyes a thousand times, must have seen the way the green of his irises got lighter towards the pupil, but this was the first time she hadn't been able to pull herself away.

Unable to move, she stood gazing up at him, feeling an unusual heat begin to rise up from her core and flood over every inch of her skin.

'This was one of the reasons I brought you here,' Guy was saying, but it took a while for the words to get through to her brain.

'Oh?'

'I know you have great plans to conquer society, but I thought you might miss the antiquities work you used to do with your father. Mr Paxton is very keen to have volunteers help with cleaning and classifying the collection. What do you think?'

'Yes,' she managed to say, still staring up at him. It was the same Guy, the same blond hair curled at the nape of his neck, the same quick smile over dazzling white teeth. It was the same man she'd known for seven years, the man she'd shared an unparalleled friendship with, yet there was something different in the way she was reacting to him.

Perhaps it was tiredness—the journey to England had been arduous and, since arriving, she had spent her time being prodded and poked at by the modiste and exploring her new home.

'Are you sure? You don't have to.'

Emma gave herself a little shake. She was being ridiculous. This was Guy, the man who had seen her fall into the Nile in her petticoats and rubbed her back when she'd felt unwell after eating some chicken that had been left out in the sun for a little too long.

'Guy, it sounds wonderful. Thank you for thinking of me.'

'Who else would I think of?'

She squeezed his arm and gave a little smile, turning at the sound of Mr Paxton's footsteps.

'I'm so sorry, I have something I need to see to. Do you mind if we continue the tour another day?'

'Of course not,' Emma said, as Mr Paxton guided them back through the maze of cabinets to the grand entrance hall.

'I will arrange another time,' Guy said, shaking Mr Paxton by the hand.

The air was cool as they stepped out of the museum and Guy saw Emma shiver out of the corner of his eye. She had a thick shawl pulled around her shoulders,

but no cloak he could see. It would have been a gradual change in temperature as she and Cecilia sailed
north from Egypt, but when you were used to the sun
on your face every day the grey skies of London left
a certain chill in your bones no matter how long the
adjustment period.

'Do you want my jacket?'

She eyed it with interest and then shook her head.
'My cloak is in the carriage, but it is such a heavy,
cumbersome thing I thought I would be able to do
without it. It seems I was wrong.'

He led her back to the carriage and reached up inside to get her cloak, placing it around her shoulders,
pausing behind her to free a few loose strands of hair
that were tucked in at the collar.

'Better?'

'Much. Thank you.'

'Cecilia should be back soon.'

'Eager to be rid of me?'

'Forty minutes is a long time, Em…'

She hit him lightly on the arm.

'I know you missed me,' she said.

'How do you know that?'

She shrugged. 'I just know. You came to the ball last
night and suggested a trip out today. Cecilia tells me in
London society two meetings in two days is quite un-
heard of unless a man is courting a woman.'

Guy laughed.

'Is it so ridiculous that people might think we are
courting?'

'No,' he said slowly, drawing the word out. Once,
a few years ago, he had thought maybe one day they
would be courting, but it wasn't meant to be. Life had

other plans for him and he and Emma were better as friends. Even if she made something stir inside him when she smiled.

She looked at him with raised eyebrows. 'Would it be *that* bad if the world thought we were courting?'

'I have my reputation to consider.'

'What reputation?'

'Ah, you're new to London, I will forgive you.'

'What reputation?' Her voice had raised a notch and he had to suppress a smile. Emma had never liked being kept in the dark about anything.

'Shall we go for a little stroll once Cecilia has returned? I think the rain will hold off for a few more hours.'

'You're ignoring my question.'

'It would be impolite to discuss this with a lady and, as much as you try to protest, Lady Emma, you *are* the daughter of an earl.'

She pressed her lips together and then let out a huffing sigh.

'Do you know, I haven't had a good quarrel with anyone since you left Luxor. Cecilia is so kind and wonderful and *forgiving.*'

'She is a saint.'

'To put up with me?'

'I didn't say that,' Guy said, holding out his hands as if to ward off Emma's next words.

'I suppose she is. I am glad she decided to return to England with me, I don't know what I would have done without her.'

'I'm sure she feels the same about you?'

'Do you think so? She is quite the best and kindest person I know.'

Guy was about to answer when Cecilia hurried around the corner and waved happily to them, carrying a couple of parcels under her arm.

'Did you have a nice time in the museum?'

'Yes, although it was cut a little short. The curator was called away.'

Guy took the parcels from Cecilia and placed them on the seats of the carriage.

'We were planning on going for a little stroll around the park. What do you say?'

'That would be wonderful.'

It didn't take long for the carriage to reach the gate to the south of Hyde Park and then they were walking arm in arm, with Cecilia on one side of Guy and Emma on the other. It had been how they had often strolled by the Nile, when Emma's father had been too unwell or too absorbed in his books to accompany them.

'How are you finding being back in England, Cecilia?' Guy knew the return would be harder for the older woman. Starting again at any age was difficult, but he was sure the older you got the more complex your feelings on change.

'Sometimes it feels as though the last ten years have been a dream. Nothing has changed, nothing except me.'

'Were there people you kept in contact with? People you are planning on seeing again?'

Cecilia grimaced and Guy felt bad for asking. He didn't know the full story of why Cecilia, as a respectable widow, had apparently fled England ten years ago, but over the years of their acquaintance he had picked up snippets of information. He knew she didn't have any family of note, at least not any who had corresponded with her while she was in Egypt. He also knew the ruse of her being at first Emma's governess and later her companion was one she had struggled with morally. She and Emma's father had lived as husband and wife in all but name.

'Mrs Willow, Mrs Willow,' a voice called out, saving her from having to elaborate further. She paused and turned, an expression of trepidation momentarily crossing her face.

'I'll be back in a moment.'

Guy and Emma watched as she hurried off to talk to the middle-aged woman who seemed so eager to renew their acquaintance.

'Shall we keep walking?'

'Is it against the rules? I actually can't fathom them out. What is or isn't allowed seems to be impossible to know.'

'A walk in the park with a chaperon close by isn't against the rules.'

'Good. What if I were to walk too close, though, or reach out to pick some dust from your shoulder?'

'Ah, then you'll be whispered about for evermore as that woman who couldn't keep her hands off the dashing and debonair Captain Fitzgerald.'

'Dashing and debonair?'

'A couple of the words I've heard describe me.'

'Hmmm,' Emma said, leaning back and regarding him as if weighing up whether the words were true. 'I suppose these mystery admirers aren't completely wrong.'

'It would be hard to argue with so many.'

Emma stepped closer again, her side brushing

against his arm as they walked. Guy was surprised at how content he felt with Emma here with him. After the previous night at the ball he'd been worried their friendship would be marred by the attraction he felt for her rearing its head, but although he couldn't lie to himself and say he didn't still feel the irresistible pull when she was near, they had slipped back into an easy companionship.

He wondered how she would feel when he told her the real reason he had left Egypt—the real reason he had been summoned home. Part of him knew he needed to tell her—keeping it secret much longer would be a betrayal of the openness they normally shared—but he couldn't bring himself to cast a shadow over their reunion.

'Did you feel that?' Emma was looking up at the darkening sky dubiously. 'I'm sure I felt rain.'

He looked up, too, taking in the dense black clouds and new chill to the air.

'Perhaps we should look for some shelter,' he suggested as the first fat raindrops began to splatter on to the path.

They began to walk quickly through the park, heading for a little gazebo perched near the edge of the Serpentine. It was wooden with the sides open to the elements, but the roof would shelter them from the worst of the downpour.

'It's getting heavier,' Emma said, as he grabbed her hand and began pulling her to the shelter in earnest.

They arrived dripping wet and laughing, glad to be out of the torrential rain.

'Where's Cecilia?'

Guy looked out, spotting her sheltering under a tree in the distance.

'She's over there with her friend, sheltering under a tree.'

Emma shivered and he quickly took off his jacket, draping it around her shoulders. Underneath, his shirt was damp and sticking to his skin, but as yet it didn't feel too uncomfortable.

'Why does anyone want to live in a country where it is cold when it is wet?' Emma grumbled.

'Wait until it snows. Come here.'

She moved up close to him and they took a seat on the bench at the back of the gazebo. It was the only side with a backing so at least they were sheltered from the wind and rain. As they sat he wrapped his arms around her, pulling her close, sharing some of his warmth. Emma stiffened for a second and then rested her head on his shoulder.

Guy closed his eyes. In a couple of months he wouldn't be able to do this any more. In a couple of months he would be a married man. A married man who would owe it to his wife to stay away from the woman he really loved.

In silence they watched the rain drip from the roof of the gazebo. The park was deserted, the few people who had been walking either fled from the park or sheltering as they were.

'Em,' he said, knowing he needed to tell her about the marriage he would soon be entering into.

She pulled away slightly and looked up at him. Guy took in her caramel-brown eyes and the perfectly arched brows above and hesitated. He knew he had to tell her, but he didn't seem to be able to find the words. She sat there, pressed against him, looking up at him with such warmth he didn't want to break the moment between them.

Guy felt the urge to kiss her, to reach out and cup her cheek and lower his lips to hers. It would be catastrophic. Over the years of their friendship he'd resisted similar urges successfully, but right here and right now he wasn't sure he could.

'Yes?' she said, her voice coming out barely more than a whisper. Her eyes were searching his, her lips parting ever so slightly, and if he didn't know better he would think she was inviting him in.

'I need to tell you something.'

She nodded, never taking her eyes off his. Guy leaned forward, closing the gap between them, focused on the rosy pink of her lips.

'The rain is easing.' Cecilia's breezy voice cut through the sliver of air between them.

Guy slowly sat back, wondering what he had been thinking. This was Emma, his friend, *not* the woman he was promised to marry.

'Yes,' Emma said, rising abruptly and handing his jacket back. 'And I am going to call on some of Mother's old friends later. We must get back.'

Wordlessly Guy offered each woman an arm and they walked back through the now light drizzle to where the carriage was waiting.

Emma looked as though she wanted to say something before she climbed up into the carriage, but seemed to think better of it, giving him a distracted smile before the carriage lumbered off down the street.

Chapter Three

'You're being ridiculous,' Emma muttered to herself. She was acting irrationally and she hated acting irrationally. It was ever since the previous afternoon when she had sheltered from the rain in Hyde Park with Guy. They'd sat there, closer than was proper, and he had turned to her as he had done a thousand times before, but this time there had been something different. Not something different on his part, perhaps, but certainly something different in how she had reacted to him. As he'd looked at her with that contagious smile she had felt her body swaying towards his. She'd had this overwhelming desire to kiss him, to close her eyes and feel his hands roam over her body.

'It's the cold,' she told herself. 'It's gone to your head and made you daft.'

She didn't have much experience with men. In fact, her experience was non-existent, but she had for a moment wondered if he'd felt it, too. There had been a spark in his eyes when he'd leaned in closer, a spark that had made her for a moment think he wanted to kiss her, too.

'Now remember to behave yourself this evening,' Cecilia said as she breezed into the room. 'Don't do anything to draw attention to yourself, at least not in a negative way.'

'I'll do my best.'

'There will be a lot of eligible gentlemen there to-night—remember, you are always being watched at the opera. Perhaps you might see someone you want to know a little more about, too.'

Emma wrinkled her nose.

'Don't be like that. You're twenty-two, Emma. You need to start thinking about it soon, otherwise you will be seen as too old for a first marriage.'

'I might not want to marry. I haven't decided yet.' She was reluctant to put her whole life into the hands of a man she barely knew. Emma believed in love, she'd seen it in how her father talked of her mother, but she also knew the pain of losing the one you loved the most. Her father had been so devastated after losing her mother he'd uprooted himself and four-year-old Emma and travelled thousands of miles while griev-ing. Emma wasn't sure she wanted to open herself up to that much heartbreak. Her father had been a broken man, brilliant in his field and an excellent father, but he had been broken by her mother's death.

Then Cecilia had arrived, gentle, kind Cecilia, and Emma had been privileged enough to witness first-hand two people falling in love. It had made her re-consider her ideas about love. Up until then she had vowed she would never marry, never open herself up to such heartbreak—but, watching her father and Ce-cilia, she had begun to realise decisions like that often weren't straightforward.

* * *

It was only a short carriage ride to the opera and
Emma found herself distracted by the beautiful dresses
and exquisite hairstyles as their carriage crawled along
the busy road, waiting for their turn to stop outside
the opera house. All the women were immaculately
turned out, their dresses made of the finest satins and
silks. Emma fingered her dark green silk dress, glad
that Cecilia had talked her into buying an entire new
wardrobe as soon as they had arrived in London. She
didn't feel out of place with her hair swept up from
her neck and pinned in place with clips tipped with
pearls or the delicate golden chain around her neck on
the end of which was her mother's locket.

The opera was one of the experiences Emma had
been most excited about. Her mother had described
it as *a riot of colour and fashion* and she hadn't been
wrong. The account in the diaries of her mother attending the opera had focused on who had worn what
and whose attention they had caught, rather than the
music itself, but Emma found she was looking forward to both.

The real reason she was here tonight, though, wasn't
to do with living the experiences her mother had so
carefully described or finding her place in London
society. The real reason was Guy.

After the moment in the park the day before Emma
knew she needed to see Guy. If she could just look at
him, remind herself he was the same man she'd been
friends with these past few years, then she could put all
this nonsense behind her. She'd done something underhand, asking her new maid to see if she could find out
Guy's schedule for the evening, and the young woman

had delivered, telling her servants' gossip could inform you of any facts in London.

Guy was planning on attending the opera, so she had asked Cecilia if they could go. All the tickets were sold out, but Cecilia had called on an old friend, Mrs Pritchard, that afternoon and secured them an invitation to have the use of the Pritchards' box as the Pritchards were engaged elsewhere. It all felt very underhand, but Emma couldn't bring herself to care. She needed to know whether the same flare of attraction was there or if it had been a simple anomaly.

Objectively she knew Guy was an attractive man and he was charming as well, although he always did her the courtesy of not using his charm all too much on her. She'd known plenty of women who lost themselves in fluttering eyelashes and giggles in his presence. Even more attractive than his physical appearance was his kindness and decency. In the course of their friendship she'd known him quietly come to the aid of dozens of people in trouble or distress. He'd calmly stepped in whether it was to help a lost foreigner in the confusing maze of Cairo streets or to fish her out of the Nile that one embarrassing time she had leaned too far over the edge of the boat.

Before long it was their turn to step down from the carriage and Emma felt a rush of anticipation. The opera house had a grand front, with ornate pillars framing the entrance. People strolled leisurely up the steps and inside Emma could see a crush of people.

'Shall we go and find the box first, then we can socialise if there is time before the first act?' Cecilia suggested, guiding Emma up through the groups of people.

It felt strange to be among so many people but to know so few. A couple of faces looked slightly familiar from the ball a few nights earlier, but as yet Emma did not really know anyone in London.

They ascended the stairs and found the right door, stepping into the plush space. Emma ran her fingers over the red velvet of the upholstery and marvelled at the twinkling of the candles in the sconces. Looking over the rail, she could see the seats filling up down below, and a few of the other boxes had guests starting to arrive.

'This is incredible,' Emma said, staring at the stage, her mind finally distracted from the prospect of seeing Guy. She had never been to the theatre before, let alone the opera.

As she let her gaze wander she spotted a flash of familiarity. It was Guy, she was certain of it, even though she could only see one shoulder and the back of his head. She would know the nape of his neck anywhere and his stance was shaped by his time in the military.

Without thinking, she leaned over the gilded rail at the edge of the box and was about to call his name when she felt a restraining hand on her shoulder.

'Remember we are not at a market, Emma,' Cecilia murmured.

Emma sagged, but obeyed. After a moment she straightened and counted round the boxes to work out which was his. Guy hadn't turned around yet, but she was able to get a look at his companions. On one side was a young woman, no more than eighteen or nineteen. She had mousy hair and a plain dress, but even from this distance Emma could see her animated expression. The young woman's whole face lit up when she laughed and Guy must have been telling an hilarious story by the number of times she giggled and used the opportunity to touch him on the arm.

'Who is that?' Cecilia said, following Emma's gaze to the box a few away from theirs.

'Guy must have many friends in London. He's been back a number of months and I always forget he grew up here, spending his youth with these people.'

'They look very close, though.'

Emma couldn't tear her eyes away from the young woman who seemed to sidle closer to Guy every minute she watched.

'He's a charming man, I don't doubt he has admirers,' Emma said, flopping into a seat in an unladylike fashion, but adjusting her posture before Cecilia could say anything. She was well aware the gnawing feeling in her gut was jealousy. In Luxor Guy had led his own life, separate to hers, but they had been the closest of friends. She hadn't known everything about his business or his daily life, but the limited company meant all his acquaintances were her acquaintances, too. Here she felt as though she was just one part of his full and complex social life.

Cecilia sat down quietly beside her. It was one of the things Emma admired the most about the older woman, her ability to be still and silent but remain a comforting presence. Emma's father had been effusive and excitable much of the time and Cecilia's calm reserve had settled him. Emma reached out and squeezed Cecilia's hand.

'I don't know if I've said thank you,' she said quietly. 'For coming with me, for always being there for me.'

'You don't have to thank me. I know I'm not your

mother, Emma, and I've never tried to be, but I love you like a daughter.'

'I love you, too, Cece. I really don't know what I would have done without you and not just since Father passed away, either.'

Cecilia looked as though she was going to say something more, but before she could a hush started to fall across the theatre, signalling the start of the opera.

Emma found it hard to follow, but the passion behind the music was emotional and meant it didn't matter if she couldn't understand the words. Every so often she would glance across to Guy's box, although he was seated with his back angled slightly towards her. The mystery woman was to his left and Emma fancied she saw her leaning in to whisper something to Guy on more than one occasion.

At the interval she decided she could wait no longer and marched Cecilia out of the box. She had to know who the young woman was with Guy. As soon as they were outside Cecilia was distracted by an old acquaintance, leaving Emma to investigate on her own.

It was busy in the corridor with many people leaving the boxes to mingle or pop in to see friends before the opera started again, but Emma spotted Guy heading in her direction long before he saw her.

When he finally noticed her he froze, an expression of near panic crossing his face.

'Emma,' he said, then quickly corrected himself. 'Lady Emma, I wasn't expecting to see you tonight.'

Next to him his companion looked Emma up and down and then smiled. Emma took in the way her arm

was looped loosely through his and the slightly preda-
tory expression on her face.

Guy cleared his throat, began speaking and then
cleared his throat again. Emma had never seen him
this unsettled and she'd watched him talk his way out
of a skirmish with a dozen armed men when they had
accidently trespassed on private land hunting for a
long-forgotten tomb.

The woman next to him was looking expectantly
between him and Emma, waiting for her introduction.

'Miss Abigail Frant, may I introduce a friend from
my time in Egypt, Lady Emma Westcombe? Lady
Emma, this is Miss Frant.'

Emma murmured a pleasantry and bowed her head,
waiting for a little more information, but Guy was un-
characteristically quiet.

'Did you know Captain Fitzgerald well in Egypt,
Lady Emma?' Miss Frant asked after a long, awkward pause.

'Oh, yes, Captain Fitzgerald was a regular guest
at our house.'

'You lived there?' Miss Frant seemed surprised.

'Lady Emma's father moved to Egypt when Lady
Emma was still very young. She spent most of her
life there.'

'How fascinating. I would love to hear about it
sometime, Lady Emma.'

Emma managed a smile and mumbled something
that sounded vaguely positive.

The three of them stood there, the awkwardness
growing until Cecilia came to stand by Emma's side.
Introductions were made again and Emma almost
hugged Cecilia on the spot when the older woman

raised a politely interested eyebrow and asked the question Emma had wanted to demand since spotting Guy this evening.

'So how do you know each other?'

Emma watched Guy, watched as he closed his eyes for a fraction of a second and exhaled slowly. To anyone else his expression hadn't changed, but she was so attuned to his moods and his demeanour she could tell when he was agitated, even when he was doing his very best to hide it.

Miss Frant giggled and then seemed to think better of it. 'We can tell them, can't we? If they are such good friends of yours?'

'Miss Frant and I—' Guy said, but he was interrupted by the young woman beside him.

'We're engaged.'

Chapter Four

Emma looked as though all the air had been sucked out of her. The shock showed on her face for a moment before she managed to pull her lips into a smile. Her eyes eventually met Guy's and for a moment it seemed as though she was calmed by the familiarity, but then the frown returned and he could see the sense of betrayal in her eyes.

He saw Cecilia discreetly lay a supportive hand on Emma's arm. He wished everyone else would disappear and leave him to explain why he hadn't told her something so important.

'Emma,' Guy said quietly, 'I planned to tell you.' Even to his ears it sounded pathetic. He should have told her, there was no doubt about it. *This* was never the way he wanted her to find out. Even though they had never been involved romantically she was his closest friend. She deserved more than bumping into him and Miss Frant at the opera.

'Well, not *quite* engaged,' Miss Frant corrected, 'but once my father has ironed out all the details with Captain Fitzgerald we will announce a date.'

Guy felt the familiar swell of nausea he always did when his impending marriage was discussed and reminded himself why this was a necessity. It was the solution to the problem of his father's gambling debts, it would guarantee his sister, Sophia, had a decent dowry when she came out next year and stop them from losing the only home his father was comfortable in as his health was failing.

He'd had a good life this past decade. His stint in the army had been challenging but rewarding and his time in Egypt had allowed him to live how he had always dreamed. Sophia was seventeen and would never get the same opportunities he'd had. Her best chance was to marry someone she actually cared for, to have some choice over at least that part of her future. For so long he had put himself first, now he needed to step up, to become the man worthy of being the head of the family.

'I think your mother is calling you over, Miss Frant,' Guy said, trying not to make it too obvious he was attempting to get rid of the young woman.

'Oh. Well, it was nice to meet you, Lady Emma. Please call on me for tea one day, I would love to hear about your time in Egypt with Captain Fitzgerald.'

Emma inclined her head and watched as Miss Frant hurried off to see her mother.

'I will leave you two alone,' Cecilia said quietly. 'I'll be in the box, Emma.' Guy was grateful for Cecilia's quiet discretion as she slipped away. He was left facing Emma, wishing he could reach out and touch her, even a friendly squeeze of her arm, but knowing after their closeness in the ballroom a few nights earlier all eyes would be on them.

'I'm sorry,' he said, waiting for her to look up and meet his eye before continuing. 'I'm sorry I didn't tell you.'

'You're really going to marry her?'

'Yes. One day. Once the practicalities are sorted.'

'The practicalities?' Her voice was unusually harsh.

'Yes, we're still negotiating.'

'Negotiating. Good Lord, Guy, what is there to negotiate? You're not buying a horse.'

He could tell how upset she was by her language. The only other time he had heard her blaspheme was when they had witnessed a small boy being beaten by a shopkeeper on one of their trips to Cairo. In true Emma style, she had marched over and demanded he stop, using a few choice words as she did so.

Gently he took her by the arm and guided her down the corridor to a quieter spot. Most people were heading back to their seats, ready for the next act to begin.

'I understand you're angry, Emma.'

'Angry—why would I be angry?' she said in a bitter voice.

'I'm sorry, I should have told you. I meant to tell you. I couldn't bring myself to spoil the time we were having together.'

'How could you not tell me you were engaged?' Her voice was rising and he placed a hand fleetingly on her arm again to remind her where they were. No matter how upset she was, they needed to remember other people were listening. '*I* thought we were friends. *I* thought we told each other the important things in life. And finding a wife is pretty important.'

'Is it?'

'Of course it is. What do you mean "is it"?'

He dropped his voice to no more than a murmur and Emma had to lean in closer to be able to hear him.

'It doesn't matter. Forget I said it. I'm sorry, Emma, you shouldn't have found out like that. I never meant you to find out that way. You are right, I should have told you sooner.'

He wasn't going to argue with her. He felt awful that she had found out about Miss Frant from a random meeting. Some of the indignation ebbed out of her and slowly her shoulders began to settle down into their normal position rather than up by her ears.

'How long have you been engaged?'

'As she said, we're not engaged really, not yet.'

'But you will be.'

He nodded, trying to keep the melancholy from his face. If he was honest, he had given up on the idea of marriage a few years ago. He had been quite content with his life until his sister had written and told him of the mess that was brewing back home. Then the years of guilt of abandoning them, of choosing to live his own life rather than return to England to prop up his father, crashed down on him.

'How long have you known?'

'Does it matter?'

'Yes.'

He considered for a moment. 'Do you remember when we returned from that trip to Cairo and there was a letter from my sister waiting for me?'

After a moment Emma nodded.

'I knew then I would have to marry *someone*.'

Emma frowned. 'What do you mean?'

Around them the corridor was almost empty now,

with the last people making their way to their boxes and seats as the first notes of the next act rang out.

'We can't do this here, Emma. You need to be seen back in that box with Cecilia. It will be noticed if you do not return.'

She looked torn, but eventually nodded.

'Tonight, then, after the opera.'

He considered, knowing he should refuse. Knowing he should insist they only meet properly chaperoned and at designated events. In the end the desire to make things right between them won and he leaned in and murmured in her ear, 'Tonight, once the household is in bed. I will meet you in your garden, away from the house.'

Emma started to reach out and looked as though she wanted to touch him, but he caught her hand and kissed it below the knuckles, then spun and walked off, back to the box with Miss Frant. Back to the box where his future lay.

Chapter Five

Emma lay on her bed, knowing she couldn't slip beneath the covers or she might risk falling asleep, and the last thing she wanted to do tonight was sleep. She needed to see Guy, needed to hear why he was getting married and why he had kept the truth from her.

When Miss Frant had announced they were engaged Emma had felt as though she had been hit by a stampeding herd of elephants. Guy had never expressed an interest in marriage, never even hinted he wanted to settle down, yet here he was with a woman he couldn't know that well, planning on spending his life with her.

If she examined her feelings more closely Emma realised a lot of what she felt was jealousy rather than betrayal and that, she knew, wasn't a nice emotion.

'He's not yours to be jealous of,' she reminded herself for the hundredth time. Guy was her friend, but that was all. She had no claim on his heart, no claim on his future. Yet she *was* jealous.

Closing her eyes, she pictured the moment in Hyde Park where she had looked at Guy as if she were seeing him properly for the first time. Something deep inside her clenched and Emma felt a heat rising up from her core. Ever since that moment she had imagined kissing him, dreamed of feeling his hands roam over her body.

Quickly she stood up, trying to distract herself with movement. Those feelings were an anomaly and she needed to push them aside tonight. Tonight was about finding out why Guy was intent on marrying Miss Frant despite seeming so reluctant to do so.

Emma listened carefully for a minute. The household had fallen quiet about half an hour earlier and she hadn't heard anything since. Already she had slipped the keys to the kitchen door into the pocket of her dressing gown. Over the top she wrapped her thickest cloak and fastened it tightly. It had a hood which she lifted over her hair, another layer of protection against the cold English nights.

Silently she made her way downstairs, thankful all the servants slept in the attic as she jangled the keys in the lock. In a few seconds she was outside, the door closed behind her, shivering already at the cool temperature.

The garden at Number Six Primrose Place wasn't tiny by London standards. It had a patio area and a stretch of grass bordered by some flower beds. There was a corner tucked away from view of the house behind some larger bushes with a little wooden bench, and this was where Emma was headed. She didn't know if Guy would be there already, but hoped so— she doubted she would be able to stay out for more than half an hour in temperatures as low as they were.

'Good evening,' Guy's low voice said from the

shadows. He was sitting on the bench, looking re-laxed and much less ruffled than earlier in the eve-ning. Emma felt her heart skip in her chest as he smiled up at her and patted the seat beside him.

Emma came and sat, her legs brushing against Guy's, and she felt a moment of warmth despite the layers between them.

'Have you been waiting long?'

'About half an hour. I saw the last candle get blown out and figured it wouldn't be too long before you emerged.'

'You must be freezing.'

He shrugged. 'You forget I spent my childhood and my youth in England. I'm not as reliant on the fiery desert temperatures as you.'

Emma sat back, trying to calm herself, trying to push down the desire to reach out and have him wrap his arms around her.

'Did you enjoy the rest of the opera?'

'Yes,' she said. 'It is a strange experience and I was surprised to understand so much of it even though I don't speak Italian, but I thought it was very emotive.'

'Opera can be quite polarising. People either love it or hate it.'

'I would definitely go again. Did you enjoy it?'

'The opera was good...' he grimaced '...the com-pany less so.'

'Miss Frant?'

He shook his head. 'Miss Frant is fine, a little young, a little naïve about the world, but she is pleasant enough. It is her parents I find hard to spend any length of time with. Her mother is kind, but a very nervous soul who frets about everything from the opera house catching on fire to whether a draught will give her pneumonia. Her father is overly effusive and gave me at least a dozen shoulder claps while I was with them.'

'How do you know the Frants?'

'They are friends of my father.'

'Ah.' She wondered if the match between Guy and Miss Frant was some sort of family arrangement, but dismissed the idea quickly. Guy had led his own life, independently, for too long to be pushed into marriage because of a family connection.

Sitting back, Guy let out a sigh and then turned to her and gave a smile.

'I'd better tell you, hadn't I? Before you freeze.'

Emma nodded.

'You said you remembered that letter I received when we returned from that trip to Cairo?'

The trip to Cairo had been amazing. They had stayed with an old friend of her father's, another obsessed with antiquities. Her father and his friend had spent their days poring over old artefacts while Guy had taken her and Cecilia to see the pyramids. When they had returned Emma had felt as though her life couldn't get any more perfect, then Guy had quickly announced his intention to leave Egypt and everything had started to unravel.

'Yes, from your sister.'

'Sophia used to write to me a lot, letters telling me of her studies and her time at our country estate, but this letter was different. I realised later that she had been hiding things from me, all my family had.' He grimaced and ran a hand through his hair. 'My father has been struggling for a while, it would appear. His memory is failing, he keeps forgetting things that he has done or have been said to him. He made some poor choices because of this, spent money he did not have, lost money at the card tables.'

'I'm sorry, Guy.' Emma had never met Guy's family, but he had always spoken of them fondly.

'He's lost all of the family money, borrowed from friends and not been able to pay them back, then took a loan from some very unscrupulous people.'

Emma started to see why Guy had been so harried in his last days before leaving Egypt.

'It is why I sold my business. I sent the money back and that, plus selling some of the land we owned, was just enough for all of his debts. All except one.'

'Oh, Guy, I had no idea.'

'My father is a proud man and it is destroying him, this loss of control. I engaged a solicitor to act on my behalf while I was out of the country and he managed to sort out most of the mess, but I knew sooner or later I needed to come home myself, to take over the responsibilities my father cannot be in charge of any longer.'

Emma reached out and took his hand, lacing her fingers between his and holding it lightly on her lap.

'I took the long route home. I think I couldn't face the idea my father, the man I knew and loved, wasn't going to be the one who greeted me on my return.'

'Is he very different?'

'Yes. He used to be a strong man, a confident man. Now he is bewildered most of the time, bewildered and confused. He forgets I have returned most days and seems surprised when I am sitting at the breakfast table each morning.'

'It must be a relief for your mother and your sister to have you home.'

'Yes. At least I can shoulder some of the burden for them.'

'And is that what Miss Frant is? Some of that burden?'

He let out a loud exhalation and then nodded. 'My father borrowed a large amount of money from the Frants. They're good people, kind people, and when they realised what a state my father was in they made very generous allowances. They're wealthy and Mr Frant agreed to forgive some of the debt if we tied our families together.'

Everything made sense. Guy's departure from Egypt when he had previously seemed so happy, and his reluctant engagement to a woman he didn't care for.

'I do have enough money to pay off the debt without marrying Miss Frant if we sold Elmwood House, but it would leave Sophia without anything for her dowry.' He grimaced, 'And it would mean my father would have to be uprooted. I'm not sure he would survive leaving the familiar and having to live somewhere new.'

Emma saw his predicament. Either he used the money to pay off the debt and left his sister without a dowry, reducing her chances of a good marriage, and unsettled his already unwell father even further. Or he married Miss Frant and allowed his sister a chance of a better future and his father some peace in his final months or years. Of course he had chosen to put Sophia and his father before himself.

'You're a good brother, a good son.'

He shook his head. 'A good brother would have been here. A good son would never have let things get this bad.'

Turning to him, she reached out with her free hand and touched his cheek, feeling the roughness of the stubble on her fingertips.

'You've given up the life you loved for your family. You are a good brother. You are a good son.'

Guy reached up and placed his hand over hers, pressing it into his cheek. Slowly he slid it towards his lips and kissed her on the palm.

Emma felt her pulse quicken and as though time slowed. All she could think of was the feel of his lips on her skin. All too soon Guy shifted, gently placing her hand back on her lap and moving away a couple of inches.

'I'm sorry I didn't tell you. It's been a hard few months.'

'Guy, you know I would help you if I could.' There was a hollowness inside her and she felt a surge of anger towards her father.

'I know, Em.'

'I would give you everything I have, but...' She trailed off, finding it too hard to tell him that her father hadn't seemed to trust her with a large inheritance.

'You don't need to explain. It's your money.'

She shook her head. 'It's not, that's the thing. My father left me an annuity—it will let me live comfortably, but not extravagantly. And he left me the house in Egypt, of course, but although it is beautiful it isn't worth all that much...' Emma paused, trying to ignore the pain she felt, the sense of betrayal when she found out her father had given away most of his fortune rather than passing it to her or Cecilia.

'He bequeathed all the artefacts and antiques he had accumulated over the years to various museums and collectors and he left a large sum of money to try to help establish a museum in Cairo or Luxor.'

Guy's eyes were wide with surprise and for a moment he said nothing.

'I'm sorry, Em, I didn't know.'

It had been one of the reasons she had decided to leave Egypt. With the house cleared of all the artefacts that had once been her father's pride and joy it felt empty and reminded her that he had chosen others to receive his life's work, not her.

'I think I can understand why he did it, if I set aside my emotions. He wanted the antiques shared with the world, he wanted the museums to be his legacy, but I still can't help feeling betrayed.'

'He didn't tell you he was going to do it?'

Emma shook her head. 'Of course I knew I wouldn't inherit the title and property in England that went with it, but I thought he would trust me enough to leave me the rest of his estate. I wouldn't have hoarded all the artefacts for myself. It just would have been nice to be able to choose what I kept and what was given away.'

'I did wonder why you were staying with your aunt rather than renting a house of your own.'

'Aunt Letitia is very generous and I am enjoying getting to know her, but it isn't very nice to be so reliant on someone else, not when my father was a wealthy man.'

'It's not a reflection on you, Em. You are not reckless or untrustworthy.'

Sometimes it was nice to have someone who knew exactly what you were thinking without having to say it out loud.

'He didn't trust me though, this shows it. I know I

am a woman, but I was his only child. I ran our household, I learned to write and speak fluent Egyptian, as well as ancient Greek and Latin. I read all the classics. I could debate with him for hours on matters of politics or ancient civilisations. Yet I was not worthy of his trust *because* I was a woman.'

Guy remained silent, reaching out and taking her hand, the gesture making some of the simmering anger settle and dissipate.

'So you see, I can't help you, not with the money, even though I would in a heartbeat.'

'I know you would. And I don't think what your father did was right or fair. I have an enormous amount of respect for him, but he has not treated you well here.'

When she had read a copy of her father's will Emma had been numb with grief and at first the enormity of what he had done hadn't really registered, but as time had passed she had felt betrayed by his actions. She wasn't greedy, she didn't feel she needed a fortune— she had been more upset about some of the artefacts that had sentimental value as well as being valuable in cultural and monetary terms. Almost a year on, it still hurt.

'You will find your place in the world, Em,' Guy said quietly.

Her head brushed against his shoulder as she looked up quickly, seeing the affection in his eyes.

'I know.'

She swayed towards him, catching a hint of his subtle cologne, and had the urge to bury her face in his shirt and let his arms engulf her.

'Miss Frant seems pleasant enough,' Emma said,

trying to distract herself from the almost overwhelming desire to kiss Guy. He was her friend and right now he was struggling with the idea of having to marry for money. The last thing he needed was another woman throwing herself at him.

'She is. She seems young and hasn't seen much of the world, but I am sure we can lead a satisfactory life together.'

Emma closed her eyes. She knew what Guy had given up already. After his time in the army, a time he didn't often speak about, but which she knew had included some harrowing moments, he had thrived on life in Luxor. He'd been happy, settled, content. It seemed cruel that he would have to sacrifice the life he loved, but even that wouldn't be enough—he still needed to marry someone he didn't want to.

'Is Miss Frant pleased with the match?'

'I think so. Her family own a number of mills up north, they're wealthy and have risen through society, but haven't been completely accepted by the *ton*. My family are well connected, if now destitute. In some ways it is a perfect union.'

Of course Miss Frant would be happy with the match. Not only would it help secure her family's place in society, Guy was the perfect husband. He was a dashing army officer, brave and selfless, and a kind man.

And attractive, the little voice in her head said. Again she was imagining him kissing her here in the darkness, laying her down on the bench and covering her body with his own.

Emma shifted uncomfortably. She needed to stop thinking of Guy this way. Soon he would be a married man, a married man whose wife probably wouldn't want him socialising with another young, unmarried woman and certainly not one who couldn't keep control of her inappropriate and salacious thoughts.

She knew Guy wasn't the sort of man to be pushed into anything, but with a pang of sadness she realised their relationship would soon change irrevocably. Guy wouldn't stop seeing her because his wife would ask him to, but because it would be the right thing to do—he was a man who had morals. They might still converse at balls or exchange pleasantries at dinner parties, but there would be no more of *this*. No more time just the two of them.

'I know it is selfish, but I feel as though I'm losing you all over again,' Emma said quietly.

Guy raised his eyes to meet her and even in the darkness she could see the glint of green. For a long moment he didn't say anything, and Emma felt the air crackle between them with a new intensity. She felt off balance, off centre, and knew if she didn't move she was likely to do something she would regret.

Suddenly she stood, stumbling in the dark as her feet hurried to keep up with the rest of her body. Guy stood, too, and gripped her by the arms, steadying her.

The time ticked past as they stood there, neither moving, neither wanting to be the first one to tear themselves away.

'You're cold,' Guy said eventually, giving her a brotherly rub on the arm. 'Get back inside, we can talk some more soon.'

Wordlessly she nodded. It was the sensible thing to do, but part of her wanted to stay out here with Guy.

He guided her back to the house, leaving her at the kitchen door.

'Goodnight,' he said and then disappeared into the darkness, leaving Emma to force herself to go inside rather than call after him.

Chapter Six

Guy picked up the magnifying glass and looked at the tiny figurine, feeling some of the tension and anxiety from the last few days leave him as he focused on the artefact. His business in Egypt had been transport and shipping, making the connections between the east and the west. It had been successful and lucrative, but to him it had been nothing more than a business. His real passion lay in the history lying buried underneath the sand. Ancient Egyptian artefacts often surfaced and he had been actively involved in searching for lost tombs and temples. He loved how each piece revealed a little about the ancient civilisation, how slowly scholars were building up a picture of the life of the people and the rulers from thousands of years ago.

It had been heartbreaking to leave it all behind, but at least here at the British Museum he could be useful while immersing himself in the artefacts he found so fascinating. Carefully he took a brush and began to clean away some of the residual sand that stuck in the little grooves of the figurine. The base was jagged, suggesting it had been broken off something else, but there was nothing else in the boxes of as yet unclassified artefacts that fitted.

'Guy,' a familiar voice called and he looked up from his work with a smile.

He hadn't seen Emma since their midnight meeting a few days earlier. Still, he could remember how the air between them had crackled with tension and how tempted he had been to kiss her. Guy wasn't inexperienced with women—he'd had mistresses before and more casual dalliances over the years. He knew when a woman was attracted to him, when she got that slightly dreamy look in her eyes and wanted to be kissed. He'd been so close to giving in to that temptation, so close to pulling her body to him and tasting the sweetness of her lips.

It would have been a mistake and one that would have changed their friendship irrevocably, but change was coming anyway. Perhaps he should have kissed her.

For a moment he thought back to a more distant memory, of the time just as he was about to leave for England when he had pulled Emma aside and asked her whether she wanted to be with him. After years of waiting, of thinking he would give her more time to grow, to find herself, he'd needed to know how she felt before he left for good. She'd given him a confused little smile and said she was confident he would be back to visit her before too long. Guy hadn't pushed—it was clear from her response that she didn't think of him as anything more than her friend.

When they had sat in the garden together at midnight a few days ago she had looked at him differently and as she walked over to him in the depths of the

Egyptology exhibition he could see the same flash of awareness, of desire, in her eyes.

'Emma, what are you doing here?'

'I offered my services to Mr Paxton. It'll be a welcome relief from the series of dinner parties and promenades in the freezing cold parks. He said I would find you here when I arrived and you could show me what to do. If you don't mind, of course?'

For a moment she stood awkwardly, as if wondering if she could trust herself to come and sit so close beside him. Giving her his most benign smile, he patted the chair next to him.

'Come and sit down. I'll show you how we clean the artefacts and then go about trying to classify them.'

She slipped into the seat beside him, her arm lightly brushing his, but then the contact was gone in less than a second.

'Many of the boxes come well packed, with ledgers of where and when each piece was found. The pieces we have here are more challenging. They've been muddled at some point during transport, or have been recovered from somewhere other than their original site.'

Emma handled the brushes expertly and they slipped into an easy rhythm, cleaning and polishing a couple of the artefacts. They had worked side by side together so many times that the familiarity soothed the tension between them.

'The idea is to clean things up and use any information we may have to build a picture of what an item is and when and where it is from. We write down our notes and then box the pieces up. The curators have a meeting once a month and I present the most interesting finds to them to see what should be added to the collection.'

'Who has the final say?'

'I've never had my recommendation turned down. Mr Paxton and the other curators are well read and sensible men, but none of them has ever been to Egypt. They are happy for someone else to make the decisions in this area.'

He watched as Emma gently ran a cloth over a chipped Canopic jar with the utmost care. Her movements were delicate, borne from years helping her father handle the artefacts that came into his house for his perusal.

'This is beautiful,' Emma said, showing the jar to Guy. It had the head of a falcon carved and painted on the green-glazed porcelain. The beak was broken halfway up and the rest of the jar had a few cracks and chips in it. It was nowhere near a perfect specimen, but Emma was right, it was beautiful.

She started to rummage through the paperwork to see if anything was noted about this particular find and Guy felt content to be working beside her. Already he mourned the loss of their friendship, even though as yet he hadn't lost her. Still, it was inevitable. He had resigned himself to marrying Miss Frant and, once he was a married man, he would owe it to his wife to keep his distance from Emma. It wouldn't be fair to spend time alone with a woman he knew he was attracted to.

'Got it,' she said with enthusiasm. 'There is reference to an incomplete set of Canopic jars found at a dig site to the west of Luxor on the west bank of the Nile. They're described as green porcelain—this must be one of them.'

She stood and went over to the box of artefacts, lifting pieces out until she found the two matching jars.

'Look, Guy.' She held up the finds, her eyes alight with enthusiasm.

He felt something tighten inside him and had to resist the urge to pull her to him for a celebratory embrace.

'Let me help you clean them.'

Carefully she passed one to him, her fingers brushing his as she transferred the delicate jar.

'Does Miss Frant know why you are going to marry her?'

Guy blinked and put his brush down carefully on the table. Emma was looking at him earnestly and he knew he had to answer her.

'I'm not sure. We met a couple of times before the subject of marriage was broached. She knows it is being arranged by her father, but I doubt she knows the reasons behind the arrangement.'

'Isn't it important that she does know?'

'It's how these things work, Em. A young woman doesn't have much choice in the matter, so why would she be involved in the negotiations?'

'Don't you think she should know you're marrying her to settle a debt?'

He sighed and ran a hand through his hair. 'What good will that do?'

'You wouldn't be starting your married life based on a lie.'

Guy fell silent. In many ways he could see Emma was right, although he still didn't think he should tell Miss Frant the only reason he was even considering marrying her was so his sister could have a decent dowry and his father wouldn't lose his home.

'When I marry,' he said slowly, trying to choose his words carefully, 'I will not love my wife, but I will do my best by her. I barely know the girl, but Miss Frant deserves my respect and consideration. I never planned to be a husband like this, Em, I've never believed in matches made for money, but I will try to be a good husband now I'm forced into it.'

Emma puffed out her cheeks and exhaled loudly. 'I know, I'm sorry.' She shook her head and he could see there were tears in her eyes. 'I'm being selfish. I don't want to lose you, not after I've just got you back in my life.'

'You won't lose me.' They both knew it was a lie.

She smiled weakly at him and Guy reached out, wrapping an arm around her shoulder and gently pulling her towards him. It was meant as a friendly, reassuring embrace, but as soon as their bodies touched he knew it was a mistake. A thrum of longing passed through him and he felt his hand move of its own accord, making his fingers dance over the material of her dress.

Emma shifted in her seat so her body was angled towards him. Guy looked down into her eyes and felt as though he were falling. Emma had always been attractive, but these last eighteen months had changed her. She'd grown up and this had brought a confidence and poise that made her shine.

'Guy,' Emma murmured, her voice barely more than a whisper.

'Emma.'

For a long moment they stayed frozen in one position, then with great effort Guy moved away.

He stood abruptly and walked over to the wooden box, pretending to look for something inside, but instead trying to silence the voice in his head telling him to go back and kiss the woman he loved and damn the consequences.

Slowly the voice fell quiet. For too long he had allowed himself to do whatever he wanted, to live the life that made *him* happy, and look where that had landed the people he loved. No, he had to think of the greater good. And the greater good did not involve kissing Emma, even if every fibre in his body was screaming at him to do so.

'Sophia is eager to meet you,' he said, hoping a change in subject would set them back on a safer course.

The light returned to Emma's eyes. 'I would *love* to meet your sister.'

'Although I have to warn you she is rather in awe of your life, your independence.'

'I hardly have that much independence.'

Guy laughed. 'Compared to her life yours seems as free as a seabird.'

'Do you know I had three people asking me where I was going this afternoon? I felt as though I needed to convene a meeting to discuss my movements.'

'Three?'

'Cecilia of course, then there was my aunt. She seems to think that because we are staying with her she has some sort of responsibility for me. Then the lady's maid my aunt has assigned me kept asking me so she could "properly plan my wardrobe".'

'You are an unmarried woman, Em. And your aunt *is* responsible for you.'

She pulled a face.

'At least you haven't got some overbearing male relative appointed as your guardian and keen to marry you off to the highest bidder.'

'Hmm. True. Well, my life certainly doesn't feel very free. Why is it Cecilia can walk through the park unchaperoned, but I would cause a scandal by doing the exact same thing?'

Guy suppressed a smile. 'It's not fair, but you don't need to understand it, Em. Stick to the rules.'

'I can see why your sister might crave a life of freedom.'

'She hasn't even had her debut yet. Don't tempt her away with stories of a carefree life abroad.'

'When can I meet her?'

Guy contemplated for a moment. It would be good to get away from London, to spend some time with Emma before the details of his marriage were settled.

'Next week. My family would love you to come and stay.'

'It won't upset your father too much?'

'No. He spends most of his time in his bedroom now, although my mother does make sure he gets out for a walk around the grounds every day. He does not know some of the servants who have been at the house for a few years, but it does not seem to distress him too much. I'm sure he will hardly notice you are there.'

'Then I would love to come. Will we travel together?'

'Yes, why not? You can try out an English horse and see if you can ride one better than a camel.'

'I seem to remember I was the graceful one on the back of a camel and you were the one who struggled.'

'Your memory is flawed, but I forgive you. It was very hot that day.'

Guy picked out a small amulet from the box and came and sat back down next to Emma. Balance and sanity had been restored and they had slipped back into their normal easy way with each other. The moment they'd shared had been an anomaly, nothing more. Perhaps to be expected when they were reunited after so long and trying to find the place they had in each other's lives now they were in England.

'I do remember perfectly how the camel chewed your hat while you were standing talking to that shop-keeper. I've never seen a camel looking so pleased with himself.'

'He did return it rather slobbery,' Guy confessed.

'I can't believe you still wore it.'

'It was a nice hat and a little bit of camel saliva never hurt anyone.'

'The rim never recovered. Every time I saw you wear that hat it made me smile to remember the camel incident.'

'Do you know I found that hat when I was packing for my return to England? I was loath to throw it away even then, but I couldn't justify bringing it all the way across Europe.'

Emma suddenly lost her smile and he realised she must be thinking of all the things her father had given away rather than passing them on to her. Lord West-combe had been a collector and their spacious house had been filled with furniture and art and artefacts from around the world. He wondered if this was one

of the reasons Emma had decided to leave Egypt—
the house must have seemed empty without all the
antiques her father had lovingly filled it with over
the years.

'I left most of my possessions in our house in
Egypt. The trinkets I'd collected as a girl, the things
my mother left for me.'

Guy regarded her for a long moment. 'It's your escape plan, isn't it? The house in Luxor.'

Emma gave a guilty smile. 'I didn't know what
it would be like here. I couldn't imagine not having
something to go back to.'

Being unmarried it would have been almost impossible for her to stay in Egypt alone, but he understood
feeling as though one needed a way back in case things
didn't work out as one expected.

'Is it as bad as you thought?'

She considered for a second before answering. 'I
didn't realise how hard it would be not knowing anyone. Not even just friends, but I don't know the servants, the man who brings the milk every day, the
people who live in the same street. In all of England
the only people I know are you and Cecilia, and my
aunt a little now, of course.'

'Give it some time and slowly you will start to feel
as though you belong.'

She gave him a sceptical look, but didn't answer,
instead settling back down to examine the incomplete
set of Canopic jars.

Chapter Seven

Emma stood on the steps outside the pristinely decorated town house and hesitated. It would be easy to turn away and get back into the carriage.

'Don't be ridiculous,' she muttered to herself. Earlier in the day Miss Frant had sent a note, inviting Emma to join her for tea and sandwiches in the afternoon, and Emma couldn't see a good reason to refuse.

Before she could talk herself out of it she knocked on the door, which was quickly opened by a footman in a red and gold livery that made him look a little like a soldier in uniform.

'Lady Emma Westcombe, to see Miss Frant.'

The footman bowed deeply and then led her through to a bright drawing room where Miss Frant and her mother were sitting with their needlework.

'Lady Emma,' Miss Frant gushed as Emma entered. 'I'm so glad you could come. I've been intrigued ever since we met at the opera. Captain Fitzgerald tells me he was firm friends with your father in Egypt.'

Emma smiled and allowed the eager young woman to guide her to a seat.

'This is my mother. Mother, this is Lady Emma, the friend of Captain Fitzgerald I met at the opera.'

'A pleasure to meet you, Lady Emma.'

'You must tell me everything about Egypt. I'm obsessed and Captain Fitzgerald, as you know, is so very quiet and stoical.'

Emma felt her eyebrows rise and quickly worked to settle her expression into something more neutral. Guy hardly knew this young woman, that was probably why he wasn't his normal talkative, charming self.

'What has he told you about his time there?'

Miss Frant tilted her head to one side and considered for a moment. 'Not much. I know he was posted there during his time in the army and then returned later. And I understand he did something in shipping and transport.' She gave a nervous little laugh. 'Not much at all, I suppose, for a man I am soon to marry.'

Emma felt a pang of sympathy for this young woman. She seemed keen on the marriage, keen on Guy, but without really knowing him.

'I first met Captain Fitzgerald seven years ago, when I was fifteen,' Emma said, smiling as she remembered the way he had listened to her opinions on the death mask he had brought to show her father even though she had still been a girl. 'He and my father were both interested in Egyptian history and antiques and he would often come to the house to discuss a find with my father.'

'How exciting. I've only read about Egypt in books, but I understand there is a whole civilisation buried under the sand.'

'Yes, and Guy—Captain Fitzgerald—loved everything about it.'

'It sounds as though you know Captain Fitzgerald well, Lady Emma,' Mrs Frant said quietly from the corner of the room. She had been sitting so still and silent Emma had almost forgotten she was there.

'I do.' There was no point denying it. 'We would talk when Captain Fitzgerald visited the house and my father and I went on a few trips with him as well. He is a good friend.'

'Would you care for a stroll around the garden, Lady Emma? It is a beautiful day.' Miss Frant threw a glance at her mother as if wanting to get away from the older woman for a few minutes.

Emma forced a smile on to her face and nodded, glad she had brought her shawl with her. She enjoyed a walk in the sunshine and heat, but people in England seemed to think it pleasant to go for a stroll in frosty temperatures.

Outside the garden was of generous proportions for such a central location. It was clear the Frants had money and good taste alongside it.

Miss Frant slipped her arm through Emma's as they walked and bent her head as if about to speak in confidence.

'May I speak freely with you? I know we barely know one another, but I feel as though we are going to be firm friends.'

It was impossible to dislike Miss Frant, she was so earnest, so exuberant.

'Of course.'

'I feel as though I barely know Captain Fitzgerald. The details of the marriage are being arranged by my father and I've only met the Captain on a couple of occasions. He seems pleasant…but a little distant. Is that unfair?'

Emma took a breath before answering, wondering how much she should say to this young woman. It would be unfair to let her believe that the marriage was for more romantic reasons than it was, but Guy *would* make a good husband. He would be kind to Miss Frant and show her the respect many women didn't receive from their husbands.

'Captain Fitzgerald is a good man, I'm sure you know that already. He is charming and intelligent and will make the best of husbands.' She paused, choosing her words carefully. 'Of course I do not know all the details, but you have to remember that until a few months ago Captain Fitzgerald's life was on a different course. He was running a business in Egypt, with plans to stay long-term. Family commitments brought him home, and now he has decided to marry, but it was not what he expected from his life.' She smiled reassuringly. 'Give him time.'

Miss Frant looked at her gratefully. 'Gosh, it is nice to talk like this. This is how I thought my first Season would be, strolling arm in arm and chatting with a friend. Alongside all the balls and dancing, of course.'

'What do you mean?'

Scrunching up her nose, Miss Frant stared off into the distance. 'For some reason I expected the Season to be more *friendly*. I thought even though all the young women were competing for attention from the same set of men, I would still make some firm friends.'

'And that hasn't happened?'

Miss Frant shook her head. 'No one has been absolutely vile, but there is a certain coolness from the other debutantes.'

'Did you know anyone before the Season started?'

'No, not really. We only arrived in London two months ago and everyone seemed to know each other already.' She sighed quietly. 'Father warned me some people would turn their noses up because of how he earned his money, but really, what is so bad about working hard and being successful?'

'Nothing at all,' Emma said quietly.

'I hope we will be friends, Lady Emma. I would like that very much.'

Emma nodded and smiled, feeling a little sick. If she was honest with herself, she had come today hoping she would dislike Miss Frant. It would make the mild sense of jealousy and injustice easier to stomach. Instead she'd found a sweet and eager young woman who it was impossible to do anything but warm to.

Emma closed her eyes for a moment and let out a slow breath. Guy might be marrying Miss Frant for the wrong reasons, but she couldn't blame the young woman for that. Miss Frant was a pawn, an innocent, in the arrangement between her father and Guy.

'Tell me about where you're from, Miss Frant,' Emma said, deciding in an instant that she would make an effort to befriend this lonely young woman.

'Please, call me Abigail.'

'And I am Emma.'

'Do you really want to know about Manchester?'

'Yes. Very much so. I left England when I was four years old, Abigail, and I barely remember anything of it. I hope to travel and visit all the places I hear people talk about: the South Downs, the Lake District, the Cornish coast. It all sounds so marvellous.'

'I'm not sure anyone would call Manchester marvellous,' Miss Frant said slowly, furrowing her brow, 'but I love it there. The city is always so busy and full of noise. Our house is right in the very centre and I love being able to look out of my window and watch the world go by.'

'That sounds…' Emma started to say, but was distracted by Mrs Frant hurrying down the steps into the garden.

'Abigail, Captain Fitzgerald has come to call on you.'

'Oh.' Abigail immediately looked flustered and Emma squeezed her hand.

'Do I look presentable, Lady Emma?'

'Call me Emma. And, yes, you look lovely.'

Emma helped her smooth down her hair and straighten her dress before Abigail nodded as if summoning up her courage.

'There's no need to be nervous,' Emma said quietly. 'For all his daring deeds and military honours Captain Fitzgerald is quite the nicest person I've ever known.'

'Really?'

'Really.'

Guy paced backwards and forward across the length of the dining room as he waited for his future fiancée to come back inside. He hadn't really wanted to come here today, but he'd realised he needed to make more of an effort to get to know Miss Frant. One day soon they would be married and it would be easier for both of them if they weren't strangers when that happened.

Mrs Frant, his future mother-in-law, bustled back through the glass doors that led to the garden and gave him an anxious smile.

'Abigail will be in shortly. Shall I ring for some fresh tea, Captain Fitzgerald? Or perhaps you'd like something to eat? A sandwich? Or something more substantial? Yes, let me go and see what Cook can prepare for you.'

Before Guy could object Mrs Frant rushed out of the drawing room, apparently forgetting she was supposed to be chaperoning his meeting with her daughter.

He looked up as the doors opened again, his whole body freezing as Emma stepped inside. It was such a shock to see her here, so unexpected that for a long moment he couldn't move, couldn't even blink.

'Emma?'

She smiled at him serenely as if it weren't completely bizarre that she was here with his future fiancée whom she had only met once before, briefly.

He barely saw Miss Frant enter the room behind her.

'Good afternoon, Captain Fitzgerald,' Miss Frant said and bobbed into a wobbly little curtsy.

'Good afternoon, Miss Frant. I trust you are well?'

'Yes, thank you.'

The conversation faltered and Guy couldn't help but turn back to Emma. He wanted to ask what the hell she was doing here, but knew he needed to modify his language first.

'I will leave, Abigail. It has been such a pleasant afternoon, but you must spend some time with Captain Fitzgerald. Perhaps we can go for a stroll later in the week?'

Abigail? When had Emma got to know his soon-to-be fiancée well enough to start using her given name?

'I would like that, Emma.'

'I will send you a note.' Emma made to leave, gently touching him on the arm as she passed. He couldn't help himself, he reached out and took her hand, stopping her from going.

'What are you doing here?' he asked more roughly than he had intended.

'Miss Frant invited me.'

He wasn't sure why he was so shocked. Emma was a friendly young woman, she was always taking in waifs and strays, always keen to nurture a new friendship. For a moment she had felt betrayed he hadn't told her about his impending engagement and then quietly she had decided she would get to know the woman who would be his future wife.

He should be happy, relieved that she was finding a way to stay in his life, albeit in a slightly different manner. Instead he felt the bitter taste of disappointment that she had adapted so easily. Not that he ever wanted her to be upset, but a little regret that soon their friendship would change for ever would have been nice.

Emma slipped her hand from underneath his and gave him a smile, then she glided from the room, leaving him alone with Miss Frant.

'Lady Emma is so lovely,' Miss Frant said after a long moment, nervously perching on the edge of one of the chairs.

'Mmm.' He didn't know why he found it so hard to talk to the young woman. Of course they had absolutely nothing in common, no shared interests, but he

had always been adept at making small talk with anyone at all, be they sailors or dukes. Something about
his situation with Miss Frant meant he struggled to
talk about even the mundane with her.

'I'm so pleased to have met her. I'm sure we will
become good friends.'

The idea made him feel vaguely sick. He could
imagine it now, his wife and the woman he had been
attracted to for years sipping tea and laughing. It would
be pure torture.

'Lady Emma does not know what her plans are.
She may not be staying in London long,' he said a little too abruptly.

'Oh.'

'In her heart she wishes to return to Egypt, but she
knows that is not practical.'

'And you?' Miss Frant said quietly.

Guy turned to face her, looking her in the eye for
the first time since he had arrived.

'And I?'

'Do you wish to return to Egypt? In your heart?'

'That chapter of my life is over,' he said stiffly. He
suddenly had the urge to get out of the house, to get
away from Miss Frant. 'I'm sorry,' he said, plucking
his watch from the little pocket in his jacket and giving it a cursory glance. 'Please excuse me, Miss Frant,
we will have to do this another day.'

She gave an understanding smile and he felt like
a complete cad. There was absolutely nothing wrong
with Miss Frant and she definitely deserved better
from him. Still, he bowed and took his leave, hurrying out of the house before her mother could return.

Guy walked briskly, catching sight of Emma after

rounding a couple of corners. It would not do to shout out to her, so he picked up his pace until he was close enough to call at a respectable level.

'Emma.'

She turned around immediately, a bright smile on her lips before the look of confusion crossed her face.

'Shouldn't you be with Miss Frant?'

'I will rearrange.'

'Oh. Are you well?'

'Yes. No. Yes.' Now he had caught up with her he didn't know what to say. Instead he took her hand and placed it in the crook of his arm as they began to walk side by side.

'I didn't expect to see you at the Frants' house.'

'I was lying in bed last night thinking about you,' Emma said with no hint of flirtation. Inwardly Guy groaned, but he managed to keep his face neutral.

'I realised that if Miss Frant is your future then I needed to make an effort to get to know her. I hope we shall be friends for a very long time, Guy, and if you are married that means being friends with Miss Frant as well.'

'Was she receptive?'

'You're very lucky, Guy. Miss Frant is a sweet young woman.'

'Mmm.'

'You don't sound convinced.'

'I agree she is pleasant enough.'

'Think what you could be lumbered with in an arranged marriage—Miss Frant is kind and caring and eager to make you happy.'

'You're right,' he said with a sigh. 'It could be so much worse.'

'She hasn't had an easy time of it.'

'What do you mean?'

'The snobbery of the *ton*. People won't let her forget she is the daughter of a self-made man. Her grandfather built the family business up from nothing and her father inherited his business acumen and paired it with the advantages of a good education to make it even more of a success.'

Emma stepped out to cross the road a pace ahead of him as a carriage came careening round the corner much faster than was safe. He felt Emma freeze in shock as the horses headed for her and pulled her back sharply by the arm. The force he used whipped her out of the path of the horses just in time, but made both of them stumble. He swung Emma round, trying to stop her from tumbling to the ground, and her body hit his chest with some force.

Luckily she was only small, but still the momentum was enough to make him stagger back. His shoulders hit the black metal railings behind him and the air was forcefully expelled from his lungs in a low grunt. Emma stayed pressed to his chest for a long moment as they both took stock of what had happened.

Without moving the rest of her body she tilted her head up so she was looking at him.

'Thank you,' she said, a slight tremor in her voice.

'You're welcome. Now, are we even from the runaway horse incident in Cairo?'

This made Emma smile and he saw some of the colour return to her cheeks.

'It cancels that one out, but you still owe me for the irate sword-wielding shopkeeper in Alexandria.'

Slowly, reluctantly, Guy pushed Emma away, knowing they couldn't stay with their arms wrapped around one another for much longer. A few seconds after a near-death experience would be forgiven or over-looked, but if he held on to her for longer someone would notice.

As she stepped back and took a moment to straighten her dress Emma looked as though she wanted to say something more, but thought better of it. Instead she laced her hand through Guy's arm and gave it a squeeze.

He resisted the urge to drop a kiss on to her head and they began walking again, this time both of them checking the road before they stepped out to cross the street.

Chapter Eight

'Come on in, dear, don't be shy,' her aunt called as Emma paused outside the door. Aunt Letitia was her father's younger sister, but ill health had aged the kindly woman, so she looked much older than Lord Westcombe had when he'd died. The curtains to the room were drawn, only a small amount of light filtering through at the top and the bottom and the room felt hot and stuffy with the fire roaring in the grate.

'How are you, Aunt?'

'It's a good day today, Emma, thank you for asking.' Her aunt patted a space on the bed beside her with crooked fingers, wincing at the pain of moving them. Emma sat down.

'Your hands look so sore... Is there nothing the doctors can do for them?'

'No, dear, just laudanum. I take it when the pain is unbearable, but I hate the way it makes me sleep all day and makes me feel groggy for the few hours I am awake. The heat helps.' She motioned to the roaring fire. 'Now, tell me what ball you're going to tonight.'

'Lord and Lady Highbridge are hosting a ball for

their daughter's debut. It is going to be a masquerade.' Emma couldn't help but smile—it was her first masquerade and she was excited.

'I thought it was the masquerade tonight, but I do lose track of time sometimes. I have something for you.'

'Oh?'

'When your father left for Egypt he declared he would never return.' She smiled indulgently. 'Henry was always so dramatic about things, so I wasn't sure if he would change his mind and bring you home one day.'

Emma could imagine her father making the declaration. He'd always loved a grand statement or gesture.

'He couldn't bring himself to pack away all of your mother's things. Together we went through her personal items and he chose what he would take with him and what he wanted you to have when you were older.'

These possessions Emma had cherished over the years—they were a precious link to the mother she couldn't really remember.

'Some things went into storage at your old house, but after a few years I realised your father was settled in Egypt and wasn't coming back. He asked me to choose a few things to rescue and keep for you in case you ever made the trip to England as a young woman.'

Emma saw the trunk at the end of her aunt's bed and felt a spark of excitement. She loved anything that provided a connection with her mother and couldn't wait to see what her aunt had chosen.

'Did you know Clara and I had our debuts the same year? I introduced her to Henry. She was so beautiful, Emma, the most beautiful of our Season.' She was fo-

cused on a point in the distance as if transported back
to the days of her youth. 'We went to a masquerade,
similar to the one you are attending tonight, and Clara
wore the most stunning dress. Her dance card was full
within five minutes of arriving and the gentlemen were
clamouring for her favour.'

'She talks about the masquerade in her diary. It
sounded magical.'

'It was. A night to remember.' Her aunt gestured to
the trunk. 'Open it and have a look inside.'

Slowly, feeling inexplicably nervous, Emma slipped
from the bed and knelt before the trunk. Here she was
closer to the fire and felt the heat burning into her
skin, but nothing could have torn her away from this
position right now.

She ran her fingers over the clasp and then opened
the lid, lifting it up to reveal the contents. Carefully
packed was something in a delicate blue fabric. Emma
ran her fingers over the soft material, already feeling
the connection to her mother.

'Take it out and have a look.'

With the utmost care she stood, lifting the dress
out of the trunk and allowing it to unfold. It was stunning. The material was light and looked as though it
would float with the slightest breeze and the colour
was a gorgeous light blue. In keeping with the fashion
twenty years earlier, the skirt was full and the bod-
ice would sit tighter on her chest than the dresses that
were popular now. It had delicate little cap sleeves and
a plunging neckline that would show off more skin
than Emma was used to.

'Isn't it lovely?'

Emma nodded, speechless.

'Look at the rest of the items in the trunk.'

Setting the dress carefully on the end of her aunt's bed, she leaned down and plucked out a pair of shoes and a mask designed to be secured with a blue ribbon. It was flimsy and would cover the top half of the wearer's face, with a hand-painted golden pattern of swirls and flowers on it.

'This is what my mother wore to her masquerade.'

'Yes. And I think you should wear it tonight.'

Emma returned her attention to the dress, not quite able to believe her aunt had managed to keep it in such pristine condition for all these years.

'Thank you,' she said quietly.

'I know what it is like for a girl to grow up without a mother. These little things, little mementos and memories, mean the world.'

'They do.' Emma was nearly in tears as she carefully held the dress to her, wondering if the slight hint of lemons was a remnant of the scent her mother used to wear. It was the scent she favoured and Emma felt a rush of emotion at the connection to her mother.

'Now take everything to your room and get your lady's maid to help you try it on. She will be able to do some simple adjustments if needed, but you have your mother's build and I think everything should fit.'

Before leaving the room Emma crossed over to the bed and gently embraced her aunt. 'I'm so lucky to have you and Cecilia in my life. Thank you.'

'Don't thank me. You've brightened up my home these last few weeks. And we're family, my dear— remember, I will always be here for you.'

Emma gave her aunt one final, gentle squeeze and

then gathered up the contents of the trunk and left the room, eager to see whether the dress and shoes fitted as she hoped they would.

Guy sipped his drink, pulling a face at the sweetness of it.

'Don't know why they insist on serving punch at these things,' Albert Peterson said as he laughed at Guy's expression.

'Can you imagine going to a ball where hard liquor was provided? The chaperons would have a nightmare of a time.' Guy smiled at the thought.

They were standing at the edge of the ballroom, tucked behind a potted plant. If anyone asked, he would strongly deny he was hiding, but in truth he and Albert were taking advantage of the cover of the thick foliage to escape from the relentless approaches from the matrons of society thrusting their unmarried daughters towards any eligible bachelor.

He had managed to make his excuses after a dance with a young woman who had giggled nervously throughout every time he'd tried to engage her in conversation. When he had gone to fetch a drink he had bumped into Albert Peterson, a friend from his school days, and they had retreated as far from the dance floor as they could.

'Who is that?' Peterson asked, his eyes fixed on someone who had entered the ballroom.

Guy turned, following his friend's gaze, and felt all the air being sucked out of him. Even from the first glimpse of the young woman he knew it was Emma. He would be able to recognise her from how she walked, how she carried herself. Dressed in a stun-

ning light blue dress that seemed to ripple in a non-
existent breeze, she looked like royalty. Her hair was
swept up and the mask that covered the upper part of
her face accentuated the beauty of her smile, all that
was visible below it.

'Emma,' Guy murmured, holding out his glass to
Peterson.

'You know her?'

'I do. Would you excuse me?' he said, knowing his
friend would not mind.

Emma was drawing a lot of attention, with people
looking and whispering and trying to work out who
it was under the mask. So far no one had approached
her yet, but Guy knew it would be only a matter of
seconds before someone broke free of the spell she
had put them under and then everyone else would follow. She would be surrounded within a minute and he
needed to get to her before that happened.

'Good evening my lady,' he said as he approached.

Emma's eyes lit up when she saw him and he
watched as she took a step forward and then restrained herself, remembering not to throw herself
into his arms.

'Good evening.'

'May I have the pleasure of the next dance, mysterious lady?'

'It would be my pleasure.'

Emma slipped her hand through his arm and allowed him to lead her to the dance floor. The dance
hadn't started yet, but the couples were beginning to
gather, so Guy took the opportunity to lean in and
whisper in Emma's ear, 'You look ravishing. The
whole ballroom stopped and stared when you entered.'

'Do you like the dress?'

Guy wanted to tell her it wasn't just the dress they had been spellbound by, but her in the dress. He held back, knowing if he said that she would then look at him with those innocent eyes and he would be lost and forget himself and be at risk of doing something he really shouldn't.

'It is lovely.'

'It was my mother's. My aunt had saved it for me.'

It explained the fuller skirt and fancier style.

'You are going to be fighting off the suitors tonight.'

Emma pulled a face. 'Can't I dance with you for the whole night?'

'It might cause a few raised eyebrows.'

'But no one knows who we are.'

'I think they might guess. These masks aren't exactly the most sophisticated of disguises.'

Lady Highbridge, their hostess, clapped her hands and called all the couples to the dance floor. The musicians took their cue from her and the music began.

The dance was a lively cotillion and although Guy had danced it a hundred times before he felt himself missing steps and moving a little out of time, all because he could not tear his eyes away from Emma. Every time they came back together he knew he held her a little too tightly or stepped in a little too close, but it was as if she was drawing him in, mesmerising him with her beauty.

They didn't have much chance to talk during their dances and Guy wished he could whisk her away at the end so none of the other gentlemen he could see lingering nearby could swoop in and spoil their moment.

'You must introduce me to your partner, Fitzgerald,'

Lord Hambley said as they stepped from the dance floor. 'I haven't been able to tear my eyes away.'

'No names tonight, Hambley.'

'Then might I request the pleasure of the next dance?'

There wasn't anything terrible about Hambley, but all the same Guy wanted to guide Emma through the ballroom, avoiding all the unmarried gentlemen, and secure her where there was only space for the two of them.

'That would be lovely,' Emma said, smiling graciously, although the smile didn't quite reach her eyes.

Guy watched as Hambley escorted Emma to the dance floor, leaning in a little too close to whisper something in her ear.

He forced down the jealousy that threatened to rise inside him. It was not a pleasant emotion and it wasn't his place to feel jealous about Emma. He had an almost-fiancée, a whole life of domesticity mapped out in front of him with someone other than the woman he couldn't tear his eyes away from.

For a moment he felt a ball of dread in his stomach. One day Emma would marry, she would find someone and fall in love and he would have to stand aside and watch. Of course he wanted her to be happy, but the idea of her in another man's arms made him feel sick.

Guy forced himself to look away. It wouldn't change anything by him standing at the edge of the dance floor glaring at Hambley. Emma had always turned away from the subject of marriage, stating she wasn't interested in tying herself to a man who would control her. He wondered if England was changing that. A lot had changed for her in the last year and perhaps she was going to start looking for a man to share her future with.

'Stop torturing yourself,' Guy muttered, making it all the way to the other end of the ballroom before he looked back over his shoulder.

Chapter Nine

Taking a sip from the glass of punch in her hand, Emma felt her head swim. She couldn't taste the alcohol in it, but she wasn't used to drinking. After a few glasses she knew her steps were a little more unsteady and she was having to lean more on Lord Romsey's arm.

'Are you sure you saw him come this way?' Emma peered around her.

They had stepped out of the ballroom on to the terrace. She was feeling light-headed and, if she was honest, a little vulnerable and had asked Lord Romsey if he would help her find Cecilia or Guy. The Earl had inclined his head graciously and told her he thought he'd seen Guy stepping out on to the terrace.

It was dark outside, despite a row of lamps set at regular intervals along the edge of the terrace, and Emma had to wait for a moment for her eyes to adjust. There were two other couples, one strolling along in the distance, arm in arm, chatting easily. Emma could tell by their relaxed posture they must be a married couple. There was no hint of intrigue or illicitness by their being outside.

The second couple were huddled to one end of the terrace and had their heads bent together, laughing and whispering. At first only the woman's face was visible, but as they stepped further out on to the terrace she felt a rush of relief that it wasn't Guy being so intimate with another woman.

Shaking her head to try to clear it, Emma knew she was being ridiculous. Guy was going to marry Miss Frant, it wouldn't make any difference if he flirted and charmed anyone else along the way. Not that he was the sort of callous cad to do that sort of thing.

'I'm sure I saw Captain Fitzgerald come this way,' Lord Romsey murmured, guiding her to the edge of the terrace where it overlooked the dark garden below. 'Isn't it nice to be out in the cool after the stuffiness of the ballroom?'

Emma's arms were bare and she was already starting to shiver.

'It doesn't look as though Captain Fitzgerald is here. Perhaps we can find Cecilia inside.'

'Stay a moment, enjoy the night with me...' He paused, leaning on the stone balustrade. 'Have you ever seen the stars shine so bright?'

Emma tilted her head back and looked up. It was a clear night and some of the constellations were visible, but it was nothing compared to stargazing in the desert. There the stars shone so bright it was like looking at perfect diamonds in the sky.

'Very nice,' she murmured.

'You're quite the enigma, Lady Emma,' Lord Romsey said, leaning in a little closer. Emma tried to shuffle away inconspicuously, not wanting to appear rude, but there was an urn to her left which in the summer would no doubt contain a plant or flowers, but now was sitting empty, blocking her way.

'Oh?'

'Everyone loves a mystery. I'd love to know more about you.'

'There's not much to know.' She glanced over her shoulder, aware of the swell of music from the ball-room as the door opened. Instead of anyone coming out, she realised the two couples that had been on the terrace had now returned to the ballroom. She was now out here alone with Lord Romsey. 'We should go back inside. There's no one else out here.'

'Perfect.' Lord Romsey stepped closer, his arm brushing hers, and Emma felt her heart begin to pound in her chest. She didn't want to be out here. Lord Romsey had behaved like a gentleman this evening while they were in the ballroom, but Guy's words of warning on the night of her first ball came back to her. If Lord Romsey was set on taking advantage of her, then she had given him the opportunity to do it.

'I'm going to take off your mask, Lady Emma,' he said, leaning forward. 'And then I'm going to kiss you.'

Emma began shaking her head, momentarily mute. She didn't want him to kiss her. She wanted to be back home, curled up in bed with Cecilia stroking her hair. Emma felt her head spin as the world seemed to lurch. She wished she hadn't had even one glass of punch and vowed if she got out of this situation with her reputation intact she would never, ever touch the foul liquid again.

'Don't be coy, Lady Emma. I can see in your eyes you want to be kissed.'

'No.' Finally she found her voice, but felt a little self-disgust at how weak she sounded.

Lord Romsey leaned further towards her, his hand coming up behind her mask.

'No,' she said louder this time, wriggling out of the tiny space he had her pinned in.

He hesitated, as if trying to work out if she was teasing him or truly didn't want his attentions. Seeming to decide to try one more time, he gripped her by the arm. Emma felt a heavy sensation in her stomach and realised this was the first time she had felt truly scared in another person's company. She hated how weak and vulnerable he was making her feel.

Everything happened at once. Lord Romsey pulled her towards him, and Emma allowed herself to be pulled for the first second, then she planted her hands firmly on his chest and pushed, shoving as hard as she could. At the same moment she heard the door from the ballroom open, the swell of the music and then Guy's voice shouting out, 'Get off her.'

Lord Romsey stumbled backwards, his legs hitting the stone balustrade. For an instant he swung his arms wildly, trying to regain his balance. Emma reached out, trying to grab him before it was too late, but she wasn't quick enough and the Earl fell back over the edge of the balustrade into the garden below.

Emma couldn't move. She felt herself shaking, unable to step forward to see if she had killed a man.

In two strides Guy was by her side, pulling her into his strong arms. Emma sank into his body, letting out a sob and feeling his strength flow into her.

'Did I kill him?' Emma whispered once she had recovered for a moment.

'Unlikely. Let me go and check.'

Wrapping her arms around her body, she hugged herself while Guy strode over to the steps that led into the garden below. Emma inched closer to the balustrade and peered over. It wasn't as much of a drop as she had feared, although it was difficult to make out what lay beneath.

Emma almost shouted with relief when she heard a groan and then saw Guy pull Lord Romsey from the bushes. The Earl looked as though he had been stunned, but was able to get to his feet with Guy's help and started staggering back towards the house.

'He's fine,' Guy called as they reached the top of the steps. Now she could see Lord Romsey didn't have any serious injuries she felt some of her initial indignation surface again and straightened her back, dropped her shoulders and raised her chin, ready to do battle with the man if needed.

'You're crazy. You could have killed me,' Lord Romsey said, starting towards Emma. He was still a bit unsteady on his feet and she began to back away at the physical threat, but held his eyes to show him she was not going to cower.

'Step back, Romsey,' Guy growled.

The Earl must have heard the warning in his voice because he stiffened and turned towards Guy.

'She pushed me off the terrace. What sort of person—'

'A scared young woman you were about to force yourself on.'

'I wasn't forcing myself on anyone.'

'You had her by the arm, pinned against that urn.'

'She wanted it,' Romsey snarled, his upper lip curling in disdain.

Emma gasped as Guy lashed out, his fist flying so quickly it was nothing more than a blur. Romsey had no chance of avoiding it, taking the full force of the blow to the jaw.

'Listen carefully,' Guy said, his voice completely calm. 'You are going to go back inside and pretend this never happened. If I ever hear a single word connecting you and Lady Emma, I will not rest until I have destroyed you.'

'How could you destroy me?' Romsey was rubbing his jaw. The question was laced with contempt, but Emma saw he was slowly moving away from Guy.

'Just as easily as Lady Emma bested a man twice her size. I listen carefully at the card tables, Romsey. I know of your schemes, your underhand dealings. I know of the mess you are in with Lockyear.'

Lord Romsey's eyes widened and he hesitated.

'Go,' Guy said, holding the other man's eye.

'You belong in an asylum,' Romsey said, pointing a finger at Emma, but then turned and stalked back inside, leaving Emma alone with Guy.

As the door closed behind the Earl Emma felt herself begin to shake again. Guy was at her side immediately, his arm slipping around her shoulders and providing her with the comfort that she so desperately needed.

'Did I overreact?' She felt so inexperienced, so stupid.

'Don't doubt yourself, Em. He pinned you, you did what you needed to.'

'I pushed him off the terrace.'

'Remind me never to get on your bad side.'

'I pushed him off the terrace,' Emma repeated, unable to believe what she had done.

The door to the ballroom opened again and an older couple stepped out. Guy moved quickly, stepping away so that when the couple looked in their direction he was a proper three feet away from her.

'Will he say anything?'

'No. I don't think so.'

'What do you know about him?'

Guy frowned and shook his head. 'Hardly anything. There are rumours that he's got in too deep with a builder and architect by the name of Lockyear. The project is riddled with problems, the houses are going up much slower than expected.' Guy shrugged. 'He must have a guilty conscience over something.'

'I'm so glad you came out when you did.'

'I wasn't sure if I was overstepping.'

'What do you mean?'

Guy ran his hand through his hair and moved towards her, still maintaining an appropriate distance if anyone was to look over.

'Lord Romsey aside, one day you might want to take a stroll with a gentleman of your choice and not have me barrelling in to interrupt.'

Emma pulled a face which made Guy laugh.

'I know you always change the subject when we talk about your future, Em, but one day you might want to settle down, to have a husband and children.'

She closed her eyes for a moment, feeling the world tilt a little. It was a subject she found hard to think about, let alone discuss. As a child she had been torn between wanting love like her father and mother had shared and not wanting the heartache of losing someone you cared for so much. She'd seen heartbreak in her father and how it had broken him, but he had talked about her mother with such affection that she wished someone would feel that way about her. Still, she had vowed not to marry, not to put herself through the pain her father had been subjected to.

Then Cecilia had arrived in their lives and Emma had seen her father fall in love. It had been wonderful to watch and for a long time Emma had hoped Cecilia might become her stepmother and complete their little family in an official capacity. Just as Emma was changing her mind about love and marriage, she had overheard Cecilia turning down her father's proposal and her reasons had chilled Emma, making her vow once again that she wouldn't ever marry.

'I don't know what I want.'

Egypt had been her father's dream. She longed to be back there, but she wasn't sure if that was because of the warmth of nostalgia she felt. If she returned, perhaps the reality wouldn't be as good as the memory.

'I feel lost, Guy,' she said quietly. 'As though I don't have a place in the world.'

He nodded, staying silent to allow her to continue.

'At the moment I have all these wonderful people around me—you and Cecilia and my aunt—but eventually life will move on.'

'Your life, too, not just other people's.'

She shook her head. 'I lived in this dream in Luxor, happy in the little world I'd created, and now it feels as though it has all been ripped away.'

'It's not a problem if you are not ready to marry

yet, Em. You still have time to work out what you want in life.'

'All these debutantes are so young. Already I'm five years older than them. In a year or two I'll be regarded as a spinster.'

Guy smiled at this. 'I can't imagine you a spinster.'

'I think part of the problem is if I marry some pleasant gentleman I am giving up on my dream of a life of more. More than dull domesticity. No husband is going to let me run away to Egypt, let alone happily accompany me there.'

'If he loved you, he might.'

Emma turned and faced Guy properly, looking up into his eyes and seeing the warmth there. In her slightly inebriated state, she nearly gave voice to the thought that was running through her head—that they should run back to Egypt together and get married. She pictured them waking up to one another every morning, strolling along the banks of the Nile hand in hand, making love late into every night.

'You're blushing.'

'No. I'm warm, that's all.'

'Nonsense. You haven't been warm since you arrived in England. What were you thinking about?'

Emma paused for a moment too long and she could feel the blush on her cheeks deepening. There was an invisible spark in the air and for a moment she was nearly bold enough to close the gap between them, then Guy coughed and looked away and Emma was left contemplating how much of a fool she had almost made of herself.

'Do you want to go home?' Guy said as he smiled

in greeting to the older couple who were now walking slowly backwards and forward along the terrace.

Emma hesitated, taking a moment to think about it. She did feel shaken and wasn't sure she could endure dancing with anyone else, let alone making conversation about the meaningless. Despite this she didn't want to leave. If she left, it would feel as though Lord Romsey had won, he'd chased her out.

'I'm not sure,' she admitted.

Guy looked at her quizzically and then nodded. She was always amazed at how well he understood her even when she didn't voice her thoughts aloud.

'What if I escort you back to Cecilia and we can take a turn around the ballroom together, pretend we're walking through Cairo arm in arm.'

'I'd like that, Guy.'

He nodded and Emma rested her hand on his arm, feeling some of the nerves at the prospect of returning to the ballroom when Lord Romsey might be telling everyone his twisted version of what had occurred lessen with Guy's touch.

'I can't wait to see Cecilia's face when she hears you pushed an earl off a balcony.'

'A terrace.'

'Still…'

'You know how protective she is of me. She'll probably drag him back out to push him off again.'

'Now that I would like to see.'

Chapter Ten

'Are you sure you don't mind if I ride with Guy?' Emma checked for the third time as Cecilia settled herself back into the carriage.

'Of course not. You young things go and enjoy yourselves. I have my book and my embroidery, and I am quite looking forward to some peace and quiet.'

'You make it sound as though you are ancient, Cece.'

'Do you know, Emma, since we've returned to England I *feel* ancient. I am very clearly pigeonholed into the role of a matriarch, a chaperon.' She smiled. 'And if I am honest I don't mind at all.'

Emma watched as Cecilia picked up her book and flicked through until she found the right page.

'Are you ready?' Guy called out, leading his horse over to her. 'Good morning, Cecilia, are you sure you wouldn't rather ride with us?'

'As I've told Emma I'm quite happy in here. You two enjoy yourselves and don't get up to too much mischief. And save me some lunch.'

Emma watched as the carriage trundled off, carrying her luggage for the week away strapped to the roof. It felt like a glimpse of the old days when Guy turned to her with his sparkling eyes and tilted his head towards the horses.

'Shall we?'

He boosted her up, his hand brushing against her calf as he helped to adjust her stirrups. Emma steadfastly ignored the warm sensation that flowed from the spot he'd touched and told herself she wouldn't tolerate any more nonsense. She was going on a trip with her friend to meet his family. Any of the inappropriate thoughts that had been filling her dreams needed to stay away.

She watched as Guy vaulted on to the back of his own horse and side by side they set off at a gentle walk through the streets.

'How far until lunch?'

He looked at her with a raised eyebrow.

'Emma, it is half past eight in the morning. You can't have had breakfast more than an hour ago.'

'I'm not saying I'm hungry yet, I'd just like to know the plan.'

'So you won't be wanting one of these?'

He held out two small pastries and raised his eyebrow again.

Emma leaned over and took one, popping it into her mouth. 'Mmm…that's delicious.'

'We'll stop for lunch once we're out of London. I've told the coachman where to pull in. Then if we push on this afternoon we should make Elmwood House later today.'

'I'm so looking forward to meeting your family.'

'My sister has written three times in the last week to make sure you're actually coming.'

'And Miss Frant?'

She saw Guy grimace and wished she hadn't brought the young woman's name up.

'Miss Frant and her parents will come down for two days at the weekend.'

'Perhaps you will feel easier about the marriage if you see Miss Frant in your home environment.'

'It is hardly my home. I've been there a few weeks in the last fifteen years.'

'It will be your home. When your father passes away you will inherit the house and the title. You will be Lord Templeton.'

'Don't remind me.'

'What do you have against the title?'

Emma had known Guy for nearly two years before she had found out that he would one day be a viscount, a member of the aristocracy like her own father. He clearly cared for his family, but every time the subject of his inheritance, of his future, came up he quickly changed the subject.

'Nothing.'

'You forget I know you well enough to know when you're lying.'

He looked at her for a long moment and then moved his horse a little closer. It meant he could lower his voice, but also that their legs occasionally brushed.

'I have nothing against the title itself,' he said slowly, 'but I shouldn't be the one to inherit it.'

'Why not? You're the bravest, most honourable man I know. You will be a good landlord and a responsible landowner.'

'Perhaps.'

'There's no "perhaps" about it, Guy. You will be a good viscount.'

He smiled at her indulgently and Emma felt herself momentarily distracted and struggled to focus on the subject in hand again. Guy was an expert at not talking about what he didn't want to talk about. He could dazzle and distract and make you forget you were ever questioning him about something. It went along with the charm. This time she refused to be pushed away.

'Why do you not believe me?'

For a long moment he was silent and Emma wondered if he might not answer her, then he puffed his cheeks and let out a breath.

'Do you really want to know?'

'Yes. Of course.' At one point she'd thought she knew Guy pretty well, but the recent revelations about his family and his engagement had made her realise that there were many things he liked to keep discreet, even from her.

'I was never meant to be the one to inherit,' he said quietly.

'What do you mean?'

'The title, the money, the responsibility. They weren't meant to be mine. *I* was meant to forge my own way in the world, not take on the responsibility of being head of the family.'

'You had a brother,' Emma said softly, a hand raising to her mouth in horror. How could she not know that? After all the thousands of hours they had spent together, never once had he mentioned he'd had a brother.

'Will. He was my twin. Older by twelve minutes.'

'What happened?'

'He died.'

'Guy,' Emma said gently, but admonishingly.

'We used to do everything together. He was quiet, witty, studious. God, I loved him. We were inseparable.'

Emma could see the pain on Guy's face and wished she could reach out and embrace him, but they were still riding through London and anyone could see. Instead she leaned over and placed her hand on his for a moment.

'My father was always very fair, but from a young age we were made aware that we had different futures awaiting us. Will would inherit the title, the estate and the money. He had his whole future mapped out for him. I would be expected to make my own way in the world. To support Will, but not expect the same. We were twins, but I was still the second son.'

'Did you mind?'

'Good Lord, no. I didn't want to be stifled, to have every decision dictated by what was best for the family, what was best for the title. I couldn't wait to get out and make my own decisions, my own mistakes.'

'That's why you joined the army.'

'A respectable path in life for a second son.'

She knew he had joined the army at eighteen, eschewing university despite being one of the most intelligent men she had ever known. Now she could understand why, at eighteen, he had been eager to mark out his future.

'So what happened to your brother?'

'He had a place at Oxford and was due to be starting the day after I left for the army. We packed our bags at the same time, said our goodbyes at the same time, even rode together as far as the place where the road split. I headed north for London, he west for Oxford. That was the last time I ever saw him.' Guy fell quiet and Emma sat as still as she possibly could, knowing now Guy had started to unburden himself he would finish the story when he was ready.

'The silly fool never made it to Oxford. He decided to follow me instead. He used the money that was meant to pay for his living expenses and fees to buy a commission. I didn't know, not at first. We trained separately—the army is a massive beast with so many regiments. Will's regiment shipped out before mine and he was killed in the very first skirmish.'

'Oh, Guy, I'm so sorry.'

He closed his eyes for a moment. 'I thought he was safe at Oxford and instead he was dying on a battle-field, a French soldier's bayonet through his gut.'

Emma looked at him shrewdly for a minute. 'You blame yourself?'

'Of course. Will might have been twelve minutes older, but I had always been the headstrong one, the leader of our pair. I should have realised he would fol-low me. I should have discouraged him.'

'He was a young man like you, capable of making his own decisions.'

'I'd always looked after him.'

Emma could see now why Guy hadn't wanted to re-turn home after his stint in the army. He'd loved Egypt and built a successful business there, but it was obvi-ous he had wanted to stay away from the house where his brother was conspicuously absent.

'Did your parents blame you?'

'No. They have always been sickeningly fair. In a way it might have been easier if they'd blamed me instead of pitying me. It made it harder to go home.' He shook his head. 'Now I am expected to step up and be the next Viscount, the role that should have been Will's.'

'People die, Guy. You can't blame yourself for your brother's decision for ever. Even if he had stayed at home he might have been thrown from a horse or suffered with a wasting disease.'

'If he hadn't followed me into the army, he would still be alive today, Emma. I *know* it, as clearly as I know my own name.'

She fell silent, realising she wasn't going to win this argument. It was too emotive and Guy's feelings of guilt too ingrained. As they rode through the streets she wondered if this was the reason Guy had not wanted to marry before this. To lose a twin must be like having part of yourself ripped away, it would make you wary of letting anyone else get close again.

'How is Cecilia coping?' Guy asked after a few minutes, clearly trying to change the subject for good.

'She's quiet, subdued. She loved my father very much, but I also think she has mixed feelings about being back here in England. I often catch her looking over her shoulder as if it is a habit, then remembering that there isn't anything to fear and slowly relaxing. She seems nervous a lot of the time.'

'Nervous, in what way?'

'I don't know. She seems jumpy. As if she is worried about running into people she used to know.'

Emma didn't know all that much about Cecilia's life before she came to Egypt. The story everyone was told was that she was a widow who had answered a call for a governess for Emma and liked the sound of an adventure in Egypt. It was true, Cecilia had been a respectable widow, but years earlier, when Emma had heard her father proposing and Cecilia turning him down, she had been shocked to learn that the older woman had married again before fleeing England for Egypt. A man who had until a few months before Emma's father's death had been very much alive.

Emma had overheard some of the awful ways Cecilia's second husband had treated her and this had in part shaped Emma's distrust of marriage. If someone as intelligent and lovely as Cecilia could get it wrong, then there was no guarantee Emma wouldn't choose a man who could beat her and belittle her.

'She loved your father very much.'

'Yes, she did. And he loved her. She was distraught when he first died.'

'Do you know why they never married?'

Emma shrugged, knowing Cecilia wouldn't want even Guy to know the scandal of her life before Egypt. She was a very private person.

'I grew up with Cecilia there—from the age of twelve she was a constant presence in our house. In many ways I know her better than I knew my own father, but I've realised since I arrived in England people are very good at keeping the different parts of their lives very separate. Cecilia never really spoke of her life before she came to Egypt, not past a few generalities.'

'Was that a dig at me?' Guy said, an amused expression on his face.

Emma grinned. 'A little. I actually can't believe in

all the hours we've spent together you never even let it slip that you had a brother.'

'I have incredible self-control.'

'Modest, too.'

Emma felt some of the normality between them restored and they slipped into an easy silence as they reached the outskirts of London. The day was mild for the time of year according to Cecilia, but the wind still whipped at Emma's cheeks and she pulled her fur hat down over her ears.

'You look like a Prussian princess in that thing.'

'Will I ever adjust?'

'To the weather? Of course. Do you know, when I first stepped off the ship in Alexandria I thought I would suffocate it was so hot? The first few days I couldn't stop dreaming of the frozen lake at Elmwood House, wishing I could dive beneath the surface and swim until my toes went numb.'

Emma suddenly had a very vivid picture of Guy stripping off his shirt and diving into the water. She'd never seen him without his shirt, but she had a brilliant imagination that could fill in the details. She pictured him tanned, despite having resided in England for the past few months, his muscles toned and defined.

'After a week I stopped dreaming about the cold and after two I couldn't imagine not liking the feel of the sun on my face.' Guy continued, oblivious to her inappropriate thoughts.

'Tell me it gets better in the summer here at least.'

'It does. This is the worst time of year. Grey, dank days, cold and wet. Even the winter is better with the promise of snow.'

'I would like to experience some snow.'

'You will.' He fell silent for a moment and then turned to her with a more serious expression. 'What are your plans, Em?'

'What do you mean?'

'After our discussion the other night I was thinking about what you said, about whether you want to get married.'

She shrugged.

'You must have thought some more on it.'

Emma was saved from answering by a commotion coming from behind them and three riders galloping past at full speed, splattering them both with mud.

'That was unpleasant,' Guy said, brushing the splatters off him.

'They were in a hurry.'

'Don't think this gets you out of answering my question.'

'Race you to the top of the hill.' Emma took off, urging her horse onwards. If asked by most people she would be able to twitter a few phrases about waiting for the right moment and the right person, but Guy knew her better than that. He could tell when she was lying—apparently he could pick up on a minute change in the pitch of her voice—and she didn't want to discuss the issue again. Especially not with Guy.

Chapter Eleven

'That was a good lunch,' Guy said, leaning back against the tree and closing his eyes.

'It'll be getting dark soon—no time for napping.'

He knew Emma had been dubious about the idea of a picnic in November, but he hated the dark, stuffy dining rooms at the inns along the road and much preferred to take his break from travelling in the open. It was a glorious day, cold and crisp, but with a brilliant blue sky that looked as though it should exist closer to the equator. They'd all enjoyed the feast Cecilia had unloaded from the carriage, but now he could see Emma was starting to shiver.

'It's only another hour and a half to Elmwood House. If you would rather go in the carriage, I can lead your horse.'

'No, I'd much rather ride. If you still don't mind, Cecilia?'

'Of course not. You enjoy yourselves and I will see you at Elmwood House for dinner.'

Guy jumped to his feet, readying the horses and helping Emma mount. He could tell she felt a little awkward riding side saddle—in Egypt she had often donned a pair of breeches under her dress and ridden like a man. He smiled at the image and at the thought of her trying to do that in England.

They set off before the carriage, waving back at Cecilia and then racing along the road to warm themselves and the horses back up. After a few minutes they slowed to a gentle trot.

'Gosh, it's beautiful out here,' Emma said, pausing to take in the rolling hills.

'This is the England the poets talk about, not the smoky rooftops of London. The true beauty of the country is in the green hills of Kent and the rocky coast of Cornwall and the rugged beauty of Yorkshire.'

'I'm already working on persuading Cecilia to go on a tour with me. You could…' She trailed off, shaking her head.

Guy felt as though he had been punched in the gut. This would be where normally she would invite him along, but already she was adjusting her expectations. Now she knew about his impending engagement there would be no more trips, no more excursions, even when properly chaperoned by Cecilia. This was their last chance to spend a week together before he would have to stamp on his reservations and ask Miss Frant to marry him. He could curse his mother for inviting the Frants at the end of the week, but he knew she had meant for it to be helpful. She wasn't aware of his true feelings about the arranged marriage and thought to turn the weekend into a little house party.

'We will still do things together, Em,' he said quietly.

'I know.'

'It isn't the end of our friendship.'

'I know.'

'It will be...different.'

'What if I don't want different?' Emma said ever so quietly after a pause. She wasn't looking at him, instead staring at the place where her hands were clasping the reins. Quickly she shook her head. 'Pretend I didn't say that. It was selfish and you don't deserve selfish.'

'What do I deserve?'

She looked at him then, a flash of something dangerous in her eyes. Guy felt all the air being sucked out of him and had to steady himself. Silently he cursed the world for how cruel it was. If Emma hadn't arrived in England for three more months he would be safely married, doing his duty, but instead she had arrived at the moment his mind was looking for any excuse not to marry a woman he didn't love.

'You deserve everything,' she said, holding his eye.

'Everything?'

She nodded and then spurred her horse forward, racing on ahead.

Guy chased her, knowing he would easily catch her. He was used to riding on English roads and he had the bigger, more powerful horse. Still, Emma was determined, and it took a few minutes before they were level.

'What do you mean by "everything"?'

'I wish...' she said, but then shook her head.

'What do you wish, Emma?' Even though he was breathing steadily, on the inside it felt as though he were holding his breath, willing her to put into words what he had been feeling for years.

Again she shook her head and spurred her horse on, but she had been looking at him too intently to notice the small branch lying across the road. Her horse took a slightly bigger step to avoid getting tangled in it and it was enough to unbalance Emma. He saw her grip tighter on to the reins and tense her body and it might have been enough if the horse hadn't whinnied and risen up in response to her tighter grip.

With a cry she tumbled from the horse's back to the ground, perilously near the back hooves. Guy moved in a flash, dismounting and gripping hold of both horses' reins in less than a second. Quietly he murmured soothing words to the unsettled horse, knowing if it moved suddenly and Emma got a hoof to the head it could be the end of her.

She was sitting in the road with her skirts puffed out around her, a slightly dazed look on her face. There was a small cut on her forehead and a trickle of blood was running down towards her eye.

Guy worked quickly, securing the horses to a nearby fence post and then turning his attention to Emma.

'Are you hurt?'

She shook her head and then winced. 'A little. I hit my head on something on the way down and my wrist hurts.'

He examined her head first, coming in close and gently probing the skin for bumps and cuts. Emma cried out when he got to a sore spot on her temple, next to where she had grazed it.

'I feel as though I'm going to swoon.'

He'd never know Emma to swoon—she wasn't the dramatic type to collapse prettily at the first sign of excitement. When he had first met her she'd been bal-

ancing on a wall outside her house in Luxor and he'd
seen her fall, scraping the skin from both her hands
and knees. Even then she had looked a little put out
by the cuts, but nothing more.

'Come here, close your eyes for a moment.' Carefully he manoeuvred himself behind her and cradled
her head in his lap, gently stroking away the hair from
her forehead. Emma sank into him and closed her eyes.
He was momentarily so mesmerised by the contrast
of her dark eyelashes on her pale cheeks that he almost bent down without thinking and kissed her forehead. He caught himself before his lips met her skin
and pulled back, silently chastising himself for being
such a fool.

'I feel a bit better,' she said after a couple of minutes. 'Sorry, I don't know what came over me.'

'You fell from a horse. You're allowed a little time
to compose yourself. Let me look at your wrist.'

A pained expression crossed her face as he pressed
over the delicate bones, but she didn't cry out and when
he asked her to move it from side to side she was able
to without too much trouble.

'Bruised or sprained, I should think, but no break.'

Emma struggled into an upright sitting position and
Guy tamped down any disappointment he felt from
her moving away.

'Ouch,' she said, holding her head.

'Do you think you can ride?'

'I'll probably be all right.'

'We can wait for the carriage.'

'How far is it to Elmwood House?'

'Perhaps twenty minutes' ride.'

Emma bit her lip and then nodded determinedly.

This was one of the things he loved about her—nothing could keep Emma down. Even when she had fallen off a felucca into the Nile she had wrung out her skirts and continued with the trip.

Carefully he helped her up and she seemed fine until she went to mount her horse, staggering backwards and giving him a sheepish smile.

'Sorry, I thought I would feel better once I was riding.'

'Come here.'

Deftly he lifted her up on to his horse's back, settling her in front of the saddle. He adjusted her horse's bridle so he could lead it easily alongside them and then mounted, settling in behind Emma and gripping her firmly about the waist.

'Tell me if you feel as though you will faint.'

She nodded and he urged his horse forward into a gentle walk, feeling the sway of her hips against his pelvis and trying valiantly to ignore the warmth of her against him.

After a few minutes they had settled into a rhythm and he could tell Emma was sitting a little straighter. She seemed a little more recovered from her fall.

'Is it terrible that I love riding like this?' she asked quietly.

'With someone behind you?'

'Yes. My father used to take me out on his horse all the time when I was little. He would sit me in front of him and we would ride all over. It is one of the memories I have of England, but he used to do it in Egypt, too. He would always complain that my hair was tickling him if I leaned back too much.'

'I didn't know that.' There weren't many things he

didn't know about Emma—she was so open, so honest with him that sometimes it had made keeping his secrets from her hard. If he was going to tell anyone about his brother, about his change in circumstances, then it would have been Emma, but some things were too painful to discuss even with someone you cared for very much.

'When we first arrived in Luxor he was restless, still mourning my mother terribly. I can remember him saying this was where we would make our home and taking me on tours of the city at dusk to avoid the worst of the heat.'

'It was just the two of you then?'

'Yes, my governess hadn't made it past Italy. She was too homesick. It was me and my father until I was twelve and then Cecilia arrived.' She half turned and smiled at him. 'Then it was the three of us until you crashed into our lives three years later.'

'It was only meant to be a quick consultation with your father.' Guy smiled at the memory. He'd been happy in Egypt, travelling between Cairo, Alexandria and Luxor, building his business and learning about the history of the country he was coming to love. On his travels he'd heard Lord Westcombe was an expert in the ancient Egyptian artefacts and wanted an opinion on a gold and sapphire necklace set that had come into his possession. One dealer had told him it looked no more than a few decades old, but Guy had been convinced it was older.

'I remember that necklace you brought to show him. My father got so excited he nearly fell off his chair.'

Guy smiled at the memory. Not long after, he had been introduced to Cecilia, who had swept him into the family as if he were a long-lost relative, giving him the warmth and companionship he hadn't realised he'd been missing when he left his own family behind. When he had met Emma properly for the first time it had felt as though he'd already known her for a lifetime.

'Look ahead,' Guy said, pointing out a turn in the road just visible in the fast-approaching dusk. 'That's the entrance to the estate.'

'Is it a large estate?'

'It was. Various portions have been sold off so now it's not much more than a house and the gardens, a little parkland. We own a number of the houses in the local village—our solicitor advised that we hold on to those—but we've sold the farms and the grazing land.'

'I'm sorry,' Emma said quietly.

He shrugged, even though she couldn't see him. 'I wasn't here to protect it so I can hardly moan now it is broken up and depleted.'

'You can still wish it were different.'

'It was never meant to be mine. It is my mother and sister I feel sorry for.'

Emma nodded and he could tell she was holding back her words, worried they would dig up too many painful memories. He was thankful and began pointing out little features of the estate as they passed.

'That lake over there was where I learned to swim,' he said as they turned into the long drive. 'William and I crept away from our tutor one hot day and goaded each other on to jump in, even though neither of us knew how to swim at that point. After nearly drowning a few times my mother decided it would be better if she taught us. It was unusual for a young woman to know how to swim, but my mother had three older brothers and I think they treated her like one of the boys when she was a child.' He shook his head in fond memory. 'It was a glorious summer when she taught us. I remember long lazy days of terrific heat.'

'It looks a little cold now.'

He grimaced. 'I fell through the ice once, trying to convince my brother it was safe to skate on. I thought my heart was going to stop, the shock of the cold so paralysed me. Will dragged me out, and I certainly cannot recommend a winter swim.'

'What's that up there?'

'The folly. My grandfather built it about forty years ago. It is meant to look like the tower from some medieval poem. It's just a shell, with some stairs up to a platform, but it looks pretty. And it is a great place for watching the stars.'

He had a sudden image of lying on a blanket with Emma at the top of that tower, her head nestled on his chest. Quickly he tried to push it away, but it had lodged in his mind and he knew that he would struggle to think of anything else whenever he saw the folly.

'I can see the house. It's lovely, Guy.'

Taking a moment to look at it properly, as if for the first time, he realised it *was* lovely. The main part of the house was old, dating from the early seventeenth century. Over the years parts had been remodelled and added on, giving it a quaint, fairy-tale look, all accentuated by the shallow moat that surrounded the house.

As they drew closer Guy's sister came dashing out the door, waving in a way he was sure his mother would say didn't befit a young woman of her place in society.

'There's Sophia.' Without a doubt his little sister was the best thing about being home. He'd missed most of her childhood and had returned to find the toddler he had left behind now a young woman. After his stint in the army he hadn't returned home before setting up his new business in Egypt. He had told his family and friends he needed to get the business established, but in truth he hadn't wanted to return to Elmwood House without Will. Fifteen long years he'd been away and so much had changed during that time.

'She looks like you.'

Guy laughed. His mother said the same, but he was unable to see the resemblance. Sophia was very fair, her skin so pale as to be almost translucent and her hair the lightest blonde. His own skin tanned as soon as he walked into the sun and his hair was blond, but a much darker shade. Perhaps there was a similarity in the curve of their lips and the shape of their eyes, but he couldn't see more than that.

'Guy,' she called out, running to meet them. 'I've been waiting for hours.'

Chapter Twelve

Emma felt herself stumble as she slipped off the back of the horse and immediately Guy's arm was around her waist, steadying her.

'Emma was thrown from her horse on the road from Westerham.'

'Oh, no, are you hurt? Shall I call a footman to carry you inside?'

'I'm perfectly fine, your brother is exaggerating. It was a little fall, nothing more, a minor bump to the head.' She couldn't think of much worse than being carried into Elmwood House in the arms of a footman. *That* entrance wouldn't ever be forgotten.

'Lady Emma,' a poised older woman said as she hurried over the wooden footbridge from the main house, 'we have been so eager to meet you. Guy talks about you so much.'

'Incessantly,' Sophia muttered with a mischievous grin on her face.

Lady Templeton gave her daughter an admonishing look before moving forward to take Emma's hands and draw her in for an embrace.

'Please view Elmwood House as your home. My tight-lipped son hasn't told me much of what he got up to in Egypt, but I do know your father made him feel very welcome in your home.'

'Thank you.'

'Shall we stop trying to embarrass me and let Emma get inside? Cecilia, Mrs Willow, will be arriving soon. The carriage won't be far behind us.'

Emma smothered a smile at the stern look he tried to bestow on his mother and sister and how they completely ignored him, bustling to her side and peppering her with questions. In the end he let them chatter for a few minutes before inserting himself into the middle and offering her his arm.

'Let me give you the tour,' he said and guided her into the house, away from his mother and sister. 'I'm sorry,' he murmured when they were inside. 'You're the first person I've ever brought to visit.'

'Surely not?'

'You forget I left when I was eighteen. Before that I was at school and in the holidays I was quite content to mess around with Will.' He shrugged. 'They'll settle down in a day or two. Let me show you the house.'

He gripped her by the hand and pulled her through the main hallway, an open oak-panelled room with a genuine suit of armour standing next to a sweeping staircase.

'Drawing room, dining room, Father's study, my study, library.'

Emma blinked, trying to take it all in.

'I'll show you the secret passages and turret rooms once we've got that head cleaned up and had something to eat.'

Her fingers flew to her forehead and she felt the streak of dried blood Guy's family had been too polite to comment on.

'I must look a state.'

He moved his head from side to side. 'I wouldn't present you to the Queen, but you don't look like you did after we got caught in that sandstorm outside Luxor.'

'I don't think I've ever looked as bad as that.'

'No. You looked awful then.'

'You weren't much better.'

'I didn't scare the schoolchildren we passed on the edge of town.'

Emma smiled at the memory and flopped into a chair in the library while Guy rang a bell and waited for a maid to appear.

'Can we have some water, please, and a towel, and perhaps some tea and cake if there is anything going.'

'Have you ever rung a bell and not asked for cake?' Emma said with a smile as Guy sat down in the chair next to hers.

'One thing the army teaches you, never take cake for granted. Or a good meal.'

'I'm not sure they should put that into a recruitment slogan.'

'No. Perhaps not. You hear tales of officers dining on wonderful banquets while the men get meagre rations, but I have to say I learned what hunger was during our Egyptian campaign.'

Guy slipped from his seat as the maid set down the water and a clean towel, and perched on the edge of her chair. His body was close to hers and Emma felt a rush of awareness. She couldn't stop thinking about reaching out and wrapping her arms around him, reaching up and tracing the contours of his face with her fingers. She relished the sting as Guy began dabbing at the scratch on her forehead and the bump on her scalp, as it distracted her momentarily, but all too soon the pain subsided and she was left sitting far too close to a man she was finding increasingly attractive.

He reached out a hand and placed his fingers under her chin, steadying her head so he could tend to her wound better. Emma felt the heat of the contact, the sparks of what felt like fire as his fingers brushed innocently against her skin. She longed for him to kiss her, to throw away all thoughts of duty and propriety and kiss her so hard and so long they both forgot their reservations.

She was so lost in these thoughts that she almost cried out when the door opened and Lady Templeton and Sophia entered the room, followed by Cecilia.

'Emma, darling, what happened?' Cecilia asked, her face a picture of concern.

Glad of the distraction, Emma took the towel from Guy and dabbed at her own head.

'Just a little tumble from the horse. All my own fault, and I haven't done any real damage.'

Cecilia inspected her, checking her over before turning to Guy.

'She has hurt her wrist and bumped her head, but nothing a day's rest won't cure.'

Perhaps she had bumped her head harder than she had initially thought. That would excuse her less than innocent thoughts about Guy, although she would be lying if she told herself today was the first time she'd felt that way.

'I'm fine. Honestly. Even my wrist barely hurts any more.'

Cecilia took the chair next to hers and Lady Templeton and Sophia sat down opposite. Guy drew up another chair and positioned it next to Emma's.

'I've asked for some tea and cake—unless you would like to freshen up first, Cecilia?'

'Tea would be lovely. I know all I've done is sit in a carriage all day, but I do find travelling exhausting.'

'Were the roads in too bad a condition?' Lady Templeton asked.

'No, for this time of year they were surprisingly good. A few rough patches, a little mud, but nothing too unexpected.' Soon Cecilia and Lady Templeton were engaged in conversation about travel around various parts of England, their heads bent together as if they were old friends.

'I was thinking we could walk into the village tomorrow,' Sophia suggested. 'If we leave it until the afternoon, hopefully it won't be too cold.'

'I've brought my thickest cloak so a walk to the village sounds lovely.'

'I'm sure you'll be far too busy, Guy, seeing that the solicitor is visiting after lunch.'

Guy grimaced and nodded. 'I'm hoping it won't take too long. I'll plan to join you after if time allows.'

'Have you shown Emma the secret passageways yet?'

'No, not yet. She's only been here twenty minutes.'

'He got distracted by the thought of cake,' Emma said, laughing.

'I got distracted, tending to your wounds.'

'This house is wonderful, there are two secret passageways that we know of and a priest's hole. Every so often I'll spend an afternoon pressing on various wooden beams to see if I can find anything new.'

'Have you?'

Sophia screwed up her face and shook her head. 'No, but that doesn't discourage me. I'm sure there are more. One day I'll find them.'

'Where are they hidden?' Emma leaned forward, intrigued. She'd never been in a house with secret passageways before.

'Come with me,' Guy said, his eyes twinkling. He seemed younger here among his family, even though Emma knew he felt the weight of responsibility of caring for them pressing down on him. She stood and he offered her his arm. Sophia trailed after them.

They made their way back through the heavily panelled hall into the little room Guy had pointed out as his study. As soon as they entered Emma could see the stamp of his personality in the details of the room. There was the requisite desk, piled high with papers, but there was also what she knew to be his favourite artefact—a beautifully preserved statue of the jackal-headed god. His armchair was turned towards the window, allowing him to chase the elusive English sun, and three books lay open on various tables in the room.

'Where do you think it is?'

Emma looked around, trying to think like a persecuted Catholic from well over two hundred years ago.

'You'll never find it. It's ingenious,' Sophia said, her face lit up with exuberance.

Emma began pressing on the wood of the panels. When that didn't work, she started tapping on the walls, searching for a different sound that might indicate a hollowness behind.

'Am I at least in the right sort of area? It's not in the floor?'

'It's not in the floor.'

She refused to give up, studying the little rose motifs in the plaster and trying out the books on the bookshelves.

'You'll never find it. You've actually already touched the switch, but it is so well hidden you wouldn't even know.'

'Show me.'

Guy walked over to the bookcase nearest the window and touched a carved flower on one of the edges. Emma heard a soft click and slowly one of the panels at the bottom of the bookcase swung out.

'It's a little narrow in there, but you must look inside,' Sophia said.

Emma crouched down, torn between wanting to go crawling on her hands and knees through the secret passage and remembering she was a guest and expected to have a certain standard of behaviour.

'Come on, I'll take you,' Guy said.

'There's room for both of us?'

'Yes, it's a squeeze, but there's room. Will and I used to crawl through here together as lads.'

Emma's curiosity got the better of her and she dropped to her knees and peered into the gap. It was dark, but not dusty. The floor was lined with stone and the gap was about two feet wide, heading off to the right down a gentle slope, and Emma realised it must go along the entire edge of the room behind the bookcases that lined the outer wall.

Guy had lit a candle and handed it to her, so with a final deep breath she crawled in.

She'd never been bothered by tight spaces or a clamber to get somewhere she wished to go. Often in Egypt she would accompany Guy and her father to some site where a local had discovered a chamber or tomb hidden underground. This had a different feel to it, however, more draughty, and more likely to have spiders or some kind of horrible insect scuttling about in it.

'Keep going.' Guy's reassuring voice came from behind her. 'The passage will turn right in a moment and open out a little so we can stand, albeit a little crouched over.'

Emma saw what he meant as she squeezed around a tight turn before the passage became a little wider. She struggled to her feet and felt Guy do the same behind her.

'We're now in between the walls of my study and my father's. It's an ingenious passageway. Most secret passageways are built as direct as possible, but where this one skirts the edge of the room it means it is less likely to be discovered.'

'Who would think a secret passageway would be on an outer wall of the room?'

'Exactly.'

'Where does it come out?'

'Keep going, see if you can work it out.'

Emma felt a thrill of anticipation and shuffled forward, bending her neck to stop her head from scraping against the ceiling.

'This must be the edge of your father's study,' she said as she ran her fingers along the wall. 'And here we turn again, with the hall on our right?'

The passageway continued with a couple more twists and turns before Emma admitted defeat.

'I don't know,' she said as they came to a dead end.

Guy was close behind her and she felt a rush of excitement as she realised they were all alone. No one would ever know if they kissed here in the secret passage, if she wrapped her arms around him and gave in to the desire that had been building these past few weeks. She knew she shouldn't, that there was no sense in it. In a month or two Guy would be married and she…well, she would be sitting at home with Cecilia and her aunt, wondering if she, too, would become a spinster.

She felt Guy's arm brush past her and for a second she thought he was going to hold her, draw her close, then his fingers continued on to a little lever on the wall in front of them. She suddenly felt very foolish. Here she was, fantasising about a man who had given her no indication he felt the same way about her. Years they'd known each other and the only time there had been a hint that he might be attracted to her was when they were sheltering from the rain in Hyde Park. Surely if he felt anything but friendship it would have been apparent much sooner.

Guy pulled the lever and there was an almost inaudible click as the panel in front of them released. Emma stepped out and looked around her, curious to see where they were, but also glad to be able to put some distance between her and Guy.

They were standing in a little alcove behind the main staircase, next to the servants' stairs that went down to the kitchen below.

'A handy escape route,' Guy said, seemingly oblivious to her discomfort.

'Mmm.'

'Isn't it wonderful?' Sophia gushed as she came bounding out of the study. She looked young with the big smile on her face, not a child, but still not quite a woman. 'The other passage isn't anywhere near as long, just a connection between two of the bedrooms upstairs, but this one is marvellous, don't you think?'

'I've never been in anything quite like it.'

'Would you like to see the priest's hole?'

'Yes.'

Guy took her by the hand again and Emma had to force herself to relax, hurrying after him as he led her up the stairs.

'Most priest holes are underneath the floor, mainly on the ground floor of houses. Ours is in the room that would have been used by the lady of the house. I think the rationale was any soldiers or searchers would be less inclined to linger in a lady's bedroom than anywhere else.'

'Fascinating,' Emma murmured, admiring the beautiful house as they dashed through it. 'Is it your mother's bedroom now?'

'No, it's a bit draughty, so it hasn't been used as a main bedroom for years.'

He stood back to let Emma enter the room first and she stepped in slowly, letting her eyes trail over the layout of the room to try to work out where this priest's hole might be.

'Is it small?'

'It's about big enough for two at a squeeze.'

She walked to the far wall and trailed her fingers

over the wooden beams. There was less furniture in
this room so it should make it easier to find, but nothing was immediately jumping out at her. The four-
poster bed dominated the room and opposite that was
a grand fireplace. There was a small alcove which
she assumed would have once been for storage, but
was empty now.

'Show her, Guy,' Sophia said, leaning against the
door frame.

'Here.' Guy led her over to the fireplace and pushed
against one of the sides. It creaked as it slid back and
Emma had to bend to see inside.

'It looks tiny.'

'Apparently enough space for two priests, although
I'm not sure it was ever tested.' He smiled. 'Don't
worry, I won't force you to go inside.'

It did look uncomfortable, but Emma was well
aware she would probably go through her life without ever going into a house with a priest's hole again,
let alone one where she felt comfortable enough to actually squeeze inside.

She bent double and shuffled in, scraping her shoulders and having to wriggle to find a comfortable position to stand up in.

'What do you think?'

'I wouldn't want to stay in here for hours on end,
but it is a good hiding place.'

'Why don't you see if two people do fit?' She heard
Sophia's voice from somewhere behind Guy in the
bedroom.

Emma thought Guy would decline, but to her amazement the little light there was suddenly disappeared as
it was blocked out by Guy's body.

'Hello,' he said as he squeezed in next to her. 'I think the priests of hundreds of years ago might have been a little smaller.'

They were pressed tightly together and it was almost completely dark. It should feel enclosed, but instead Emma felt a thrill of excitement.

'I'm going to close the door,' Sophia said and before either she or Guy could protest Emma heard the scrape of the priest's hole door closing.

There was no light whatsoever and Emma was pinned in place by Guy's body. She could feel his heart beating in his chest through their clothing.

'Sophia,' Guy shouted. 'Open the door right away.'

'What's the matter?' Emma asked, sensing his agitation. She knew he wasn't afraid of confined spaces, had watched him wriggle into tight spots before without even breaking a sweat.

'Sophia, open it up now.'

'Guy, I'm sure she will open it in a second.'

'Sophia,' he shouted again. There was only the sound of their breathing.

'She can't have gone,' Emma said quietly.

'Don't do this, Sophia,' Guy muttered.

'Do what? Guy, explain to me.'

'She's trying to ruin us. You.'

'What? Why would she do that? She only met me an hour ago. Surely she can't dislike me that much in such a small amount of time.'

'She doesn't dislike you, Em. She thinks she is doing us a favour.'

'I don't understand.'

She felt Guy try to bend his knees and reach down

behind him and wondered if the door could be opened from the inside.

'Sophia doesn't want me to marry Miss Frant. She thinks I am throwing away my future to secure hers and has told me numerous times that if she had known what I would insist on doing she would never have called me back.'

'I don't understand why she is trying to ruin me, though.'

'Think about it, Em. She shuts us in here together, in very close proximity, alone. If it got out, your honour would be compromised and I would have to marry you.'

'She doesn't want you to marry Miss Frant, but she doesn't mind if you marry me.'

Even in the dark she knew Guy was grimacing.

'Apparently I talk about you a lot. Sophia has got it into her head that we would be better suited.'

'Even if that means she will have no dowry, no advantage when it comes to finding a husband.'

'She's seventeen and hopelessly romantic. You remember what it was like to be that age. You have this unswerving optimism that everything will go your way in life, that only good things will happen to you.'

Emma could remember the time when it seemed as though her life was charmed, as though nothing bad that happened to other people could ever possibly happen to her.

'Surely it won't work,' she said, refusing to panic. 'It's only your mother and Cecilia downstairs and they are hardly going to say anything.'

'Save me from the warped logic of seventeen-year-old girls,' Guy muttered.

'We can get out of this, I'm sure we can. Can you slide the door with your foot?'

A minute passed as Guy tried to move the secret door.

'No. It's impossible.'

'Have you got enough room to turn around?'

'No, but I think if I crouch down I might be able to reach behind me and move it.'

Emma was glad that the darkness hid the expression on her face. Crouching down would involve a lot of close contact, but she knew it needed to be done.

'Do it,' she said quietly.

Chapter Thirteen

Guy took a moment before he moved, trying to distract himself from the knowledge that Emma's body was pressed up so close to him he could feel every breath, every miniscule movement. He tried listing all the ways he was going to punish Sophia for this prank, but even that was not enough to tear his mind away from what he was going to have to do.

He braced himself against the walls and then slowly started to slide down, feeling the tickle of her breath on his face as he passed her lips. The urge to kiss her was almost overwhelming and his body paused involuntarily. With a great effort he pushed onwards, having to suppress a groan as his chin caught the material of the neckline of Emma's dress, the resulting jolt pressing his face momentarily into her cleavage. He felt her take a sharp breath in as he hurriedly pulled away, hitting his head against the wall behind him and letting out a low curse.

As he sank lower he tried thinking of anything but the anatomy of the woman in front of him. Crop cycles, military manoeuvres, the life cycle of a frog. It wasn't working. He was acutely aware of her body separated from his lips by just a few thin layers of material.

He held his breath as he steadied himself in a crouch before starting to try to move the secret door from the inside. There was a tiny gap that he could almost work his fingers into and he was sure if he could do that the door would slide open. Again and again he scrabbled with the edge of the door, not wanting to admit his fingers were too big, that it was futile.

'I can't fit my fingers in the gap.'

'There's a gap?'

'Yes. Tiny, but I think if I could work my fingers in there I could slide open the door.'

'Let me try. I have smaller fingers than you.'

'How?'

'Stand up.'

Slowly he complied, as aware of her body on the way up as he had been on the way down. He paused again when he was level with her lips and had the sense she was breathing more heavily, as if as agitated as he was by their close quarters.

When he was standing fully, Emma pressed her body into his even tighter and together they began to shuffle round in a half-circle so now her back was to the secret door.

Even though it was dark Guy had to close his eyes and bite his lip as Emma began sliding down his body. Her delicate hands gripped on to him for balance, holding on to his clothing and reminding him how close she was. As she settled into a crouch her head was level with the waistband of his trousers and it was all he could do not to groan in frustration.

'I can feel it,' she said, her voice brighter. 'I think I can...'

There was a scraping sound as the door opened and Emma shuffled backwards, falling out of the priest's hole and into the room beyond. Guy bent low and followed her out, helping her to her feet.

'You're covered in dust,' he said, unable to stop himself from smiling. He was sure he looked a state as well, but Emma looked as though she had walked through a derelict house thick with dust. Carefully he plucked the biggest pieces from her hair and brushed off the material of her dress.

As he did so he felt Emma go completely still, her eyes on his.

'Guy...' she said softly.

She looked so beautiful, so perfect that he ached to kiss her, to admit his feelings for her had for a long time been more than friendship, no matter what he'd told himself over the years.

'Emma.'

His hand lingered on her shoulder, his fingers edging off the material of her dress to caress the smooth skin at the base of her neck. He knew he couldn't kiss her, it would only hurt them both, but he'd never wanted something more in his life than he wanted to kiss Emma right now.

He allowed himself one more second and then stepped away, turning his back to her in the pretence of brushing off the dust from his jacket, then closing the secret door to the priest's hole.

Guy wasn't one to lament the injustice in the world. He was aware that many, many people had it worse than he did, but right now things did seem unfair. Just when Emma was showing that first flare of desire, when she was looking at him as something more than a friend, he was tied in to a marriage he did not want but couldn't escape.

'Please excuse me, Emma, I need to go and reprimand my sister.'

He didn't trust himself to linger or look back, so instead strode from the room and made his way back downstairs, already regretting not kissing her.

'Sophia,' he bellowed as he reached the bottom of the stairs.

His sister sidled meekly from the drawing room, biting her lip.

'You are in trouble, young lady.'

'I did it for you, Guy.'

'What you did was reckless and cruel. For all you knew Emma might have been afraid of enclosed spaces.'

'She didn't have any qualms about going in. I thought it unlikely.'

'Don't try to be clever, Sophia.'

He saw his sister squirm and felt some of the anger drain from him. *This* was a role he'd never asked for, never expected to be his. Head of the family, responsible for his mother, his sister. This should have been Will's responsibility. It wasn't as though he and Will had been raised differently, but in everything they had done they had been aware that one day Will would step up and run the estate, take care of the family. And he... well, he would not.

'You don't like Miss Frant.'

'No,' he said slowly, knowing it would be pointless

to lie. 'I don't know Miss Frant, but I am sure when I get to know her she will be perfectly pleasant.'

'Why settle for perfectly pleasant when you could have true love?'

'What are you talking about, Sophia?'

'Lady Emma. She's your one true love, the woman you are destined to marry.'

Guy laughed and then saw the slightly hurt look on his sister's face and quickly turned it into a cough.

'I see how you look at her. How you look when you talk about her. She is in every one of your stories.'

'Not every one,' he murmured, knowing that it probably wasn't true. He and Emma had spent a lot of time together in Egypt and had a lot of fun. She did feature in most of his anecdotes in one form or another.

'Why would you marry Miss Frant when you can have Lady Emma?'

'One,' he said, holding up a single finger, 'to pay off this family's debts and give you a fighting chance of a happy future. Two...' he held up a second finger '... Lady Emma has no interest in marrying me. Three...' he held up a third finger '... I am a gentleman and a gentleman does not go back on his promises.'

'One, I don't need a dowry. I don't want a dowry if it means you are trapped in an unhappy life. Two, of course Lady Emma would marry you—even I can see you're perfect for one another and I'm a naïve seventeen-year-old with no real world experience. And three, I don't believe you've never broken a promise before. Anyway, it would be kinder on Miss Frant in the long run to break things off now than to spend your life married to her and in love with someone else.'

Guy tried not to let how much his little sister's words were affecting him show on his face.

'And Father? What of him? If I do not marry Miss Frant, we lose the house and just think how unsettled he would be if forced to move somewhere new.'

Sophia looked uncomfortable.

'All of this is beside the point. Whatever your views on my courtship and future engagement, you do not shut me or any of our guests in a priest's hole. I suggest you take a moment to think of a suitable apology and then go and find Lady Emma.'

'Of course I'll apologise,' Sophia said, already starting past him and making her way up the stairs. 'But that doesn't mean I think you're right.'

Guy watched his sister go, shaking his head in incredulity. She was his blood, his sister, but he barely knew her, not really. He hadn't been there for any of her formative moments, he wasn't part of any of her memories. Despite that he knew that she truly meant what she said, she valued his happiness as highly as her own. If only she could see that she wasn't guaranteed a happy future and it was his responsibility to make it more likely that she was contented in her choices.

Deciding he couldn't face going back to the library with his mother and Cecilia, he headed instead to his study, determined to think about anything but the memory of Emma sliding down his body, her hands gripping him.

Emma was sitting on the wide windowsill, looking out over the beautiful gardens when she heard the knock on the door. She felt unbalanced, disconcerted, and had asked one of the servants to show her to her room so she might have a few minutes to sort through the raging emotions inside her.

'Come in,' she called, trying to suppress the surge of anticipation she felt as she wondered if it were Guy. He'd had the perfect opportunity to kiss her in the old mistress's bedroom, but instead he'd stepped away. He wouldn't turn up at her door now.

Sophia stepped into the room, looking sheepish, dawdling by the door.

'Come in, Sophia, join me.'

Slowly Guy's sister walked over the thick rug that covered most of the floor and stopped when she was a couple of feet away.

'I'm sorry for shutting you into the priest's hole,' Sophia said quietly. Emma was reminded how young she was really, little more than a child, pushed into becoming a young woman by society's expectations of her.

'Why did you do it, Sophia?'

The young woman bit her lip and fidgeted on her feet.

'Come and sit down with me and tell me. I'm not angry, I'm curious.'

Sophia perched on the other end of the windowsill and fiddled with the latch that secured the window.

'Guy hasn't been happy since he's been home,' she said slowly. 'I know I don't know him, that he left when I was not much more than a baby, but I am good at watching people, at working out what they're feeling.'

'It must be hard for him, for all of you, with your father.'

'Yes. It's horrible to watch Papa become a shell of

his former self, but for Guy it's more than that. He doesn't want to be here. He doesn't want this life.'

'I'm sure that's not true, Sophia. It's an adjustment, that's all.'

'When he talks about his time in Egypt his face lights up. When he talks about you he is always smiling. *That* is the life he wanted.'

Emma nodded. Sophia might be young, but she was obviously very perceptive. It would be condescending to try to deny what she had picked up from her brother.

'We can't live our lives solely doing the things we want. Everyone has responsibilities.'

'I know. I am aware Guy *had* to come back here and sort out the mess we were in and he *has* to run the estate, but surely I should have a choice as to whether he throws away his chance of a happy marriage for me.'

Emma considered for a moment. 'It is a big responsibility he places on you, if he does this for you.'

Sophia nodded. 'What if I don't make a good match? What if no one ever proposes? Then we'll both be unhappy and it'll be all my fault.'

'Guy doesn't care about whether you marry a duke or an earl or a man with no title. That isn't what he is doing this for. He is doing it so you might have a choice. So that you can choose the man who might not offer so much, but you care for more. Or the man who might not consider you without a decent dowry who turns out to be the perfect match for you.'

'I know.' Sophia turned to her and tilted her head to one side, seeming to change tack. 'What do you think of Guy marrying Miss Frant?'

'Miss Frant seems pleasant, sweet even. I think once they know each other they will be happy.'

'They won't. He won't, not really.'

Emma closed her eyes. Sophia wasn't the right person to confide in, to tell about the blossoming feelings she was having for Guy. She would seize upon even a hint of attraction and build it up to more than it was.

'There are many things in this life that we worry about before they happen, but a year or two on and we can't see a different present to the one we have.'

'I'm sorry I shut you in the priest's hole together. I thought...' Sophia shook her head. 'It was foolish. Can you forgive me?'

'Of course.'

The younger woman stood and smiled. 'I'll leave you to rest, you must be tired after your journey. Dinner is always at eight. Do let me know if you need anything.'

Emma watched Sophia leave and then turned back to the window, waiting for the door to close before she allowed herself to let out the big breath she was holding in a loud sigh.

In truth, she wasn't completely sure why she was so upset, but everything felt a little overwhelming. She yearned for her father, for his gentle smile, his wise words and his practical outlook. She wanted to curl up on a chair beside him and listen to his stories, to let him distract her with one of his tales. Even though it had hurt when she had heard his final wishes in his will, she still would do anything to have him back with her.

'I miss you,' she whispered, resting her head against the cold windowpane.

Everything had changed this past year and she wished for the comforts of her home.

'What should I do?' Even as she asked the question she realised it was the wrong one to ask. Guy was marrying Miss Frant. He believed that was what was best for his family and she had to respect that. Her real question should be—what did she want from her life? For a long time she had been wary of love, wary of giving herself to someone. Her father had felt the loss of her mother so deeply and then the snippets she'd heard about Cecilia's second husband hadn't made her feel any more positively about marriage. However, she couldn't deny that even though both her father and Cecilia had been hurt by their relationships, they had allowed themselves to fall in love with one another and found happiness.

Marriage wasn't something she had ever seriously thought was in her future. She'd imagined growing older surrounded by the people who loved her—her father, Cecilia, Guy—but in the past year everything had changed.

Since coming to England she had started to realise what the alternative to the life she had assumed would be hers was. Guy soon would be gone, her friend only at a distance. And who knew if Cecilia would look to marry again now she had returned to England? She was certainly attractive and still in the prime of her life.

'I don't want to be alone,' Emma said quietly, but she knew instantly that no man would ever be able to live up to Guy.

With a sigh she tore herself away from the window, knowing it was no use sitting here moping. This week was for enjoying. She and Guy were getting to have one last adventure together and, instead of mourning what she was about to lose, she was determined to enjoy their last few days together.

Chapter Fourteen

Emma had always found it difficult to sleep in new places. At home, in her own bed, she fell asleep within minutes and slept soundly until morning. However, whenever she spent the night in a strange bed she often tossed and turned into the early hours.

Tonight it was impossible. Dinner had been a pleasant affair—none of the strain from the events earlier in the day had carried over and she could see Lady Templeton's calming influence in that. They'd laughed and talked long after the desserts were cleared, the only conspicuous absence Lord Templeton.

Guy had told her quietly that his father got overwhelmed by new faces and the routines of daily life, so spent most of his time in his set of rooms. So far Emma had not even caught sight of the old man, but she could see the strain on Lady Templeton's face every time a servant came in to whisper some information about her husband.

With a sigh of annoyance Emma flung back the covers and reached for her dressing gown, pulling it around her shoulders. A wonderful blazing fire had been lit in her bedroom earlier in the evening, but the heat from that had completely dissipated and now there was a chill to the air in the room.

Quietly she slipped out of her bedroom, deciding to head downstairs to find a book to read from the library. Hopefully half an hour of reading and her lids would start to droop and she would get at least a little sleep before dawn.

The house was big, but not so big you could get lost in it. As she walked down the stairs she was aware of the creak of the old boards under her feet, sounding as loud as a breaking branch of a tree to her ears in the silence.

The library was dark even with her candle casting shadows on the walls. She had to stand close to the shelves to peer at the titles on the books, running her fingers along the leather-bound spines.

Emma spent a few minutes selecting a couple from the shelves, deciding she would take two or three upstairs and decide there which to read.

A soft noise behind her made her stiffen and she turned quickly, holding her candle out and hating the way the flame flickered as her hand shook. She reminded herself it was an old house—it was natural for it to groan and creak in the wind. With her heart beating a little harder, she gathered up the three books she'd selected and held them to her chest with one hand while lifting up the candle with her other.

She felt uneasy and suddenly had the urge to be back in her bed, tucked under the covers, warm and safe. Walking quickly, she left the library, but as she stepped out of the door a hand shot out of the darkness and grabbed her by the wrist.

Emma screamed. The books fell from her arms and clattered loudly to the floor, narrowly missing her toes. The candle flickered and died, adding to her panic.

'Got you,' a deep voice said, the tone part-menacing, part-gleeful.

It felt as though her heart was going to burst through her chest. Every single muscle in her body tensed, as if preparing to run, but the hand that gripped her wrist held on even tighter.

'Creeping about in the dark and stealing my valuables. I'll see you handed over to the magistrate. You'll hang for this.'

Emma was too petrified to take in the words at first, but as she struggled and wriggled, desperate to free herself, she felt some of her initial blind panic ebb away.

'What's going on?' Guy's comforting, familiar voice rang out through the hall. He wasn't carrying a candle, but Emma had never been so pleased to see someone's silhouette before.

'Guy,' she called, hating the fear in her voice.

He was at her side in an instant, laying a hand on her shoulder and making her feel immediately more in control of herself.

'Father,' he said gently, 'let go of her.'

'She was sneaking about in the dark. Trespassing. Stealing.'

'This is my good friend Emma. She's a house guest. She wasn't trespassing and she wasn't stealing.'

'House guest? No one told me about a house guest. It's my damn house and no one tells me anything.'

'I'm sorry, Father, it was late and I didn't think you would mind.'

Lord Templeton mumbled something inaudible, but Emma felt the pressure on her wrist releasing and watched as Guy guided his father a few steps away from her.

Lady Templeton appeared at the top of the stairs, candle held in front of her and a maid trailing behind.

'What's happened, Guy?' she said, descending the stairs as if her heels were on fire.

'Father thought Emma was a burglar.'

'I couldn't sleep so I came to choose a book from the library,' Emma explained, her voice still shaky.

'I'm so sorry, my dear,' Lady Templeton said, rubbing Emma's upper arm in comfort. 'Lord Templeton does sometimes wander at night. He struggles to sleep. I'm sorry he shocked you.'

'No need to apologise. I'm sorry for all the commotion.'

'Come, Father, let's get you back to bed.'

Emma watched as Guy led his father back upstairs, Lady Templeton beside them lighting the way with the candle. Quickly she gathered the books she had dropped and hurried up behind them, turning right where they turned left.

She re-lit her candle with the tinderbox that sat on the mantelpiece in her bedroom, not wanting to sit in the darkness yet. Her body was still on edge, as if prepared for another shock. With her candle placed on the little table beside the bed, she wriggled under the covers, too shaken to even open the books she had gone downstairs for.

Lord Templeton had been very strong—there was no way she would have been able to prise herself from his grip. The impression she had of him, from what she could make out in the shadows, was a physically impressive man, but she would never forget the look of utter bewilderment on his face as Guy had explained she was a guest, not a burglar.

As she was contemplating blowing out the candle and attempting to sleep there was a quiet knock on the door. She called out for the person outside to some in, expecting it to be Cecilia or perhaps Lady Templeton.

Guy slipped into the room, closing the door quietly behind him.

'You can't be here,' she said quickly. 'We're in your house, with your parents along the corridor, and your fiancée is coming to stay in a few days.'

'Almost-fiancée. I needed to check on you.' Even though half his face was in shadows she knew exactly what his expression would be—she would know in any scenario. 'Although I am impressed by your consideration of propriety.'

'Even I know a man cannot visit a lady's bedroom,' she grumbled.

'I'm sorry about my father.'

'You don't need to apologise for him.'

'Your scream…' He shuddered. 'I thought the worst.'

Emma pulled the bedcovers a little higher as Guy advanced further into the room, sitting down on the end of the bed as if they were on a park bench, not in her bedroom. She couldn't focus on his words, felt too distracted to do anything but nod and hope some of her sense would return soon.

'I should have warned you—' He broke off and rubbed a hand across his eyes. 'He wanders at night. Sleeps for most of the day, but come nightfall he becomes restless. We have a servant who sits with him, but she must have drifted off.'

Emma saw the pain in Guy's eyes and pushed away her own feelings to focus on his. 'It must be hard, coming home to a different man from the one you left.'

'He used to be so strong, so knowledgeable. He knew every variety of plant in the garden, every type of bird, every insect that might spoil the crops. Now he barely knows who my mother is.'

'You're mourning him.'

Guy closed his eyes for a moment and then nodded. 'I can't tell if I should feel guilty for mourning him when he's still alive.'

'You can mourn what you have lost, that relationship, that spark that made your father who he was.'

'Then I feel selfish. What right do I have to mourn when I wasn't here for so many years? My mother, Sophia, they have had to watch him slip away.'

'It doesn't mean you can't miss him, Guy. He is still your father, you still love him, you still have those fond memories of time with him in your childhood. Just because you haven't been here the past few years doesn't mean you have any less right to miss the man he was.'

Guy fell silent and Emma moved to take his hand, shuffling down the bed with the bedcovers still pulled up to her chin.

'I should go, leave you to sleep.'

She nodded, knowing there was nothing else they could do tonight. Guy had risked both their reputations by coming to check on her and every moment longer he stayed increased their chance of discovery.

'Goodnight, Em. Sleep well.' He raised her hand to his lips, his kiss lingering for a second longer than it should, but before Emma could see the expression on Guy's face he'd stood and strode from the room, closing the door with a soft click behind him.

Chapter Fifteen

Guy leaned back in his chair, swinging on the back legs as if he were still a child. There was something about being back in his childhood home that made him regress to some of his youthful behaviours.

He couldn't suppress a smile when Emma eventually emerged, yawning and still looking half-asleep despite it being after nine. She'd never been a morning person, even in Egypt where the most productive time was often in the hour or so after dawn when it was still cool from the night. Instead she would do things when the sun was at its height and wonder why everyone looked at her as though she were crazy.

'Good morning,' he said. 'Did you sleep?'

'A little, thank you. It took me a while to drop off after the excitement of the night.'

'I heard all about it,' Sophia said, hurrying in. For someone whose life revolved around Elmwood House his sister always seemed to be in a rush, as if she was worried the world was getting away from her.

'Did something happen?' Cecilia asked. She looked

well rested and fresh, obviously undisturbed by the night's events.

'I came downstairs to get some books from the library and was surprised by Lord Templeton, that's all.'

'Our father wanders at night,' Sophia said, taking a slice of toast even though Guy knew she had already had breakfast.

'There was a commotion?' There was concern in Cecilia's eyes.

'I screamed,' Emma admitted quietly. 'In my defence it was very dark.'

'Woke the whole household up—I'm surprised you didn't hear it, Cecilia,' Guy said.

'Henry always said I could sleep through anything.' The smile slipped from Cecilia's lips as she realised what she had said. Although in Egypt Emma's father and Cecilia had often walked arm in arm, heads bowed together showing the intimacy of their relationship, Cecilia had always been careful when among people they didn't know to keep up the pretence that she was first Emma's governess and then her companion.

Luckily it was only Sophia and she was too caught up in her buttery toast to notice the look of panic on Cecilia's face.

'Right, I've got the solicitor coming later today, but I have time this morning to give you a tour of the estate if you would like.' He directed his words to Emma and Cecilia, but he knew his sister would join them. She'd been so excited about the prospect of guests she wouldn't be left behind.

'We can show them the gardens and the old dairy and the lake and the woods,' Sophia said in one great gush of breath.

'Is your wrist too painful to ride?'

Emma flexed it a few times, smothering the grimace.

'It isn't too sore. Let me change into my riding habit and I'll be ready to go.'

'Can I tempt you, Cecilia?' Guy asked.

The older woman shook her head. 'I think I'll keep my feet firmly on the ground if your sister is going to accompany you. Your mother promised me a tour of her garden.'

Guy stood, meaning to go and tell the stable boy to prepare the horses, only realising Sophia was trailing after him once he had taken a few steps from the room.

'Put on a coat,' he admonished his sister as she went to follow him out of the front door.

'You're not wearing a coat.'

'True, but I have a shirt, a waistcoat and a jacket. You are wearing a flimsy dress.'

'Don't let Mother hear you call it flimsy. It cost enough. She was at her wit's end when I grew out of all of my dresses last year.'

He glanced at his sister and grinned. She wasn't quite his six-foot height, but she was certainly tall for a young lady.

'You have enough dresses?' He was suddenly aware that it wasn't an area of the household budget he knew much about. After he'd paid off most of his father's debts things were tight, but not dire. They could afford a few dresses for Sophia if needed.

'I have enough dresses. That wasn't why I wanted to come with you, to beg for more clothes.'

'I assumed you wanted the pleasure of my company.'

'Mother *really* likes her,' Sophia said, ignoring his last statement.

Guy frowned, knowing exactly who his sister was talking about, but not wanting to have this conversation again.

'Lady Emma. Mother thinks she's wonderful. I overheard her talking to Mrs Willow last night and she was saying how nice it is to see you smile.'

'I smile a lot.'

Sophia cocked her head to one side and considered for a moment. 'You're not foul tempered, that is for sure, but you've smiled more since you arrived yesterday with Lady Emma than you have in the last month.'

'Lady Emma is my friend. A good friend. We've shared many good times together,' he said slowly.'

'I know you love her,' Sophia blurted out.

'And how do you know that, little Sister?'

She bristled at that and straightened, hurrying to catch up with him as he rounded the side of the house and headed towards the stables.

'I just know.'

'From your years of experience?'

'Don't be condescending. I may be young, but I'm observant.'

Guy paused and turned to his sister. 'No more tricks today, Sophia. I mean it. I want to enjoy my last few days with Emma before...'

'Before you get married?'

He strode off quickly, not stopping until he reached the stables, only to find Sophia had turned back and disappeared inside the house.

Emma looked elegant in the bright red riding habit lined with black fur, her eyes sparkling in the sunshine. It had started as a bright day, but in the last half an hour the clouds had begun to build and Guy wasn't sure the rain would hold off until they returned. Still, he much preferred being out in the fresh air and was willing to take the chance.

'Would you help me mount, Guy?'

'Of course.' He moved over to Emma, wondering how many times he had boosted her up on to the back of a horse. It must be hundreds. Thousands, perhaps.

'To the lake?' he suggested when both Emma and his sister were settled in their saddles.

'I think I might go and find a hat,' Sophia said, looking up at the black clouds that were gathering. 'You go ahead. I'll catch you up.'

Giving his sister a firm look that she promptly ignored, Guy turned to Emma.

'The lake we passed to the side of the drive on our way in?' She had a familiar gleam in her eyes.

'Yes.'

'I'll race you there. Last one has to dip a toe into the water.'

Before Guy could protest she had urged her horse forward and was racing down the drive, bent low over the horse's neck.

He couldn't help but smile, adjusting his position and speeding off after her.

It wasn't all that far down to the lake and with a few seconds' head start it would be hard to catch up, but this was familiar territory for him and he was confident it wouldn't be him dipping his toes in the freezing, murky water of the lake.

Emma's hair was whipping out behind her, trying to

break free from its pins, and he could hear her laughing as he drew level with her.

'You're never going to win this one, Em,' he called over.

'The race isn't over yet.'

He saw her bend lower and then to his amazement she urged her horse into a spurt of speed before jumping over a low hedge to continue on a more direct path to the lake.

Guy refused to give up, picking out a spot to jump the hedge a little further down the drive and trying to encourage every last bit of speed from his faithful horse.

He arrived at the lake five seconds after Emma had slowed to a stop, looking very pleased with herself.

'That was crafty,' he said.

'Not crafty. I chose the best route to get to where I wanted to go. It's not my fault you're slow.'

'Crafty. You waited until I drew level to take the jump so I couldn't follow you over.'

'I have no idea what you are talking about, Guy, but I do know you are trying to distract me so you don't have to paddle in the lake.'

'Paddle. You said dip a toe.'

'I think paddling is a more fitting forfeit.'

He slipped from the back of his horse, looping the reins loosely over the branch of a tree, and held a hand out to help Emma down.

'Do you promise not to pull me in?'

'I am a gentleman.'

'That didn't stop you pulling me into that fountain in Cairo.'

'You looked hot, as if you were about to swoon.'

'Nonsense. I've never swooned in my life.'

'I promise I will not pull you into the lake. Although you might want to join me.'

Emma laughed. 'Why on earth would I want to do that?'

He shrugged. 'Perhaps you're not brave enough.'

'Do not try to goad me into it, Guy. It's your forfeit, stop wasting time and get on and do it.'

He leaned down and pulled off his boots and socks, feeling the cool grass underneath his toes.

'Last chance,' he said, reaching out for Emma's hand. She slipped her fingers into his and for a moment Guy felt as though the world slowed. For the last few months, the time he had known he would need to marry Miss Frant, he had tried to forget how happy he was when it was just him and Emma. He felt complete, as if all his worries lifted, when her hand touched his.

'Stop it,' he told himself quietly. There was no point in torturing himself. His future had been decided.

The water in the lake was high so the step down was only a few inches from the bank, but even so the coldness of the water took his breath away. After a second he sucked in a sharp breath as the water lapped over his feet to his ankles.

'That's cold.'

Emma was still holding his hand, peering into the lake.

'Is that ice over there?'

'Most likely. Do you know in some of the cold countries they bathe in ice lakes? They say it is good for the circulation.'

'Please don't try to persuade me to take a swim in your lake. Perhaps in the summer...' She trailed off.

They both knew she wouldn't be coming to stay in the summer.

'I won't ask you to swim, but come for a paddle. It's quite pleasant when you get used to it. Unless you're too scared.'

Emma gave him her superior gaze, but he was amazed when she perched down on the edge of a fallen tree trunk and began to unlace her boots.

'You're really coming in?'

'I'm coming in and what's more I will go deeper than you.'

'You won't last five seconds.'

She stayed silent as he watched her pull off her boots and lift up her skirts to unhook her stockings. If he were a gentleman he would turn away, but he was mesmerised, unable to move, his body shot through with desire as she rolled down the silky white stockings and revealed her creamy skin underneath.

He held out his hand as she approached the lake, waiting while she gathered up her skirts so they wouldn't get wet.

Emma made a high-pitched squeaking sound as she stepped down into the icy water and gripped his hand even harder. He knew she wouldn't jump out again immediately—she was too competitive for that. Instead she stood there, skirts in her hands, her body all stiff and tense.

'You can get out.'

'I don't need to,' she said through clenched teeth, taking a step further in.

Guy followed her, drawing level, making sure his feet were firmly planted on the muddy bottom of the lake so he didn't slip over. A full body dip wouldn't be pleasant this time of year.

'My toes are going numb,' she said after a minute.

'I don't think I can feel mine any more.'

'Remind me why we thought this was a good idea?'

He laughed. This was one of the things he loved about Emma, her desire to live life, to try new things, even if ultimately they didn't turn out to be things she enjoyed.

'Want to get out?'

'Yes.' She spun too quickly, her feet losing grip on the slippery mud, and Guy felt her grip his hand tighter as she fought to keep her balance. He had a steady base and didn't think he would be pulled over, but he was more worried about Emma falling into the water. He tried to steady her, but her feet were slipping away from underneath her and she had nothing else to hold on to. Making a split-second decision, he pulled her closer to him and then whipped her up into his arms, then once he was steady taking the two steps out of the water on to the bank.

Guy didn't set her down immediately, enjoying the weight of her in his arms, the way her body was pressed against his.

'Thank you,' she murmured and he looked down into her eyes. For a moment the rest of the world seemed to recede and there was nothing but the rich brown of her eyes and the pink curve of her lips. He had the overwhelming urge to kiss her, to give in to the desire that was coursing through his body. Somehow he knew she would taste sweet.

Emma was looking back at him, her eyes fixed on

his, her lips slightly parted. She clung to his neck and he knew there in that moment she wanted to be kissed.

Before his common sense could talk him out of it he bent his neck and kissed her gently on the lips. For a second she stiffened in his arms and then he felt her relax and begin to kiss him back. Guy felt hot sparks of desire shooting through his body and kissed her harder, feeling her respond in his arms, pulling him closer still.

'You taste like strawberries,' he murmured as he set her down on to her feet. Emma's eyes were glazed slightly, her arms still looped around his neck. She didn't let go and he couldn't help but kiss her again, taking his time to enjoy the softness of her lips and the feel of her body underneath his hands.

Even as he was kissing her Guy knew he had to stop. His future was mapped out and it didn't involve a romance with the woman in his arms. As much as he would wish for it, a life with Emma was impossible.

It was a cruel trick of the universe, to finally bring them together in this way when he couldn't take it any further. Two years ago, if they'd kissed like this, if Emma had *wanted* to be kissed like this, he would have dropped to one knee and asked her to marry him. Two years ago, he'd been free to put his own desires first. Now he wasn't.

Slowly he pulled away, wishing even as he did so for one more kiss, one more second in her arms, but knowing he had to put a stop to it or he wouldn't be strong enough to make the decisions deep down he knew were right.

'I'm sorry,' he said quietly, searching her face for signs of regret.

For a few seconds Emma looked dazed, as if still reliving the kiss in her head. Then a hand flew to her mouth and she let out a little gasp.

'What did we do, Guy?'

'We kissed.' He closed his eyes, willing himself to be strong. 'I'm sorry, Emma, it shouldn't have happened.'

She nodded vigorously, but wouldn't meet his eye. It was the first time in years of friendship that she wouldn't look directly at him.

'I don't know what came over me.' It was the truth. Hundreds of times he'd thought about kissing her, but had been able to resist. He wasn't sure what had been different this time.

As he thought about it he realised that wasn't quite true. Hundreds of times he'd wanted to kiss her and she'd looked at him in the same way as she always had, as her friend. Today there had been something different in her eyes, something primal and irresistible. She'd desired him.

'Guy...' She reached out to him, but he knew if he took her hand now he would be lost.

It felt as though he had been stabbed in the heart as he half turned away, not wanting her to see his expression. He couldn't look at her, couldn't see the betrayal on her face.

'We should get dressed,' he said quickly. 'I need to prepare a few things for when the solicitor arrives. Perhaps we can continue the tour tomorrow.'

'Guy,' Emma said more insistently, and he glanced up as he sat to pull on his socks.

'I'm sorry, Em, I shouldn't have kissed you.'

'Why did you?'

He blinked, stunned by the question and he was sure it showed on his face.

'You owe me that at least, even if you can't bear to look at me.'

Taking a deep breath, Guy pulled on his boots before returning her gaze.

'I kissed you because I wanted to. No…' He shook his head, changing his answer. 'I kissed you because in that moment I couldn't *not* kiss you.'

'Oh.'

'I know I shouldn't have, but I did, and I can't take it back. I'm sure one day we'll laugh about this.' He wasn't sure of any such thing.

'Do you want to take it back?'

Emma was pulling on a stocking with such force the material ripped and a ladder began running down its length. Quietly she cursed and he saw she was trying to hide just how upset she was.

'No. Yes. No.' He ran a hand through his hair. 'You're my best friend, Em. The one person I enjoy spending the most time with. I don't want to jeopardise that.'

She looked a little mollified at his answer and nodded abruptly before pulling on her boots and hurrying over to her horse.

Guy knew she couldn't mount on her own and he felt a swell of desire as he came in close behind her and caught a hint of the lemony scent of her hair. Quickly he boosted her up and handed her the reins, crossing to mount his own horse, but before he could settle into the saddle Emma had started forward.

'I would like some fresh air. If you are returning to the house, I think I'll ride out for a while before lunch.'

'Would you like me to accompany you?'

'No,' she said quickly and before he could offer again she was gone.

'Idiot,' he said quietly to himself. He was a complete idiot, firstly for kissing her and then for how he'd handled the situation afterwards. Shaking his head, he set off at a more sedate pace, crossing over the grass to the drive. When she'd asked why he'd kissed her he couldn't have told her the absolute truth. It served no purpose to confess he'd been in love with her for years, had wanted to kiss her for years. No purpose except to make them both pine for what could have been.

Guy had never resented the fact that Emma had only ever seen him as a friend. They had a wonderful friendship and he truly believed that sometimes things were not meant to be. He had silently loved Emma for a long time and had resigned himself to his love being unrequited. It was one of the reasons he had so readily agreed to marry Miss Frant. He'd known he would never love anyone else but Emma, so it didn't seem too much of a sacrifice to enter a loveless marriage. It wasn't as though he was denying himself a future with a woman he loved by marrying for money.

He thought back to the time in Egypt, just before he'd left for England, when he had asked Emma if she wanted to be with him. When she'd told him she was sure he would visit her soon it had felt as though his heart was being squeezed until it was about to burst. If only she had thought of him then as she did now.

Life could be cruel sometimes. Silently he tried to forget the hot desire in Emma's eyes as she'd looked at him, the eagerness to her kiss, the way she'd pulled him closer. It would do no good to torture himself with what ifs now.

Chapter Sixteen

Thankful that no one was around to see her as she dashed through the halls of Elmwood House to her bedroom, Emma firmly closed the door behind her before flinging herself on to the bed. The tears had started as soon as she had left Guy, tears of embarrassment along with tears of pain. Now she allowed herself to sob into the pillow, the complete outlet of emotion feeling cathartic.

She couldn't believe Guy had kissed her. It seemed surreal, as if she had watched it happen to someone else. No, that wasn't quite true. If she'd watched it happen, she wouldn't be able to remember the spark as his lips had brushed hers, or the deep longing she'd felt as he'd pulled her into his arms.

After a couple of minutes she stopped crying, drying off her face and sitting up, wondering why she felt so hollow inside. It was a kiss, nothing more. They'd been friends for a long time, Guy was a very attractive man and she was aware that, although not classically stunning, she had a pleasant face and a nice figure. In a way many people might find it strange they hadn't felt this attraction before.

She'd always known Guy was good looking. He was charming and kind and funny, too, but until recently she'd seen him as nothing more than her friend. It was confusing to feel her pulse quicken every time he came near her now or to feel her heart thump in her chest.

'You're being contrary.' She didn't really believe she had only started noticing her attraction to Guy because he was now unavailable, but she couldn't explain why it had happened now.

Shaking her head in frustration, she told herself it didn't matter. Guy was an honourable man. He was going to marry Miss Frant to settle his father's debt and that meant that the kiss would never be repeated. It had been a moment of weakness, one that she could see he regretted immediately after.

'Emma.' Cecilia's voice accompanied the knock on the door.

Quickly Emma checked her face in the small mirror on the dressing table as she called for Cecilia to come in.

'Is something wrong?' Cecilia looked at her with concern etched on her face.

Shaking her head, Emma tried to summon a smile, but knew it was futile. Cecilia had never tried to be a replacement for her mother, but she knew Emma better than anyone else.

'Oh, darling, what has happened?'

With a soft click Cecilia closed the door behind her and came and sat on the bed next to Emma, taking her in her arms as if she were still a little girl.

'Nothing. It's nothing, honestly. I'm being silly.'

Cecilia stroked her hair and Emma felt some of the tension she'd been holding in her shoulders start to disappear.

'Love is hard, Emma,' she said after a few minutes.

'I'm not in love, Cece. I was being foolish.'

'You forget I know you. I've watched you grow up. I've loved you for years.'

Emma fell silent. 'Was love hard for you?'

'Not with your father.' Even though Emma couldn't see her face she knew Cecilia was smiling at the memory. 'He made everything easy—those nine years were the happiest of my life. I had love and I had a family.' She seemed to be lost in thought for a few minutes before continuing. 'I've never told you much about my life before I came to Egypt, have I?'

'No.' Emma had always been interested, especially when she had overheard snippets of conversations between her father and Cecilia, but even at a young age she had realised that some things you didn't probe, didn't ask about, as it might rake up painful memories.

'You know I was married quite young. My parents arranged the match, but Mr Willow was a very kind gentleman. He was a fair bit older than me, but he treated me well. He loved the countryside, so we spent most of our time in his beloved Yorkshire.'

'He died a few years into your marriage, didn't he?'

'Yes. I mourned him, but mostly I mourned the loss of the family I had always wished for. We weren't rich, but we had been comfortable and I inherited the house and a small pot of savings, enough to keep me living modestly, but comfortably, for a very long time.'

Emma couldn't imagine Cecilia in a lonely house in Yorkshire. She always thought of her in the sunshine, smiling and happy, walking with her arm in arm by the Nile.

'Is that when you decided to come to Egypt?'

'No. I lived quietly for a couple of years, observing the mourning period for my husband, then I was invited to stay by some friends in London.' She shook her head ruefully. 'I wasn't sure what I wanted from my life at that point. I was only twenty-six, yet it felt as though my life was over.'

'What happened in London?'

Cecilia didn't answer immediately. When she did her voice was more strained than usual and Emma realised it was hard for her to tell this story.

'I enjoyed myself. I went to balls and dinner parties and socialised. I had never had a proper debut, my family arranging the marriage to Mr Willow rather than needing to fund the expense of a Season in London. Then I met Lord Greyson.'

Emma wondered if this was Cecilia's second husband, the one she had been fleeing from.

'I fell in love with him. I was completely besotted, the sort of romance you read about in books. He was gallant and handsome and charming, and I felt as though I was waking up from a long sleep and finally living my life.'

'What happened?'

'He told me he loved me, too.' Cecilia closed her eyes for a moment and took a breath before continuing. 'He did love me, I know he did, but not enough. He was the heir to an earldom, expected to marry within the upper echelons of society. I was a respectable widow, but certainly not good enough for his family.'

Emma took her friend's hand and squeezed it. She'd had no idea Cecilia had experienced such heartbreak.

'I could see he was torn between me and his duty to his family—he found it impossible to make the decision. I was heartbroken, but I loved him, so I made things easy for him. I accepted another man's proposal.'

Emma blinked in surprise. She had known about the second marriage, but not about the man Cecilia had loved in between.

'It was rash, too hasty. I knew next to nothing about the man I was about to marry, Mr Hudson. We married in a small ceremony in Brighton and travelled straight after to his estate in the Sussex countryside.' Cecilia took a deep breath, the tension showing in her posture and the angle she was holding herself at. 'He was cruel, malicious. He hurt me physically, but more than that he spent every moment of every day belittling me. It gave him pleasure.'

'Oh, Cece.'

'I spent six months as his wife, six months where he isolated me from everyone else, made me doubt my worth as a person and made me question whether I wanted to be alive.'

Emma reached out and drew Cecilia to her. She'd never imagined things could have been that bad for Cecilia. She was so kind, so wonderful, it made Emma angry to think of anyone mistreating her in such a way.

'I knew I had to get out, so for weeks I planned my escape, hiding away money and possessions and waiting until Mr Hudson was away for a night, out gambling in Brighton. Then I ran.'

It was impossible to imagine how Cecilia must have felt, running into the unknown.

'I knew my husband would come after me if I stayed in England, so I went to Southampton and bought a passage on the first boat available. I don't think I relaxed until we rounded the south of Spain.'

'That's when you came to us?'

'The boat was sailing to Egypt. When I arrived, I heard of the position of governess to a little girl. It seemed as though for once something was going right, that something was meant to be.'

'Did you ever hear from your husband again?'

'No. I have no doubt he searched for me and, if he knew I was in Egypt, I think he would have come to drag me back. Your father promised me his protection and slowly, very slowly, I allowed myself to forget my life in England.' She smiled warmly. 'You and your father were the best things that ever happened to me, Emma. You saved me, healed my broken heart.'

'So that's why you and my father didn't marry?'

'Yes. We received news Mr Hudson had died a few months before your father became ill. We planned to marry then, but time was not on our side. I would have dearly loved to have married your father, Emma.' Cecilia took her hand and squeezed it.

'You've seemed nervous since we've been back.'

'It's not something that I can control. I know my second husband is dead, I read the announcement, but I still feel jumpy when someone comes up behind me. Not many people in society know or remember I was married a second time. We married away from London and were never in the city as a couple, but after I left I didn't know what lies Mr Hudson had spread about me. I didn't know whether I should call myself Mrs Willow or Mrs Hudson when we returned, but a few acquaintances addressed me by my first husband's name and it is the one I'm more comfortable with, so I thought I would stick with it.'

'No one has said anything?'

'No, no one. It makes me wonder if Mr Hudson didn't just try to sweep the whole thing under the carpet to save his having to explain why his new wife fled just months into the marriage.'

'I hope you can start to relax soon, Cece.'

'I know it isn't quite the same as your situation…'

'My situation?'

'With Guy.'

Emma felt her cheeks grow warm as the blood flooded to them.

'There is no situation with Guy.'

'Oh, my darling,' Cecilia said, wrapping Emma in her arms. 'No one else could upset you like this.'

Biting her lip, Emma considered what she wanted to tell Cecilia, then realised the older woman knew her so well she could probably guess most of it.

'Guy has always been the best of friends and, until we returned to England, that was all I had ever thought of him as.'

'But since our return?'

There was a long silence as Emma tried to put into words the blossoming desire and attraction she felt for a man who was no longer available.

'I look at him and I feel different,' she said eventually.

'As though you want him to kiss you?' Cecilia was normally quite reserved, but Emma realised she had

fallen in love twice and been happily married as well.
She would know about these feelings.

'Yes. As though all I can think about is him kissing me.'

'I'm not surprised, Emma. He's a very attractive
man and he's kind, charming, fun and adores you.'

'He doesn't adore me.'

Cecilia smiled softly. 'He adores you.'

Emma thought of his reaction after their kiss. He'd
made it clear it was definitely a mistake. Certainly he
cared for her, but he didn't adore her.

'I want to go back to how we were.'

'Do you? Is that really what you want?'

What she really wanted was for Guy to come striding through the door, scoop her up into his arms and
carry her to his bedroom where he could do all manner of unspeakable things to her. She swallowed before trying to form a reply.

'He is going to marry Miss Frant. He needs to marry
Miss Frant.'

'Yes, that is a problem.'

'That's not the problem. The problem is how do I
go back to thinking of him how I used to.'

'I don't think you can, Emma.'

Cecilia stroked her hand and, even though she had
solved nothing, Emma felt comfort at being able to
share her distress at the change in her feelings.

'Don't push him away. You rely on your friendship
with Guy so much, he is good for you. Don't focus on
what you worry might or might not happen, focus on
enjoying your time with him.'

Emma nodded glumly. Her limited time. Perhaps

it was the sense of panic that she was losing him that had fuelled these new feelings.

'I had better get back to Lady Templeton. I abandoned her when I saw you dashing through the house. We'll talk later, when you've had a chance to let everything settle.'

Giving her a tight hug, Cecilia then stood and glided silently from the room. Emma remained in the same position on the bed for a while longer, thinking about everything Cecilia had said. She was shocked at the details of Cecilia's life before she had arrived in Egypt and surprised that she had been married twice and in love with a third man all before coming to live with them a decade ago.

More pressingly she wondered whether to take Cecilia's advice, whether to put the kiss and Guy's reaction to her after from her mind and focus on enjoying the next few days in his company.

'You have a few months at most until he is a married man,' she murmured to herself. She wasn't going to waste it moping.

Chapter Seventeen

Pulling the hood of her cloak up around her ears, Emma peered out into the gloom and wondered how her companion remained so cheerful despite the biting wind and ominous clouds above their heads.

She was with Sophia, having walked into the village of Overhampton earlier in the afternoon. They had wandered through the streets, popped into the modiste where Sophia had asked Emma's opinion on the couple of dresses she was having adjusted for the winter and stopped to talk with a few villagers along the way.

Now the November evening was drawing in and Emma was sure she'd felt the first flurries of snow on her face. It was about half an hour's walk back to Elmwood House and Emma was already dreaming about warming her toes in front of a roaring fire.

'You've been to some balls in London, seen what the Season is like—is it really all everyone says it is?' Sophia had grown serious and Emma sensed there was more than just casual interest behind her question.

'One of the reasons I was keen to return to England

was to experience a London Season, to twirl through ballrooms, gossip with friends, choose dresses at the modiste. My mother died when I was very young, but I have her diaries from when she was a debutante and she painted a wonderful picture.'

'Was it everything you hoped?'

Emma considered. The balls were fun and she loved the fashion and elegance of the *ton*, but she hadn't been completely swept away, and the memory of the masquerade and being cornered by Lord Romsey still made her shudder.

'I think it all depends whom you share it with.' She smiled and then hurried to explain further. 'There are two big balls this week, *unmissable events* if you talk to anyone in London, but I would much rather be here in Kent with Cecilia and your brother.'

Sophia nodded, her eyes fixed on the horizon as if deep in thought.

'Are you excited for your debut next year?'

The young woman shrugged and Emma wondered what was the cause of her reticence. She didn't know Sophia well, but normally she was bubbling with enthusiasm. Before she could ask she saw a figure approaching on horseback in the distance and felt her body tighten in anticipation as she realised it was Guy. She hadn't seen him since she'd fled after their kiss earlier in the day and even though she knew she needed to make this right, to show him they could move past the kiss, forget about it even, she felt nervous to talk to him.

'Good afternoon,' Guy said, raising his hat in a mock formal greeting. 'What a lovely afternoon for a stroll.'

'I think my fingers might fall off, Guy,' Sophia said, showing him her red hands. 'I forgot my gloves.'

Quickly Guy dismounted and pulled his own gloves from his fingers, handing them over to his little sister.

'But you'll get cold.'

'I will live. Take them, I insist.'

Sophia gave a little sigh of contentment as she pulled the warm gloves on and then threw herself at Guy and gave him a hug.

'Everything is better now you're back,' she said, her voice muffled in his thick coat.

'You're frozen, Sophia.' He looked across in concern at Emma, frowning as he took in her cold visage. 'How long have you been out?'

'A couple of hours.'

He shook his head. 'You ride back on Hercules. I'll walk back with Lady Emma.'

'I couldn't take your horse.'

'I'll never hear the end of it if your fingers drop off from the cold. Go, I shall make sure Lady Emma doesn't get stuck in the snowstorm.'

In unison they all looked up at the dark clouds. It had begun to snow in earnest now and there was no sign of it relenting. Luckily there was a good road back to the gates of Elmwood House and then the drive was level and well maintained up to the house.

'If you're sure…' Sophia said, eyeing the horse as if wishing she could jump on its back and gallop home to the warmth.

'I'm sure. Tell Mrs Harvey we'll want hot tea to warm us when we get in.'

'Thank you, Guy,' Sophia said, smiling as her brother

helped her up on to the back of Hercules and handed her the reins.

They watched as she drew away from them, before Guy turned and held out his arm for Emma to take.

'Shall we?'

For a few minutes they walked in silence and Emma could tell Guy was building up to saying something he felt was important. Suddenly she didn't want to hear it, she didn't want him to say something that might pull them apart for good.

'How was your meeting with the solicitor?' she asked quickly, hoping it would be enough of a distraction.

'Fine. He is going to stay overnight and travel back to London tomorrow. Good Lord, Emma, you're freezing. I can feel the iciness of your hand even through your gloves and my coat.'

It was true, her fingers felt like little icicles, ready to shatter at the slightest pressure.

'We've been out a while.'

'Sophia is loving having you here. I hadn't realised how lonely she was.'

'She doesn't have many friends close by?'

'Not really. There aren't many local families with children of her age.'

They fell silent and Guy took a deep breath.

'I'm sorry about earlier,' he said quickly. 'I reacted poorly.'

'There is nothing to apologise for, Guy. I shouldn't have run away from you. It was nothing, I overreacted.'

'Nothing,' he murmured and then nodded forcefully.

'I don't want it to come between us. I feel as though

I've only just got you back and I'd hate for there to be any awkwardness between us,' Emma said, wondering why she felt hollow inside as she uttered the words.

'No, we don't want that.'

He turned to her and seemed about to say something and then shook his head. Emma cursed her irrational brain as she had the sudden urge to kiss him, to wrap her arms around him and feel the firmness of his body against hers. Instead of this stilted apology they were giving each other she wanted to admit to how she felt when he looked at her, how she wanted to be more than his friend.

They walked along in silence for a while longer, both bending their heads against the increasingly heavy snow. The wind was whipping it into their faces and as they reached the gates of the estate Emma knew she couldn't stand much more.

'Do you want to shelter for a while?'

She looked up, confused. 'Is there somewhere?'

'The old gatehouse. It hasn't been used in years, but I know where the spare key is hidden.'

Emma eyed the stone building to one side of the gates and nodded. It might not have a roaring fire, but even a few minutes out of the biting wind and snow would allow her to recover a little of the feeling in her face and fingers.

She watched as Guy reached high above the door, picking up a key that had been hidden in a stone groove, then putting it in the lock and letting them inside.

The relief to be out of the wind and cold was immediate, even in the darkness of the disused gatehouse.

'No one has lived in here for decades,' Guy said as

he closed the door behind them. 'I doubt we'll find any candles or a tinderbox, but we can shelter for a few minutes before we push on up to the house.'

Emma was shivering, her whole body shaking. Guy frowned and then drew her to him. It was an innocent gesture, but all the same Emma felt her body respond to his proximity, to his warmth. She hesitated, then wrapped her arms around his waist, feeling a peculiar sense of calm as she buried her face in his shoulder.

'Put your hands inside my coat,' he said, his voice a little gruffer than usual. 'No one will know and you'll warm up much quicker.'

Even though at least three layers still separated her from his skin Emma felt an illicit thrill as she threaded her hands under his coat. He was right, she felt much warmer that way, but she couldn't deny the other feelings that flared and burned as she stepped even closer.

'Do you think the snow will settle?'

'Yes, it's cold enough. You might be lucky to see Kent covered in a layer of pure white snow tomorrow. It is beautiful when that happens, Em.'

'I'd like that.'

'Although I warn you I have a strong arm and brilliant aim when it comes to snowball fights.'

She smiled at the thought and realised some of her fears had been wrong. Despite the kiss, despite her changing feelings for Guy, they would be able to return to some normality. They enjoyed one another too much to allow the awkwardness to remain.

'If conditions allow will you take me to the folly tomorrow?'

'Of course. Although it is a bit of a trek in the snow.'

She'd stopped shivering now and felt some of the

feeling return to her hands and feet. It had been a good idea to shelter for a few minutes. Slowly she pulled away a little, her hands still wrapped around Guy's torso, but now her face wasn't nestled into his shoulder and she could look up at him. He shifted, then looked down, their eyes meeting in the darkness.

Emma felt a sudden urge to stand up on her tiptoes and kiss Guy and for a long moment she wasn't sure if she would be able to suppress that desire, but gradually she was able to force herself to pull away.

'We should get going otherwise your sister will raise the alarm, thinking we've got lost in the snow.'

'Yes.' Guy's voice sounded strained, but Emma made herself concentrate on making sure she was all bundled up before they stepped back out into the cold.

They walked briskly the rest of the way to the house, Guy aware that every minute that passed meant that the temperature would fall a little more.

When they got inside he could see Emma's cheeks were pink from the cold, the tip of her nose was red and she was shivering.

'Dear me, what an evening,' Lady Templeton said as she ushered Emma into the drawing room. Guy was pleased to see his mother fussing over Emma and ensuring her chair was close to the fire. He passed his coat and gloves and hat to a footman and followed them in. For a few minutes he stood, enjoying the warmth of the flames thawing out his frozen skin until he felt warm enough to back away from the fire and sit for a while.

'Tea and cake,' he observed. 'Good girl, Sophia.'

'I knew you'd want cake. You always want cake.'

'A man has to be well sustained after an afternoon of battling the elements.'

Emma scoffed. 'You'd want cake if all you'd been doing was sitting in the library reading a book.'

'I do not deny it.'

He took a sip of the tea and felt his insides begin to warm, settling back into the chair.

'Will you play for us, Sophia?' Lady Templeton suggested.

Sophia obliged, taking her place at the piano and playing a slow, relaxing tune very proficiently.

'What an afternoon,' Cecilia said as she came to join them. 'I was worried you would be stuck in the snow.'

'Guy came to find us,' Emma said with a smile.

'Of course he did.'

'We have a couple of hours until dinner. I was wondering if perhaps we might play a game or two. What do you think, Mrs Willow? Lady Emma?' Lady Templeton suggested.

'Cards or something else?'

'How about that one we used to play with Papa?' Sophia suggested from her position at the piano.

Lady Templeton smiled at the memory.

'You'll remember it, Guy. We used to play it with you boys as well before...' She trailed off and then forced a smile on to her face.

'Me and Father against you and Will,' Guy said.

'Yes. You and your father always used to win, if I remember correctly. But we are five, Sophia, and that game only works for four.'

'I am quite happy to observe,' Cecilia said, sipping on her cup of tea.

'How do you play?' Emma was intrigued. She and her father had often played games together when she was young, passing long evenings when it was just the two of them happily laughing and talking as they played.

'Each team writes ten words—people or places or objects—on pieces of paper. They then exchange the pieces of paper with the other team. Only one person can look at them, then they have to describe what is written without using the word itself. You time for a minute or two minutes and see which team can guess the most within that time.'

'That sounds fun.'

'You had better pair with Lady Emma, my dear,' Lady Templeton said to Guy. 'You have more shared experiences. I will partner Sophia.'

Sophia stopped playing and helped her mother find some paper and two pens and then they went off to discuss word choices.

'What shall we put down?' Emma moved chairs so she was sitting next to Guy and he caught a hint of her scent, which momentarily distracted him. It had been so hard in the gatehouse to feel her hands on his body and not respond how he wanted to and now he seemed to be responding to even the slightest provocation with a surge of desire.

'Places are easy to guess, people, too, unless you choose carefully. Objects are harder, I think.' They discussed in hushed tones for a couple of minutes until they had a complete list of ten words. His mother and sister took a few minutes longer before returning to the room with their pile.

'Do you want to go first and show Emma how it is

done?' he suggested to Sophia and his mother, handing her the slips of paper he and Emma had written down the words on.

'Good idea. Would you like to guess, Sophia, or shall I?'

'I'll guess.'

'How long are we having?'

'A minute?' Guy handed his pocket watch to Cecilia and Sophia stood in front of their little group. Guy was struck for a moment at how comfortable he felt. When he had first returned he had felt awkward in his own home, his father a stranger, his beloved brother a ghost of a memory and a sister he barely knew. Only his mother had stayed the same. Even a few weeks ago he'd felt uncomfortable to spend long periods of time there, caught between guilt for having stayed away for so long and the desire to flee so he wasn't assaulted by the memories of what his family had once been.

He knew it was having Emma here that made the difference. She made him relax, feel more like himself. In the last couple of days his mother had commented a number of times on how much more he was smiling, how much happier he looked.

'Go,' Cecilia said, and his sister turned over the first piece of paper.

'Something you cook with.'

'A spoon. A bowl. A saucepan.'

'Yes,' Sophia shouted, her eyes sparkling with excitement. 'Oh…erm…a collection of countries. A continent.'

'Europe.'

'No. Hotter. They have lions.'

'Africa.'

'Yes, Mama.'

Guy found himself grinning at his sister's enthusiasm and glanced over at Emma. She was smiling encouragingly at Sophia, clapping her hands together when Lady Templeton guessed the correct answer.

'An animal. Big teeth.'

'Tiger. Lion.'

'No, lives in the water.'

'A shark?'

'No, in rivers. Scaly.'

'A crocodile.'

'Yes, Mama.'

'Time is up,' Cecilia called and Sophia groaned as she looked at the pile of words still remaining.

'We're out of practice, Mama,' she said.

'Let's see what Guy and Lady Emma can do.'

'Do you want to read or guess?'

Emma considered for a moment and then said she would guess. Guy stood and took the little pile of paper his mother and sister had written the words down on, signalling to Cecilia he was ready.

'Pulls a carriage.'

'Horse.'

'Eat soup with it.'

'Spoon.'

'Comes from clouds.'

'Rain.'

'City of canals.'

'Venice.'

'Wear on your feet in the winter.'

'Boots.'

'Food your father hated.'

'Carrots.'

'My favourite animal.'

'Monkey.'

'Most evil military dictator.'

'Napoleon.'

'You got one of these stuck in your hair in Cairo.'

'Comb.'

'Sweet red fruit.'

'Strawberries.'

Guy put down the last piece of paper and tore his eyes away from Emma to see his mother and sister looking at them with open mouths.

'Ten seconds left,' Cecilia said and Guy could see she was trying to suppress a smile.

'How did you do that? Could you see the answers, Lady Emma? That's impossible, no one has ever got ten in less than a minute before.'

'Even your father and I used to struggle to get more than eight when we used to play together,' Lady Templeton said, giving Guy a strange look.

Guy shrugged. He knew Emma so well he knew exactly what to say to make himself completely clear.

'You two know each other so well,' Cecilia murmured.

'I can't believe it,' Sophia said. 'How do you know each other so well?'

Guy saw Emma was looking a little uneasy from the attention.

'Did I tell you about the time I was trapped at Lady Emma's house with her and her father and Cecilia for three days straight due to a sandstorm?'

'A sandstorm, how exciting,' Sophia said, her focus already pulled from Emma.

'We played so many games to pass the time, Lady

Emma and I became quite the team.' It wasn't the real reason, although he wasn't lying about the sandstorm. The real reason he and Emma had scored so highly was that they were so compatible.

Quickly he suppressed the thought. He had abandoned his family for far too long, now was the time to make amends. Thoughts of compatibility with Lady Emma would not be helpful.

'That was fun,' Emma said, rising from her seat. 'But I think I will go and freshen up before dinner. My dress is a little damp from the snow.'

She hurried out, catching his eye on the way. Guy waited for a moment and then made his own excuses, following her into the hall.

'Guy,' she whispered, peeking out from behind a suit of armour. She looked so ridiculous hiding behind the metal artefact he couldn't suppress a laugh. 'What's so funny?'

'You hiding behind the suit of armour. Is something the matter?'

'No. Yes. Well, I don't know.' It was unlike Emma to be so unsure of something. She was normally very decisive and always seemed to know her own mind.

Guy looked behind him to check no one else was following them out of the drawing room, then motioned for her to step into his study.

He knew it was foolish to close the door behind him, but Emma looked so forlorn, so dejected, he wanted to make sure she told him exactly what she was thinking and why she looked so low.

'What's wrong?'

'They know,' she whispered.

'Who knows what?'

'Your mother, your sister. They know about the kiss.'

Guy started to laugh, but caught himself when he saw Emma's completely serious expression.

'They don't know, Em. No one knows but us.'

'But they looked at us as though they knew. And Cecilia...' She trailed off, shaking her head.

'What about Cecilia?'

'Nothing.'

'You're worrying too much.' He shrugged. 'And what does it matter if they do?'

'Of course it matters. You're going to be married soon.'

'Don't remind me,' he muttered.

Emma's expression changed to one of concern and she stepped forward, as if about to say something.

'I wish...' she said eventually, then trailed off. For a moment her eyes met his and he knew exactly what it was she wished for, without her having to say it. Guy felt as though he had been stabbed as a sharp pain ripped through him. All these years of secretly wanting something he thought would never happen and now, when it had become impossible, she wanted it, too.

'I wish, too,' he said quietly.

For a long time they didn't move, locked together by some invisible force, not touching, but still not able to break free. Then Emma closed her eyes and took a deep breath, looking as if she were trying to compose herself, before turning and fleeing from the room.

Chapter Eighteen

It felt strange to knock on the door to his father's quarters and have a servant answer, rather than his father's strong voice calling for him to come in.

'Is he awake?' His father often slept much of the day now, his body seemingly confused by when it should be awake and asleep, meaning he was up and restless as everyone else was heading to bed.

'Yes, Captain Fitzgerald, he's sitting in his chair, looking out over the garden,' Daisy, one of the maids charged with looking after his father, said, gesturing into the room behind her.

'Is he…lucid?'

His father's state of mind seemed to fluctuate. He was always confused, always forgetful, but some days seemed better than others. Some days he could sit quietly and reminisce about the past and to the casual observer it might seem as though nothing were wrong. Of course Guy still could tell there were only fragments of the father who had once been so vibrant, so engaging, left, but at least there was something recognisable there. Other days when Guy visited his father looked agitated and dishevelled. He would get worked up over the slightest thing and it would be more damaging to stay than to leave him to rest and hope for a better day soon.

'He's had a good day today, although he is a little tired. Lord Templeton was up most of the night last night.'

Daisy stepped aside and let Guy into the room, closing the door behind him and turning the key in the lock. Even though it seemed cruel to keep the old man locked away, it was safer for him. Although much frailer than he was in his prime, Guy's father was still a strong man physically and would easily be able to overpower Daisy or the other two maids who had been employed to care for him. Keeping the door locked meant he didn't wander out into the cold or head for the kitchens and burn himself on the fires.

'Hello, Father,' Guy said as he approached slowly, giving the old man the chance to register his presence before he sat down. 'It's Guy.'

A brief flash of recognition swept over Lord Templeton's face and he smiled. Guy felt a flood of relief—at least it wouldn't be one of those days where his father thought a stranger was impersonating his son.

'How are you?'

'Damn terrible. Look at this snow. I need to go and check the tenant farmers are prepared for winter and instead I'm stuck in here.'

'The tenant farmers are all prepared, Father, I checked myself.' Over the last few months Guy had found it was less distressing for his father if he went along with whatever time period his mind told him he was in, rather than disputing it. The farms had all been sold off a few years earlier to pay some of the debts, but reminding his father of this would cause unnecessary distress.

Lord Templeton looked at Guy and then nodded his approval.

'Good.'

They sat in silence for a few minutes, both looking out at the falling snow. Guy was secretly pleased— snow would mean Miss Frant and her parents would be less likely to be able to make the journey from London, which meant more time before he had to propose and make everything official.

'Can I ask your advice, Father?'

'Of course.'

'I have to do something I really don't want to, but it is my duty. It will secure the future of this family. How do I silence the selfish voice inside me that wants to say no, to do what will make me happy instead?'

'Duty or happiness,' his father mused. 'Can you have one without the other? Choose duty and you will be content that you have done what is right by the family, but you may not be *happy.* Choose happiness and there will be the guilt that you put yourself above the others you are meant to care for.'

Guy closed his eyes, letting his father's words sink in. They were surprisingly coherent and sensible. Choose duty and be content or choose himself and be laden with guilt. He already lived with more guilt than he could handle with Will's death always hanging over him—he knew he would crumble under the weight of any more. He felt the pressing need to live up to his brother's memory, to do the best by his family as Will would have done as its head.

'Thank you,' he said quietly to his father, reaching out and patting a leathery old hand with his own. It had confirmed what he needed to do. When Miss Frant arrived at Elmwood House he would stop delaying and propose, suggesting a quick wedding. He had a good set of morals and knew once he was married he wouldn't be tempted by Emma's sweet smile or beguiling kisses, at least not enough to act on them.

'Where's Will? Normally you two are thick as thieves.'

'Will is away, Father. He'll be back soon.' Feeling the familiar lump in his throat he always had when talking of his brother, Guy gave his father a forced smile and turned the conversation to more mundane topics. His father loved to talk of the estate, of the farms and fields and parkland, and Guy liked to listen, to hear the stories that were familiar from his childhood.

The snow had stopped falling a few minutes earlier and Emma was enjoying looking out of the window at the glistening white in the moonlight. She was enthralled, unable to tear her eyes away. Even though she had lived in England until she was four she had no memory of snow and growing up had never visited anywhere to see it. It looked magical, surreal, and she could quite happily watch the little flakes falling for hours. She'd been sitting there, wrapped in a blanket from the bed, for twenty minutes when she saw a figure striding across the lawn. She would know Guy's gait anywhere and watched with interest as he moved away from the house. It was late, the hands on the clock on her mantelpiece slowly edging towards midnight, and she wondered what he was doing outside.

As she watched he turned slightly and even though she was a fair distance away she caught sight of the expression on his face and it made her heart leap in her chest. He looked distraught, more unhappy than she had ever seen him before. Without hesitating she pulled the curtains closed, rapidly dressed, donned her thick cloak with the fur-lined hood and hurried downstairs. She knew Guy could move quickly in all terrains and might be too far away for her to catch up with him, but she also knew she had to try.

It was icy outside, the sky clear now it had rid itself of the snow that had fallen earlier in the afternoon. Everything looked beautiful in the moonlight and Emma was glad to see Guy's footprints clearly in the fresh snow. It would be easy to follow him, although as the wind whipped around her, pushing her hood back, she wondered at the folly of her traipsing through the cold in a place she barely knew.

Bowing her head, she pushed aside her doubts. Despite her confusing feelings for Guy these past few weeks he was still her friend and still worthy of her care. The expression on his face that she had seen through the window had worried her and that meant she needed to forget about her own discomfort and seek him out to see what she could do to help.

As quickly as she dared Emma hurried through the formal gardens, treading beside Guy's footprints, every so often peering up to see if she could spot him in the distance. The trail headed out into the parkland, off to the right of the house, and after Emma had been walking for about ten minutes she realised where Guy was going. For a moment she paused. It was quite a trek to the old folly his grandfather had built up on the hill behind the house, but she was certain that was where he was headed.

Emma quickened her pace, eager to catch up with Guy and persuade him back to the warmth of the house, but she was almost halfway up the hill to the folly before she caught sight of him in the snow. He was almost at the tower, head bent against the wind, and he hadn't once looked back.

Emma must have reached the tower five minutes after him, her legs aching from the climb up the hill in the snow. She took a moment to rest as she poked her head through the door and saw the winding stair-case spiralling above her.

Once she had her breath back Emma started the climb, turning round and round on the spiral staircase until she emerged through the door at the top. An icy wind hit her as she stepped out and at first she couldn't see Guy. Confused, she looked around. The parapet was only small, with nowhere obvious to hide a man. If Guy wasn't up here…she shook her head. She hadn't imagined him or his footsteps in the snow.

'Emma.' The voice came from behind and above her and Emma spun quickly. She looked up to see Guy sitting on the roof of the tower, above the door she had emerged from. He held out his hand and pulled her up and she was glad to see there was a small alcove he had been sitting in to shelter from the wind. 'What are you doing here?'

She got herself settled first, wishing she had taken the time to don more layers before rushing out. Guy saw she was shivering and quickly handed her his gloves and wrapped his thick scarf around her neck.

'I saw you in the snow. You looked upset and I knew I had to check on you.'

'You're crazy. You could have got lost in the snow, fallen into a ditch and frozen to death.'

'I followed your footprints.'

It was warmer up here, sheltered from the wind, and now Emma had Guy's gloves and scarf on she felt some of the tension release from her shoulders.

'What's wrong, Guy?'

For a long time he was silent and it seemed as though he might not answer her question.

'Do you ever wonder how you got to this point in your life?'

Emma looked at him, trying to work out what was going through his mind.

'There is so much I am grateful for. My health, my family, my friendship with you, all those years I spent in Egypt doing what I loved.'

'There's a lot to be grateful for.'

'It feels churlish to be so discontented.'

'You've always been the maker of your own destiny, Guy. You chose to join the army. You chose to settle in Egypt and build your shipping business. You chose to take an interest in Egyptology.' She smiled up at him softly. 'For the first time in a very long time the choices are being taken away from you.'

He nodded. 'So many people are in a worse situation.' He laughed, but there was a touch of bitterness to it. 'Do you know when I heard Will had died I made a promise to him? I promised I would live enough for the both of us.'

'You're still living, Guy. Even if you're married, it isn't the end.'

'Why does it feel like it?'

Emma didn't have an answer. Instead she reached out and took his hand.

'This was my favourite place to come when I was a boy. I was always sneaking off here at night to look at the stars.' He pointed up at the clear sky. 'That's Ursa Major, can you see?' Carefully he traced the outline of the bear with his fingers over hers, pointing to each star in turn. They'd often gazed at the skies in Egypt, with Guy always pointing out a constellation or two.

'Who taught you about the stars?'

'My grandfather, the one who built this folly. He was old when I was a boy, but sprightly. He used to bring Will and me up here to look at the stars. It was a passion of his.'

Emma shivered and she saw Guy frown. 'We should get you back to the house. It's icy up here.'

'I can go alone if you need time to think.'

'Don't be silly. It was a self-indulgent moment anyway.' He stood and offered Emma a hand, pulling her to her feet. As she rose the momentum meant her body bumped into his, only softly, but the contact was enough to make them both pause.

For an instant the hundreds of reasons they couldn't be together rushed through her head, then were pushed out by the irresistible pulse of desire that swept her body.

'Guy,' she murmured, wanting to feel his lips on hers more than she had ever wanted anything before.

He looked pained, as if trying to do the right thing but unable to deny himself one last kiss. With a groan he relented and kissed her so tenderly Emma knew this would be a moment she remembered her whole life.

Even as he pulled away, brushing her cheeks with his fingertips, she knew she wanted more, needed more.

'One last time,' she murmured.

He looked powerless to refuse her and kissed her again, wrapping her in his warm embrace. Even through her thick cloak she could feel his hands roaming over her body, pulling her closer, making her feel as though she wanted him to slip his hands inside her cloak, inside her dress and touch her where no one else ever had.

When he finally pulled away Emma could see how hard he was finding it to restrain himself. Silently she took his hand and closed her eyes. In that moment she hated her naivety, her hesitation. If only she had seen what they could have had a few years ago, if only she had realised what she truly wanted from him then.

'Let's go back,' Guy said, his voice a little hoarse.

They descended the tower, Emma feeling as though they were leaving behind their last chance of being together, even in a very limited way. Once they returned to the house it would only be two days until Miss Frant arrived, only two days until Guy's future would be irreversibly set.

'Guy,' Emma said as they hurried back down the hill, the wind whipping at their faces. 'What if...?' She trailed off, knowing she had no right to ask him to choose her over his duty, his family.

'What if what?'

Emma shook her head, biting her lip to try to stop herself from saying something she shouldn't. They walked the rest of the way without uttering another word. As they reached the kitchen door Emma had the urge to flee, to run ahead up to the sanctuary of her room.

As they stepped inside Guy caught her hand and waited until she turned to face him.

'I wish I could, Em. If I had a choice, if there was a way, then I would make it happen, I would choose a future with you, but it is impossible. You must see that?'

She did. She didn't blame him for the choice he had to make—if she were in the same position she knew she would make the same decision—but it didn't mean it hurt any less.

It was the first time he had voiced that he wanted a future with her, however impossible the reality, but in a way that made things worse. This wasn't a passing desire, it was true and deep, and by not realising soon enough Emma had allowed the man she cared for more than any other to slip through her fingers.

'We will still have our friendship,' he said, giving her a sad smile. 'That's been enough for us until now.'

Emma nodded, not trusting herself to speak.

'Sleep well, Em. I'll see you tomorrow.'

'Goodnight, Guy.'

Emma could feel his eyes on her back as she hurried up the stairs, loosening her cloak but not ridding herself of any of her outer garments until she was in her bedroom with the door closed behind her.

Chapter Nineteen

Guy sat at the breakfast table with his head bowed, frowning into his cup of coffee. Luckily he was the only one up so far—he didn't think he was capable of polite conversation yet. Last night had been a disaster. He'd climbed up to the folly in the snow, hoping for some clarity, some peace of mind, and instead he'd done what he had promised himself he wouldn't ever again: he'd kissed Emma. Now all he could think about were her soft lips and inviting glances and he wondered what he had done to deserve such torture.

'Good morning,' Sophia said far too chirpily for Guy's gloomy mood as she slipped into her seat. 'Did you sleep well?' There was a glint in her eye that made Guy pause, his cup of coffee halfway to his lips.

'Fine, thank you.'

'I went out to look at the snow this morning,' Sophia said, oblivious to Guy's curt tone. 'Can you imagine my surprise to find someone, or rather two people, had already been out. There were footprints heading through the garden and up to the folly.'

'Oh?' Guy felt tension begin to rise inside him. It

was only his family here, along with Emma and Cecilia, and none of them would do anything to sow the seeds of scandal, but it only took one slip of the tongue, one word said at the wrong moment.

'It hasn't snowed since last night, so the footprints were still visible.'

Guy glanced out of the window, but they were on the wrong side of the house to see into the garden and up to the folly.

'Don't worry,' Sophia said, leaning in. 'I wandered all over the trail through the gardens. Most of it is obscured or looks as though it was just me this morning.'

'Thank you,' he said gruffly. He still wasn't sure how he felt about his sister having grown up into the intelligent young woman sitting across from him. Sometimes he still imagined her as an infant, or the child his mother had written to him about in the long letters he received from England, but here she was, happily helping him to cover the illicit midnight meeting with Emma.

'I'm thinking about running away,' Sophia said as she buttered a piece of toast, scraping it loudly with the knife.

'What?'

'I'm thinking about running away. It would solve your problems, wouldn't it? I wouldn't need a dowry and then you could marry Lady Emma.'

'Keep your voice down. And don't even joke about running away, Sophia. You would be eaten alive on day one.'

Sophia pouted. 'I'm not as naïve as everyone makes out.'

Guy didn't answer, instead taking a long, slow sip of

his coffee before setting the cup down. 'Do you know how to find a lodging house in the city? Or which areas are safe for a young woman walking alone? Or how to generate an income for yourself?' He shook his head. 'Anyway, it isn't all about you. Remember, if I don't marry Miss Frant we will have to sell the house and Father may not survive the disruption.'

Sophia crinkled up her nose, but was saved from answering by the arrival of Emma and Cecilia. He couldn't help but lock his gaze on to Emma, but she studiously avoided eye contact and he wondered if she had sought out Cecilia to save her from having to come down and face him alone.

'I didn't realise how much I had missed the snow,' Cecilia said as she walked over to the window and looked outside. 'I wasn't sure about coming back to England, but in some ways it does feel good to be home.'

Emma threw him a quick look and he knew exactly what she was thinking. To her, and to a lesser extent to him, Egypt was home. This was the foreign land that didn't feel quite right.

'I can remember snowball fights when I was a child with the other children in the village. We would line up girls on one side and boys on the other and pelt each other with snowballs as if it was a proper war.' Cecilia was smiling at the memory.

Guy could remember dozens of winters with his brother, both of them wrapped up in coats and scarves until they could hardly move, running out of the house and diving into the snow. They would launch snowballs at each other and sometimes their father would join them, with Guy and Will forming a team to beat the older man.

'Good times,' he murmured. He felt surprised—in the last few months he'd been bombarded with memories of Will as he visited their childhood haunts. At first it had been almost unbearably painful, but in the last few days he had actually enjoyed reminiscing.

'Have you ever had a snowball fight, Lady Emma?'

Emma shook her head, but Guy could see the excitement burning in her eyes. Already the awkwardness of a few minutes earlier was lifting and she glanced at him as if asking a question.

'I promise to be gentle with you,' Guy said, smiling.

'I don't promise to be gentle with you.' She turned to Sophia. 'I have excellent hand-eye co-ordination.'

'Please say we can form a team against my brother.'

'Of course.'

'Cecilia, can I tempt you into joining my team?' Guy asked, wondering what he had let himself in for.

'I think I will stay right here and watch the fight. I'm sure you can handle two young ladies.'

'Hmmm.' Already he had visions of being pelted with snowballs. At least it would distract him from the inappropriate thoughts he kept having about Emma.

Guy eyed Emma as she gathered the snow into a snowball. She and Sophia had spent the last two minutes whispering about their tactics and now he had the feeling he was going to get pummelled with snowballs from all directions. Emma had a gleam in her eye and he was glad they could move past the kiss of the night before and return to having fun together. Even if they both had to work hard at not looking as though they wanted to pounce on one another.

Emma grinned as she approached him, snowball held high, and he was so fixated on her that he nearly didn't see Sophia approaching his flank and flinging the huge snowball in his direction. He dodged, ducking his head at the last moment so the snowball went sailing over it, some of the loose flakes of snow flying off and dripping down the back of his neck. As he was straightening up Emma threw hers. He sidestepped, grinning at her. Already her cheeks were flushed from the cold and her eyes were sparkling.

Quickly he saw it was going to be almost impossible to gather his own snowballs while both his sister and Emma were pelting him, but he did his best, scooping up handfuls of snow and pressing them together. He aimed his first one at Emma, watching as she ducked, but a little too late, the snowball glancing off her shoulder and exploding into a shower of snow. Luckily her head and neck were protected from the worst by her cloak, but Guy saw the determined glint in her eye. He knew that expression and knew it meant she would not give up until she had scored a similar hit.

He'd turned, ready to throw his next snowball at his sister, when he felt the blow of one landing between his shoulders. From then on it was relentless, both young women laughing and crying out in victory as they landed snowball after snowball on him. A few minutes in Guy stopped trying to defend himself, he was so covered in snow, and focused on attacking, hitting both Emma and Sophia with a series of snowballs.

Emma was giggling too much for her snowballs to

have much power behind them now, although Sophia was continuing her bombardment.

'This is so much fun,' Emma called out, running towards him and using her momentum to throw one much harder in his direction. It hit perfectly on his collar, some of the snow slipping down his jacket and making him shiver.

'Shall we finish him, Lady Emma?' Sophia asked, her tone slightly menacing. Guy looked at his sister and saw she was enjoying this far too much. He supposed for a very long time she'd had only their mother for company and, as wonderful as Lady Templeton was, she wouldn't ever suggest a snowball fight, let alone throw a snowball herself.

He turned to see Emma racing towards him, snowball in hand, but instead of throwing the snowball she launched herself through the air, knocking him to the ground. Sophia came running and began pelting his supine form with snowballs, a few of them bouncing off Emma. Eventually Sophia ran out of snowballs and stood panting above them. Emma was still in his arms, sitting to the side of him, looking happier than he could have ever imagined her to be in the cold weather.

'I think I concede defeat.'

'You were well and truly beaten,' Sophia said with a grin.

Emma leaned back into him ever so slightly and Guy had to focus hard to be able to resist pulling her on to his lap right there in the snow in front of his sister.

'You both look happy,' Sophia said, shaking her head. 'So happy together.'

'Sophia…' Guy shot her a warning look.

Emma struggled to her feet, brushing the snow

from her dress and looking around her with a contented smile. 'I feel happy,' she announced. 'When I arrived in England and everything was so *different* I doubted whether I would ever feel happy here. There seemed to be so many rules and expectations and all I wanted to do was run straight back home, straight back to Egypt.' She shook her head, 'But here I do feel happy. There is something wonderful about your home, Guy, and being with people who love you.'

Guy nodded slowly, looking around him and trying to see Elmwood House through the eyes of Emma. She wasn't haunted by the history of it, haunted by the memory of his brother everywhere. She saw a charming estate in the most beautiful part of England, filled with people who loved him. Sometimes it was enlightening to see things through another's eyes.

'I am lucky,' he murmured. For a second an image of them happy together flashed through his mind. They were married, surrounded by a brood of children, strolling hand in hand through the formal gardens. Perhaps if he had Emma by his side he would be able to build some more happy moments at Elmwood House, not to replace the memories of his brother, but to dull the pain he felt whenever he was here.

'I wish…' Emma said slowly, pausing for a moment as if gathering her thoughts, 'I wish my father had kept our house in England, the one where I was born. I can see how important a family home is.'

'You're thinking of your mother?'

Emma nodded. 'I wish I knew more about her. Father told me stories, but he was always so sad when he spoke about her that I never pushed him, I never asked everything I wanted to. I have her diaries, of course, which are wonderful, but I wish there was somewhere here in England I could go to feel more connected to her.'

'Did she have any family?'

'No, not really. No one she was close to.'

'Did your father sell the house before you left England?'

'No, initially I think he thought it was the grief driving him away. He sold the house once we were settled in Egypt and it became clear we were never coming back. He used to say it wasn't fair on the tenants on the estate to have such an absent landlord, but I think in part he wanted to rid himself of the place where my mother had died.'

'I'm sorry, Em,' he said, laying a hand on her shoulder.

'Could you go and visit?' Sophia suggested, hopping from one foot to another in the snow.

'I don't know who my father sold it to. A second cousin inherited the main estate along with Father's title after he died, but that wasn't where we lived when my mother was alive. The house I grew up in he sold via a solicitor when we were settled in Egypt. I don't even have a name.'

'Perhaps you could write via the solicitor first.'

Emma tilted her head to one side and considered. 'I suppose it wouldn't do any harm to write to them. They may not mind me visiting for an hour or two and I would love to see the place my mother describes so vividly in her diaries.' She considered for a moment.

'Write to them,' Guy urged, knowing how much it would mean to Emma to feel this connection to her mother. 'The worst that can happen is they say no.'

'Sophia, darling, come inside. You look freezing,' Lady Templeton called from the glass doors, looking out at her daughter with concern.

Guy grinned as his sister rolled her eyes, but dutifully made her way back to the house. 'Do you want to go back inside?'

Emma shook her head. 'Do you know, I don't even feel that cold? It's lovely with the sun on your face, but with the crisp bite of the air.'

'Shall we go for a stroll?'

'Yes. I'd love to see some of the estate in the daylight.'

'Your wish is my command.'

Brushing off the last of the snow from his coat, Guy offered Emma his arm. They had just rounded the side of the building when the door from the drawing room opened and Guy's father stepped out.

'Lovely day,' Lord Templeton said, rocking backwards and forward on his heels, gazing up at the sky.

For a moment Guy could see his father as the man he had been twenty years earlier: sharp, witty and always quick to join a discussion and give his opinions.

'You'll get cold, Lord Templeton,' Daisy said as she hurried out after him.

'Nonsense. I've lived in England my whole life. A little snow isn't going to do me any harm.'

Chapter Twenty

Emma felt an irrational bubble of fear as she looked at the old man stepping out of the drawing room. She remembered the strength of his grip two nights earlier as he had caught her coming out of the library, but as she regarded him she felt the fear slip away.

He was smiling warmly at Guy, brushing off the maid's attempts to get him to come back inside.

'Your mother told me we had guests,' Lord Templeton said, turning his attention to Emma. 'Don't think she mentioned your name, though. Introduce me, Guy.'

'Father, this is Lady Emma Westcombe, a dear friend of mine from Egypt. She has recently come to live in England after her father died. Lady Emma, this is my father, Lord Templeton.'

'A pleasure to meet you,' Emma said, noting how the old man's eyes flitted over her, assessing her.

'My sympathies for the loss of your father, Lady Emma. I knew Lord Westcombe in my youth. Fascinating chap. Always had something to say on any subject.'

Emma paused, surprised at how lucid Lord Templeton seemed this morning.

'You'll catch your death, my lord,' Daisy said, wringing her hands. 'At least let me get you a coat and some proper shoes.'

'What if we come inside, Father? It is time we warm up after being out in the snow.'

'Everyone fusses too much,' Lord Templeton grumbled, but allowed himself to be guided inside. 'Don't just stand there, Daisy, get one of the kitchen maids to make hot chocolate for my son. Both my boys love their hot chocolate.'

Daisy looked nervously at Guy, but he nodded quickly and the maid hurried off downstairs.

'Why don't we sit by the fire, Father?' Guy stepped forward and guided the older man to his seat, plumping the cushions and making sure he was comfortable before he sat down. Emma hovered, not wanting to intrude on a family moment, but Guy motioned for her to join them and soon she was warming her toes in front of the roaring fire.

'Where's Will? Did he come home for Christmas with you? I sent the carriage to school to pick you both up.'

Emma watched as Guy swallowed and a momentary expression of sadness passed over his face before he composed himself.

'You were going to tell Lady Emma about her father, how you knew him when you were younger.'

'Ah, yes. Fascinating chap. Two years below me at Oxford, but I can remember drinking together at the end of term. He was one of those men who had an interesting story about everything, whether you were talking about smugglers or the latest law passed by Parliament.'

'I used to love listening to him talk,' Emma said quietly, a lump forming in her throat.

'He was witty, too, had us all rolling about with laughter with his observations of our tutors.' Lord Templeton smiled as if remembering happy times. 'How is the old chap?'

'He died last year,' Emma said quietly.

Lord Templeton's face fell and he turned towards Emma. 'I am sorry for your loss, my dear.' He reached out and patted her on the hand and Emma could see there were tears in his eyes. 'Of course it is the natural order of things for a child to outlive his or her parents...' He trailed off, a tear slipping from his eye and on to his cheek. He stood abruptly and wobbled. Guy was by his side in an instant, a guiding hand under his elbow.

'Would you like to go back upstairs, Father?'

Lord Templeton didn't answer, so after a few seconds Guy led him gently away, leaving Emma staring after them.

The maid appeared with steaming cups of hot chocolate just after Guy had left with his father and Emma reached for one, wrapping her fingers around the warm cup and trying not to think of the look of desolation on the old man's face when he had remembered he had outlived one of his sons.

'Sorry,' Guy said as he returned to the drawing room a few minutes later. 'He's settled back in his bedroom.'

Guy picked up his cup of hot chocolate and sat down into the seat next to hers. For a long while they sat in silence, both lost in their own thoughts.

'I was surprised he remembered my father.'

'Me, too. Although the events from forty years ago seem to be much clearer in his mind than last week.'

'He remembered, didn't he? When we were talking, he remembered your brother had died?'

Guy nodded. 'Sometimes he gets lost in certain time periods. A lot of the time he seems to think Will and I are still young lads, fifteen or sixteen perhaps. Still at school. Still both alive. Then when he does remember, when he does realise Will isn't here any more, it is like losing him all over again.' Guy paused, staring into the fire. 'These moments of lucidity are getting fewer, though. When I first arrived home he would have as many good days as bad. Now...' He shrugged, toying with his cup. 'Now I find myself worrying one day soon he will be permanently confused, permanently bewildered and scared.'

'You have everything set up so well for him here, though. If that does happen, he will be safe and cared for and loved.'

Guy nodded grimly.

They drank in silence for a little longer, Emma feeling the warmth from the fire suffuse through her body. She could feel Guy's sadness, see how hard it was for him to lose his father in such a slow and cruel way. She wished there was something she could do, some way to show him she would be there for him no matter what, but it wasn't quite true. Soon he would have Miss Frant to comfort him, to take some of this burden, and Emma would have no place trying to be the one to buoy him up.

Guy sat back, looking into the fire, lost in his thoughts. One of the things he loved about his relationship with Emma was their ability to be together without feeling the need to fill the silence. It was comforting to have her there with him as thoughts of the past and the future collided and he tried to make sense of them, but she wouldn't push him to tell her about them until he was ready.

Over the years Will had always been at the forefront of his thoughts. Every time he made a decision there would be the little voice asking what Will would do, what Will would think. For a long time he had tried to suppress it, to forge his own path, but that had taken its toll. Now he was back home the reminders of Will were more frequent, more poignant.

He felt Emma's eyes on him, a look of concern in them, but she remained silent, waiting for him to be ready to talk.

'Have you ever felt torn in half, Em?'

She shook her head, letting him continue.

'I feel torn between the man I want to be and the man I am.'

'What do you want to be?'

'Better. More worthy, more considerate of the others around me.'

'Guy, you couldn't be more considerate. Look at what you've already given up for your family and what else you are prepared to sacrifice.'

'I wish I wasn't so reluctant to do it.'

'You can't berate yourself for having feelings.'

'Will would have been better at this.'

'That is something you can never know. You were boys when you were last together. He would have been moulded and shaped by his life experiences as you have been. You can see what sort of man you have become, but I don't think you could ever know exactly how your brother would have been after half a lifetime.'

Guy stood, pacing towards the fire and leaning on the mantelpiece. He would give anything to have his brother standing there with him.

He felt Emma approach behind him and felt her hand on his back, a soft touch between his shoulder blades. Slowly he spun until they were face to face. His eyes flickered to her lips, remembering the kiss of the night before. It was an intoxicating memory, one he wanted to repeat so badly.

'Em,' he said, lifting a hand from the mantelpiece and running his fingers down her cheek. He didn't know what else he wanted to say and for a long moment they just stood looking at one another. Then she raised herself up on tiptoes and brushed a kiss against his lips.

Guy was lost. If she hadn't kissed him he could have kept his distance, could have ignored the deep pull he felt whenever she was close, but as her lips met his he felt something primal swell and roar inside him, washing away all conscious thought, all sense of reason.

The first kiss was gentle, hesitant, but as she began to pull away Guy caught her by the arms and stopped her retreat. He kissed her deeply, as if she was his only lifeline to the world, his arms wrapping around her back and pulling her to him.

He heard her moan as she surrendered, her body melting into his, her hands coming up and tangling in his hair. In that moment Guy didn't care that they were in the drawing room where anyone could walk in, the door ajar. All he cared about was kissing the woman in his arms. He wanted to make her his, to lay her down in front of the fire and make love to her until they both collapsed in exhaustion.

His fingers trailed up her back, caressing her neck and then down over her shoulder to the velvety soft skin of her chest. He felt her gasp against him as he dipped a finger below the neckline of her dress and loved how she pressed herself against him in encouragement.

'Guy,' she murmured in his ear, her voice husky and filled with desire. He kissed her again, wishing this could be their reality, their future.

With that thought the present came crashing back and Guy stiffened. As much as he wanted it, as much as Emma wanted it, this could not be. He wouldn't compromise her, not when he couldn't marry her. Slowly, knowing this would be the last time he kissed the woman he loved, he pulled away.

Emma looked flushed and beautiful and it was almost impossible to resist the urge to kiss her again. He took a step back and then another, only trusting physical distance to stop him from acting on his desires.

She was looking at him wide-eyed, as if the kiss had surprised her as much as him, even though she had initiated it.

'I'm sorry,' she whispered, biting her lip.

'Don't apologise, Em.'

'I shouldn't have done that. You were feeling bad enough as it was about the future.'

'Don't apologise,' he repeated. 'Whatever happens, I will always have the memory of our kiss.'

Emma nodded, looking as though she wanted to say

more, but was trying her hardest to bite her tongue. She shuffled from foot to foot and then gave him a nervous smile before quickly hurrying from the room.

Chapter Twenty-One

Guy couldn't help but smile as Emma entered his study after dinner. He'd needed to sit down with some estate papers the solicitor had left behind, documents that had been long neglected by his father as he'd slipped into his confused state. Her cheeks were rosy from spending most of the day in the cold winter's air, but she looked healthy and happy despite all the turmoil she must be feeling from everything that was soon to change.

'Am I disturbing you?'

'You know I would never say no to you disturbing me. Sit. Do you want a drink?' He gestured at the bottle of brandy sitting on one of the bookshelves.

'Yes, please.'

Emma was silent while he poured the two glasses, handing one to her before taking his seat behind his desk again.

'Your mother and sister have gone to bed and Cecilia retired an hour ago.'

'You didn't feel tired?'

'I feel restless.' She bit her lip and then looked up at him. 'I have this ache in my heart, Guy.'

'A physical ache?'

Emma shook her head, but remained silent. He knew there would be consequences of them kissing both the night before and earlier today, but the last thing he wanted was to make Emma hurt.

Guy sat without saying anything for half a minute, then rose and moved to take the chair next to hers. The house around them was quiet, but even so he lowered his voice when he next spoke.

'I think I know what you mean, Em.'

'I need to say it out loud, to tell you how I feel, even though I think you know.' She looked down at her hands resting in her lap and began twisting at the material of her dress. 'I feel as though the clock is ticking down. There is only one more day until Miss Frant arrives and I feel as though then I lose you for good.'

'You'll never lose me.'

She gave a sad smile. 'We keep telling each other that, don't we, but it won't be the same. You will be married to Miss Frant and we won't ever be able to do *this* again.'

Guy fell silent. He knew exactly what Emma meant—he felt as though the minutes were racing by and at the end of it he would lose her and gain a wife he didn't want.

Emma took a deep breath. 'You are the most important person in my life, Guy. You make me smile when no one else can, you make me feel as though I'm the only one in a room. I feel…' She trailed off and then seemed to steel herself. 'I feel as though there is an invisible force pulling me towards you. I want to touch you, to kiss you, even though I know it is impossible, that we cannot be together.'

This was what Guy had once hoped for, that Emma would feel the same about him as he did about her.

'Do you…?' She let the question hang in the air, her eyes filled with nervousness and a sliver of hope.

'Do I feel the same?'

She nodded.

Guy took a breath, wondering if he would be a fool to reveal how long he'd loved her for.

'Do you remember that day four years ago? We were walking along the banks of the Nile and we saw that family of turtles dropping off the river bank into the river and swimming back and forth. We watched them for ages.' He smiled at the memory. 'That was the day I realised I loved you, Em.'

She frowned, looking up in surprise. 'But that was four years ago.'

'It was. And I've loved you every day since.'

'You never said anything.' She was shaking her head as if she didn't quite believe him.

He blinked and shook his head.

'I did. Just before I left Luxor. I asked you to marry me.'

It was Emma's turn to look confused and she frowned, crinkling up her nose.

'I would remember that, Guy.'

'Not in so many words, I admit, but I asked you if you wanted to be with me.'

'No,' she said after a moment. 'I remember, but you weren't asking me to marry you.'

Guy could remember the day clearly, the day he'd had his heart broken.

'We were sitting together, watching the sun set, and I asked if you wanted to be with me.'

'I thought...' She trailed off, shaking her head again. 'I thought you were just asking me if I would miss you.'

He thought back to his words, trying to remember exactly what he had said. In his mind it had been clear, his purpose obvious, but had that been because he knew he was in love with Emma? Perhaps to her his words had been more ambiguous.

'You never asked me directly to come with you, to marry you.' She sounded distressed, as if only just realising the consequences of the misunderstanding.

'What else could I mean?'

'I just thought you were saying you wished I could come with you, or you could stay. I never imagined you were actually asking me.'

Guy closed his eyes, cursing his assumption and wondering what her answer might have been if he had been clearer. He decided he didn't want to torture himself with the answer.

'You wanted me to come with you?'

He nodded. 'I loved you, Em, and I wanted you to be my wife.'

Emma's hand flew to her mouth as if she couldn't quite believe what he was saying.

'You love me?'

'I do.'

'And it's my fault we can't be together.'

'No, don't think that. It wasn't to be. The timing wasn't right. Perhaps if my father hadn't become ill, if I had stayed in Egypt, if I had been clearer when I asked you to come with me...' He knew he shouldn't obsess over the what ifs.

Emma tore her eyes away from him and looked down, as if trying to work through everything he'd told her. Her eyes were flicking from side to side, her whole body tense.

She let out a cry of distress, trying to smother it with her hand, and Guy felt like a cad. He shouldn't have told her. This was his burden to bear. She didn't need to know that he had loved her for a long time and that, if she had realised her feelings sooner, the issue of his marriage to Miss Frant wouldn't be a problem.

Reaching out a hand, he gripped hold of her fingers, gently uncurling them until her hand rested in his. Emma looked up at him and then shook her head.

'I need to think, Guy, I need some time.' Slowly, as if in a daze, she walked from the room and a few seconds later he heard her footsteps on the stairs.

Guy sat where he was for a long time, wishing he could go after her, but knowing that even in his own house he couldn't stand outside her door in the middle of the night knocking and knocking.

He gulped down the rest of his brandy, closing his eyes and slumping back in his chair.

Lying on her bed, Emma buried her face in the pillows, wanting to hide away from the world. She was reeling from Guy's admission that he had been in love with her for a long time. Surely she should have known, should have seen that he saw her as more than his friend? Surely she should have realised sooner?

It was so cruel and it was all her fault. She thought of the hundreds of times he'd taken her hand, all the times he'd put her comfort above his own. Now that she looked back it seemed obvious and she felt ridiculous that she hadn't realised before. If she had… Shaking her head, she tried not to think about it. It would involve a very different future from the one facing her now. A future of happiness and love and family.

'I wish…' she murmured, finishing the wish silently in her head. She wished to turn back time, to make different decisions, anything that would mean she and Guy could have a life together. He would make the perfect husband.

Emma sat up, knowing there was nothing to be done now. One of the qualities she loved most about Guy was his sense of right and wrong, his moral compass, and the part of him that put others before himself. She couldn't ask him to choose her above his family, above his sister. It would destroy him.

Without really thinking, Emma stood and started to get undressed. She wanted to curl up beneath the covers and lose herself in the oblivion of sleep. All the time she was awake she would not be able to stop thinking of all that could have been and the future that now faced her, without Guy.

She struggled off with her dress, not wanting to call a maid, not wanting to see anyone, and quickly slipped on her nightdress, blowing out the candle before she wriggled under the bedcovers.

For a few minutes she squeezed her eyes tight and tried to think of anything but the pain in her heart. It was impossible. Even when she instructed her mind firmly to think of something else, soon images of Guy crept back in, taking over everything else.

* * *

After half an hour she sat, knowing sleep would not come any time soon. She thought about lighting the candle and trying one of the books she had brought up from the library a few nights earlier, but immediately knew she wouldn't be able to concentrate on the words.

You need to see him.

The little voice in her head was getting louder and more insistent. Emma lay down again, refusing to listen, but as she lay looking at the ceiling she knew she wouldn't be able to sleep without talking to Guy. She'd left so abruptly, just after he had told her he loved her. Suddenly she wondered what he was feeling... whether he was hurt by her sudden departure after his confession.

Throwing the covers back, she made the decision to go to him, even though it must be past midnight. They could talk, clear the air between them, then perhaps she might sleep.

She listened carefully at her door, wondering if Guy was still down in his study or if he had gone to his bedroom. The house was silent and dark, with only the odd creak of the old beams in the wind.

Quietly she crept along the corridor, her heart pounding in her chest, half expecting Lord Templeton to jump out at her from the shadows as he had a few nights earlier.

Pausing outside Guy's door, Emma hesitated. This was foolish, beyond foolish. Guy was probably in bed, trying to sleep, and here she was disturbing him. She almost turned back, but something rooted her to the spot and before she had made the conscious decision to knock on the door her knuckles were rapping gently on the wood.

The door opened almost immediately, as if he'd been expecting her, and for a long moment Guy stood there in the shadows. He looked as though he were debating whether to invite her in.

'You can't be here, Em,' he said finally, but stepped aside at the same time.

Emma slipped into the room and closed the door firmly behind her. The rest of the household were asleep, there was no one to catch them. She would be a couple of minutes, nothing more.

Guy had a candle burning on his bedside table. It looked as though he had been sitting in bed, reading. The flickering light cast shadows around the room, but it meant Emma was able to see at least a little of Guy's expression.

'I needed to see you.' Now she was here she didn't know what to say, but something was compelling her to stay. Nervously she crossed the room and perched on the edge of the bed. Guy didn't move. He stood completely still, watching her. 'I'm sorry I ran off earlier.'

'I understand. You can't be here, Em,' he repeated.

'Come and sit with me.'

For another few seconds he didn't move and then finally he relented, coming to sit on the end of the bed at least a foot away from her.

Emma waited for a second, then shuffled round so she was next to him. She reached out and touched him on the hand and as their fingers met Emma knew the real reason she had come to his room tonight. It shocked her, both the act and that she could have been so in denial of her own thoughts that she would only realise it now.

'Kiss me,' she said softly.

'No.'

'I want you to, Guy.'

'We can't do this, Em. If we start…'

'We won't stop. I know. What if I don't want to stop?'

'You don't mean that. If anyone found out, you'd be ruined.'

'No one is going to find out. I want this, Guy. I want you. Just one night.'

'And then what?' he asked, a hint of bitterness in his voice. 'I go and marry Miss Frant and we forget this ever happened?'

'Then we will always have tonight.'

For the first time since he'd sat down he turned and looked at her properly, studying her face, staring into her eyes, and Emma knew it was only a matter of time before he agreed. He wanted this as much as she did. She knew it wouldn't be easy after, stepping away and waving him off to his new life, but she meant what she had said to Guy: at least they would always have the memory of tonight.

He groaned and pulled her to him, kissing her deeply, and Emma felt as if she were floating off the bed. His lips were soft but insistent, making her want more and more as he tangled his hands in her hair and pressed his body to hers. Tentatively Emma reached out and ran her fingers over Guy's back, feeling the warmth of the skin through his shirt, and then, before she could think too much about what she was doing, she tucked her hands inside his shirt so they were directly on his skin. For a moment Guy stopped kissing her and then began again in earnest.

She was wearing a cotton nightdress and a robe over the top, more practical than attractive, and Guy expertly rid her of the robe as he kissed her. His lips were moving from her lips over her cheeks to the sensitive patch on her neck, a spot an inch below her earlobe, making her shiver and dig her fingertips into his back.

'Somehow I knew you'd like being kissed there,' Guy murmured in her ear, then returned to kissing her. All the time Emma felt the desire building inside her, making her want more and more. She inhaled sharply as Guy lifted the hem of her nightdress, pulling it up her body and lifting it over her head, exposing her skin to the cooler temperature of the room. Before she could even think about feeling self-conscious Guy pressed her back into the bed and covered her body with his own. Quickly he pulled off his shirt and their bodies were skin to skin, feeling as if they were made for one another.

Emma trailed her fingers over his back, his neck, tangling them in his hair and then starting the descent down. All the time she was having to bite her lip to stop herself from crying out as Guy began to kiss her body, starting at the very base of her neck and working his way down, teasing her as he kissed her breasts, but circled around her nipples and then moved on.

It felt as though her body was on fire. Her hips kept pushing up involuntarily, begging for his touch, but Guy continued the exquisite torture, kissing and stroking her until Emma wasn't sure she could recall her own name.

'You don't know how many times I've had to stop

myself from imagining this,' Guy said as he dipped a
finger into her most private place, making Emma gasp
and writhe under his touch. 'You're even more perfect
than in my dreams.'

'What are you doing to me, Guy?'

'Do you want me to stop?'

The idea was painful. 'No. Never. Don't stop.'

He smiled at her and then slid away, down her body.
For a moment Emma was about to protest and then she
lost her ability to string two words together as Guy put
his lips over her. She let out a low moan, pressing her
hips up. It felt exquisite, as if a jolt of pleasure were
being sent through her body. As he teased her she felt
a tension begin to build deep inside her and she knew
if Guy stopped she would cry out in disappointment.

He didn't stop, kissing and stroking, making Emma
writhe on the bed, until she cried out and tensed, waves
of pleasures rippling through her body. For a long moment Emma felt as though her heart was going to burst
through her chest it was thumping so hard. Slowly she
began to recover, finally able to prop herself up on her
elbows to look at Guy.

'I can stop,' he said, looking as though he really
didn't want to stop. 'If you want me to, I can stop.'

Emma knew he was offering to step away, to let
her keep some of her virtue, even though he looked as
though it might half kill him if she said yes.

'Don't stop,' she whispered. 'I want this, Guy.'

He didn't need telling twice, lowering himself over
her and catching her lips with his own. Emma sank
back on to the bed, already lost in the wonderful sen-
sations shooting through her body as Guy started trailing his hands over her skin.

Tentatively Emma gripped the waistband of Guy's trousers, running her finger along the edge. He let out a low moan and encouraged Emma as she dipped her hand lower. Guy quickly unfastened the waistband and pushed his trousers down, moving out of them while still managing to keep kissing her. Now there was nothing between their bodies and it felt wonderful. With his hand guiding her Emma reached down and gripped his manhood, making Guy shudder in pleasure. She liked the way he writhed on top of her as she moved her hand backwards and forward, feeling as though she had the power after being rendered senseless by his touch minutes earlier. Her movements were tentative at first, but as she saw how Guy reacted to her she grew in confidence, making her strokes bigger and bolder.

After a minute Guy moved her hand away and pressed himself into her. Emma gasped and Guy started to pull back, but she gripped hold of him.

'Don't go.'

Slowly he pressed again and Emma felt a sting of pain and then the first jolt of pleasure as Guy began to move. Emma looked up into his eyes and saw the love there and felt a momentary sadness that this was not going to be her life. This was going to happen once and once only, no matter how much she wanted more. Refusing to let the idea take hold, Emma allowed all thoughts of the future to float away and be replaced by the pleasure of the moment.

Emma's hips were responding instinctively, meeting his thrusts as he bent down and kissed her hard on the lips. She could feel the wonderful build-up of tension again, mounting with every second until it felt as though she were going to explode. Her whole body tensed and then she was engulfed in wave after wave of pleasure. Vaguely she was aware of Guy tensing above her as they climaxed together and then Emma allowed herself to float on the happy sensation, closing her eyes to try to prolong it even longer.

Guy pushed himself off her and for a moment she was worried he would walk away, but then he manoeuvred in beside her, pulling her gently on to his chest.

For a long time neither of them spoke, not wanting to bring the dream crashing back to reality.

Emma squeezed her eyes tight shut, enjoying the heaviness of Guy's arm slung across her waist and the firmness of his body against hers. If she shut out all thoughts about the future, all worries about being alone, in this moment she was happy.

'Em,' Guy said eventually.

'Don't apologise.' She said it sharper than she had meant, but she couldn't bear the thought of him apologising for something that meant so much to her.

'I wasn't going to. I was going to ask you to stay for a while.'

She wriggled and turned over so she was facing him in the darkness. The gleam of his eyes was visible and she thought she could make out the curve of a smile on his lips.

'I shouldn't...' She shouldn't, but she wanted to. Emma was aware this was the only time she would get to lie in Guy's arms, the only time it would be acceptable for her to move forward and brush her lips against his. It was illicit, but *they* were allowing it for tonight.

'Why did you come to me?' he asked the question

gently, running a hand down her back and cupping a buttock as he did so.

'I was in my room and I knew I had to see you. I couldn't admit to myself what I wanted, not until I actually saw you.'

'Some part of you knew you wanted this?'

She nodded, knowing he would sense the movement in the dark even if he didn't see it.

Emma didn't want to talk, didn't want to tell him how much she regretted not realising earlier what they could have together. All she wanted was a couple of hours of happiness, lost in Guy's arms, making memories that would have to last her a lifetime.

Chapter Twenty-Two

It was before dawn when Guy woke, his body stiff from lying in one position for most of the night, his arm still wrapped around Emma's body. For a long time he didn't move, even though he knew they needed to discuss a lot before the rest of the household awoke. Emma looked peaceful, her dark hair spread out on the pillow, her eyelashes resting on her cheeks. He wanted to enjoy one more minute of this bliss, pretending this was his reality, before he had to face the consequences of what they had done.

Emma stirred and nuzzled into him, her eyes flickering open and a soft smile on her lips. He saw she was truly happy for that one instant before she was fully awake.

'Good morning.' He couldn't help but lean over and kiss her. She tasted sweet and Guy felt desire swell within him.

'Good morning.' She pushed herself up on her elbows, a faint look of panic dawning in her eyes as she realised where she had spent her night. 'How late is it? Are people up?'

'No, not even the servants yet. We're fine, we have time.'

'I should get back. I need to get back. What if one of the maids comes in to light my fire and I'm not in bed?'

'I doubt her first thought would be you're here in bed with me.'

'It might be.'

'We'll get you back in a minute, Em, but I think we need to talk first.'

She sank back down into bed, but still looked a little agitated.

'I think I should perhaps get dressed first.'

He followed her line of sight across the room to where he had flung her nightdress. As much as he would like to watch her get out of bed and walk over to fetch it, he could see she felt uncomfortable to be naked around him in the light of day.

Without another word he got out of bed and walked over to the nightdress, picking it up and returning to slip between the sheets. Emma's eyes had followed him the whole way and now her cheeks were turning a beautiful pink.

Quickly she slipped the nightdress on, wriggling so she could tuck it beneath her bottom.

'Perhaps you should put something on,' she suggested.

'I'm not cold.'

'I was thinking so we could concentrate.'

Guy raised an eyebrow, but then obliged, reaching for his shirt and pulling it on.

'Thank you.' Emma took a deep breath. 'Perhaps it

is best if I make an excuse to leave before Miss Frant gets here.'

Guy blinked, surprised at the direction of the conversation.

'I don't think I can be here when you propose to Miss Frant.'

'Em,' Guy said slowly. 'I can't propose to Miss Frant. Not now.'

There was a flicker of hope in her eyes, but he couldn't begin to feel excited about the future. Last night he had been overcome by passion, overcome by desire, and he'd given in. A stronger man, a better man, would have turned Emma away, sent her back to her bedroom. He had invited her in.

Guy closed his eyes for a moment. *This* was what he'd always wished for, but not like this. It felt bitter, wrong and he knew he would regret this night even though it was what he'd always wanted.

'We will have to marry.'

'What do you mean?'

'Em, we've spent the night together. You might be pregnant. If anyone finds out, you will be completely ruined. We have to marry.'

'You don't want to marry me?'

Running a hand through his hair, Guy knew he was going about this wrong, but his own emotions were overwhelming him. He didn't seem to have the capacity to put this in a better way to Emma.

'Of course I do, Em. I've loved you for years, but...'

'But?'

'But I've failed my family again. I've put my needs first *again*.'

'Guy—'

He shook his head, cutting her off. 'I will arrange the details.' He started to stand up.

'No.'

'What do you mean *no*?'

'I won't marry you.'

Guy sank back down on to the bed, unable to take in what Emma was saying.

'That wasn't why I came here last night. I know we can't be together. I know you have to marry Miss Frant.'

'I have to marry you after last night.'

'You're a gentleman, Guy, I understand that, but you have an impossible choice. The right thing to do here is to marry me because of what happened between us last night, but also to marry Miss Frant because of your duty to your family. That is obviously impossible so I will make this easy for you. I will not marry you.'

'Don't be ridiculous, Em.'

'I'm not. No one knows what we did. I can be back in my bed before the household wakes up and if we are careful no one will notice a change in us today.'

'What if you're pregnant?'

Emma scoffed. 'After one night? I hardly think it is likely.'

'It may be unlikely, but it is possible.'

'I doubt it. And if it is, then I will flee in disgrace to Egypt.'

'With my child.'

'I'm not going to be pregnant, Guy.'

'I will do the right thing by you, Emma.'

'What about me doing the right thing by you?' she said quietly. 'You already feel the strain of responsibility for your family, for your father, for your sister.

I do not want to marry you if it means making you feel guilty, unhappy. I will not be responsible for that.'

Guy felt a pain deep inside his chest. In the woman sitting across from him he had everything he'd ever wanted. If his family didn't need him in the way they did and he was free to marry Emma, he knew they would have the happiest of lives together. Emma was right, though, it wasn't those circumstances and marrying her would make him feel as though he had abandoned his family again, put his own needs above theirs again.

'I love you,' he said quietly.

Emma looked devastated and he reached out, squeezing her hand.

'We had last night,' she said, her voice catching in her throat.

'We had last night.'

They fell silent and Guy wondered if he was making the biggest mistake of his life. In a year's time would he regret this? Would this be the mistake he lamented about on his deathbed forty years from now? He could see now Emma was already pulling away from him—it was impossible for her not to. They wouldn't be able to be normal together any more and the thought of losing her in more than one way was like a knife to the heart.

'I need to go, Guy.'

'I know.' He still couldn't let go of her hand. Surely there was some way, something he could do to make this work.

His mind was blank. There was no way. If they sold everything including the house, then he would have enough to pay the debt to Mr Frant, but his father would lose the only place he felt safe, the only sanctuary he had as his mind failed him, and Sophia would be left with no dowry.

He shook his head. He couldn't ask his parents to sell the house. His father was disorientated enough in a place he had spent his whole life—moving him would be devastating.

There was no other option. He *had* to marry Miss Frant.

Emma pulled her hand from his and he knew he had to let her go. She stood, hurrying to the door, but pausing before she opened it, hand on the handle.

Slowly she turned, looking back over her shoulder at him, and then seemed to make up her mind, running back to the bed and kissing him as if she were dying and it was her last act on earth.

Guy felt her take a few deep shuddering breaths and held her tight and close, as if he were trying to tie her to him, but eventually Emma pulled away and this time when she reached the door she didn't look back, slipping out into the hallway and disappearing into the darkness.

He sank down, his head in his hands, feeling as though he had made the wrong decision, even though it hadn't really been his to make.

Emma ran down the corridor, aware if anyone saw her they would know exactly where she had come from, but unable to walk calmly with all the emotions roiling inside her.

Thankfully Guy had been right and the servants weren't even stirring yet. She was able to slip back into her bedroom unobserved, locking the door behind her. She didn't want anyone coming in and seeing her distraught on the bed.

Last night had been wonderful and she didn't regret it. She had decided to give every bit of herself to Guy and he had responded. For a few hours at least they'd been blissfully happy in one another's arms.

She'd always known this morning would be difficult, but she hadn't expected Guy to propose. It was the first time ever Guy had treated her as though she were a duty, something to be taken care of, and she didn't like it. A small part of her had wanted to accept. Spending a lifetime with Guy would be amazing, but not with him resenting her. However much he would tell her he didn't feel bitter about how things had come about it would be unescapable that she was the reason he'd had to disappoint his family.

'This is your doing,' she muttered into her pillow. She had known leaving would be painful when she'd gone to Guy's room the night before.

For a long time she lay on her bed, first with her face buried in the pillow to stifle her sobs. Then, as she calmed, she turned over and stared at the ceiling. She knew she couldn't stay, not to watch Guy propose to Miss Frant. She would not be able to congratulate them, her face would betray her. Everyone would know she wanted Guy for herself.

She would ask Cecilia to help her to come up with an excuse and hopefully they could be away from Kent before the Frants arrived. Perhaps she would forget about the Season in London this year, persuade Cecilia to travel around the country with her instead. What she really wanted was to go back to Egypt, go back to her home, but she knew that wasn't possible.

She wished she could creep into her father's study, find him sitting in his favourite chair. He would always be up early, never needing much sleep. He would gather her in his arms and tell her some story from classical history that would be only vaguely related to her predicament, but still manage to make her feel better.

It had been light for about an hour when Emma slipped into Cecilia's room, finding her sitting up in bed reading a book. Cecilia looked relaxed—this spell in the countryside seemed to suit her—and she smiled when Emma climbed into bed beside her.

'Can I ask you a favour?'

'Of course, my darling. What is it?'

'Can we make up an excuse to leave?'

Cecilia immediately looked concerned, setting down her book and turning to face Emma fully.

'What has happened?'

'Nothing. I think we should leave.'

Cecilia nodded, her eyes flicking from side to side as they did when she was thinking.

'You want to leave before Miss Frant arrives.'

Emma nodded. Cecilia knew her too well. She was attuned to every one of her moods. It was impossible to hide anything from her.

'Has something happened between you and Guy?'

Emma didn't say anything.

'Oh, Emma.'

'It doesn't matter, Cece.'

'Of course it matters. Guy is a gentleman, Emma, and the best man I know. He will do what is right.'

'That isn't the issue.'

Cecilia remained quiet for a minute and then nodded. 'I see.' She left a long pause and Emma could see she was struggling to find the right words to express what she wanted to say without causing too much upset. 'Sometimes, Emma, things happen for a reason. Take my story as an example. I told you of my second husband, the terrible time I had with him, but it all worked out for the best. If I hadn't needed to flee the country I wouldn't have met your father. I wouldn't have had those most wonderful years with him and you.'

'You're saying leaving here might lead to something good.'

'No. No. That's not what I'm saying. I'm saying that even if it isn't how you hoped, how you planned, something good might still come out of what has happened. It might not have been the proposal you wanted, but do you really want to turn it down? You and Guy, you're made for each other.'

Emma shook her head. 'He needs to marry Miss Frant, Cece. It will break him if he doesn't, if he puts himself above his family.'

'There must be a way.'

'There isn't.' Emma forced a smile. 'It hurts and it will hurt for a while, but I will survive.' They were brave words but right now Emma wasn't sure she believed them herself. 'I need you to help me get away from here before...' She trailed off. She couldn't bring herself to say *before the proposal.*

'Of course. I will think of an excuse and perhaps we can leave early tomorrow before the Frants arrive.'

'Thank you.'

Cecilia wrapped her arms around Emma and Emma sank into her, glad of the comfort.

Chapter Twenty-Three

Emma took breakfast in her room, eating little, and afterwards went back to pacing backwards and forward in front of the window. She needed to be away from here, away from Guy. Every inch of her body was on edge and she wanted to be somewhere she could collapse in bed for a few days and hide until everything stopped feeling so raw.

A little after ten there was a soft knock on her door. She expected it to be Cecilia, so called out for her to come in. Instead it was Lady Templeton, looking tired but elegant.

'Mrs Willow said you were feeling out of sorts today. I thought it would check on you.'

'Thank you.' Emma summoned a smile. 'I'm fine. Just a little wearied, I think. The travelling is catching up with me.'

'I'm glad to hear you are not unwell.' Lady Templeton paused and then sat down on the chair in the corner of the room. She waited patiently for a minute until Emma perched on the edge of the wide windowsill.

'It has been so lovely having you here, Lady Emma.

You cannot imagine the worry I have felt over the years. Worry about Guy.'

Emma nodded. It must have been awful for Lady Templeton to have one of her sons killed in battle and her other still serving in the army.

'He seemed unhappy when he returned...' Lady Templeton paused as if trying to choose her words carefully. 'Not exactly unhappy to be home, but as if he blamed himself for the mess we find ourselves in.'

'Do you blame him?'

'Good Lord, no. All young men need to go off and live their own lives. Guy even more so after he lost his brother. He and Will were so close. No, the blame lies squarely with my husband and myself.'

Emma waited for Lady Templeton to continue, sensing there was more she wished to say.

'Lord Templeton knew he was making bad decisions at the beginning, but, proud fool that he was, he kept thinking that the next *big thing* would be the one to save us. Of course I should have seen earlier what was happening, but I was so preoccupied with Sophia I didn't realise until it was too late.' She shook her head. 'Whoever is to blame, it certainly isn't Guy.'

'It won't be easy to persuade him of that.'

'My son is very stubborn, I'm sure you've seen that, Lady Emma.'

Emma smiled at some of her memories.

'Guy has been distant since he's been home. I know he wishes he was still in Egypt, however much he tries to hide it—' Lady Templeton smiled at her '—but since you've been here, Lady Emma, I've seen a different side to my son. A happier side, more carefree.'

Looking down at her hands, Emma remained silent. She didn't know how to respond.

'I have always loved all of my children equally and I want them all to find happiness. I also value all of their futures equally.' She spoke slowly, as if wanting to make sure her point was getting across. 'And I love my husband dearly and of course do not want him to be unduly upset in his final years, but I hate the idea of Guy throwing away his entire life when Lord Templeton only has a few more years at most on this earth.'

Lady Templeton stood and gave Emma a smile, then sailed from the room, leaving Emma completely bewildered. She wasn't quite sure what had happened, but she thought Lady Templeton had given her blessing to Guy choosing Emma over Miss Frant.

Emma shuffled further back on to the window-sill, looking out of the window, wondering if everyone could see the smouldering attraction between her and Guy. It was another reason to leave before Miss Frant arrived—she didn't want the nice young woman to think there was something going on between her and Guy, because there wasn't. No matter what Lady Templeton said, Guy *did* value his sister's and father's happiness over his own. His own conscience wouldn't let him abandon his family.

She heard footsteps outside in the hallway, recognising immediately it was Guy, and felt her whole body tense. The footsteps paused outside her door and after almost half a minute there was a knock on the wood.

'Come in,' she called, even though she didn't trust herself to see Guy.

'Em,' he said, standing in the doorway. 'I wanted

to talk to you. Cecilia said you are going to leave tomorrow.'

He looked drawn. His normally tanned skin was
pale and he had dark rings under his eyes. It looked as
though he had the weight of the world on his shoulders.

'It's for the best.'

Guy shook his head. 'None of this is for the best.'

Emma took a deep breath and tried to force a smile,
stopping when she realised it felt more like a grimace
than anything else.

'In three months, maybe four, we'll be together in
London, perhaps at a ball or a dinner party, and you
will sit down next to me and we will be all right. You
will make a joke and I will laugh and things will be
comfortable.'

Guy closed his eyes and nodded.

'We're still friends, Guy, nothing will ever change
that.'

The words that were unsaid flew between them.
Emma knew neither of them wanted to be just friends,
but she realised it *was* better than nothing.

'I...' Guy said, then trailed off, his eyes flicking
to something over her shoulder. Emma followed his
gaze. 'No, no, no.'

'Who is it?' A carriage was visible round the side
of the house, pulling into the stable yard.

'The Frants.'

'They're not meant to be here until tomorrow.'

'I know,' he said grimly.

A maid knocked quietly on the door behind them
and both Emma and Guy spun around.

'Sorry to disturb you, but Lady Templeton asked

me to inform you Mr and Mrs Frant and their daughter, Miss Frant, have arrived.'

'Thank you,' Guy said, his voice flat.

'They're early. Too early.' All Emma's plans of escaping before Miss Frant arrived were dashed in a single instant. Now she would have to smile at the young woman, knowing she was getting the life Emma dreamed of.

'I should go and greet them,' Guy said, his face devoid of any emotion. Emma hated seeing him like this, hated seeing the emptiness inside him. Guy was so vibrant, so happy, yet here he was, a shell of his normal self.

'I will follow in a few minutes.'

Guy nodded and then disappeared through the door. Emma needed a few minutes to prepare herself, pinching her cheeks to give them colour and checking her appearance in the mirror. She needed to appear as though everything were normal, as if she hadn't just made love to the man she loved and pushed him away all within the last twelve hours.

Guy felt as though he was walking to his execution. His boots felt extraordinarily heavy, his legs as though he had climbed a mountain and was now faced with another.

He summoned a smile, knowing anyone who knew him would be able to tell it was fake, and then descended the stairs to his fate.

'Good morning,' he said as he reached the entrance hall, where the Frants were still divesting themselves of their coats and gloves.

'Good morning.' Mr Frant stepped forward, giving

his hand a hearty shake. Mrs Frant greeted him in that timid way of hers and then Miss Frant was in front of him, waiting with an air of expectation. He reached out and took her hand, bending over it and seeing her blush as he lowered his head. He didn't kiss her knuckles, pausing just a few inches away, and then straightened.

'We're sorry we have arrived so early. We thought it best to set out with plenty of time with the snow and then the roads were surprisingly clear,' Mr Frant said.

'We're delighted to have you,' Lady Templeton said, coming up next to Guy and gesturing for the Frants to go through to the drawing room.

Guy was about to follow when he saw Miss Frant was lingering.

'I am very pleased to see you again, Captain Fitzgerald.'

Guy nodded and smiled, not trusting himself to speak. Miss Frant was perfectly pleasant, but somehow that made all of this worse.

'Abigail.' Emma's voice came from behind him. He turned to watch her descend the stairs gracefully. She looked beautiful as always and as if the last twenty-four hours had never happened.

'Lady Emma, I'm so happy you're here.'

'You look well, Abigail. I hope the journey was not too arduous in the snow.'

'It was not a bad journey at all, thank you. Are you well? You look a little tired.'

For an instant Guy saw the mask on Emma's face slip, but he doubted Miss Frant did. 'I do not sleep well when I am in a strange bed,' Emma said with a self-deprecating smile. 'But Cecilia and I will be returning to London soon and I will be able to catch up on my sleep when I am back at my aunt's house.'

'Oh, you will stay a few more days, won't you? I was hoping you and Captain Fitzgerald would tell me all about your adventures in Egypt.'

Emma didn't answer and Guy could see the pain in her eyes. She wanted to be gone, right now, and not have to face this horrible situation.

Miss Frant was distracted by her mother momentarily and Emma took the opportunity to slip away. Guy wished he could follow her.

Emma had successfully avoided both Guy and the Frants for most of the day, spending a few hours reading peacefully in her room and then bundling herself up in multiple layers before venturing out into the cold. It had been a refreshing walk around the gardens and then up through the parkland to the folly, and Emma had climbed to the top of the tower, allowing the wind to batter her. By the end of her walk her cheeks felt sore, but some of the more despairing of her thoughts had been blown away at least.

'Lady Emma,' Miss Frant called as Emma reached the edge of the formal gardens. 'I was hoping to find you.'

Emma summoned a smile. Whatever awful situation she and Guy were in, Miss Frant was the innocent party here. She deserved Emma's kindness.

'Please, do call me Emma. How are you settling in, Abigail?'

'Very well, thank you. Captain Fitzgerald's family home is delightful and his mother so kind. Sophia…'

she started to say, but trailed off, then gave a sunny smile. 'Sophia asks a lot of questions, doesn't she?'

Hiding a grimace, Emma could imagine the sort of interrogation Guy's sister had put Miss Frant through.

'She is young and has been kept sheltered here. I understand she will have her debut next year. She probably wants to find out as much as possible from someone in a similar position as her. I think you are of a similar age.'

'Perhaps that is it.' Miss Frant paused for a moment and then regained her sunny disposition. 'I'm so glad you're still here, Emma. I was very nervous on the journey, but you being here makes everything so much better.'

Emma felt a pang of guilt as the memory of the night she spent with Guy flashed into her mind. She doubted Miss Frant would think the same of her if she knew how close Emma had got to her future husband.

'I think Cecilia and I will leave soon. Give you some time with Captain Fitzgerald and his family.'

'No, please don't, not on my account.'

'Surely you want to get to know him a little better?'

Miss Frant screwed up her face and shrugged. 'Captain Fitzgerald is very handsome and gallant, but I get the impression he doesn't much enjoy my company.'

Emma was about to say Miss Frant was mistaken and then forcibly pressed her lips together to stop the words from slipping out. Lying to the young woman would be wrong, instead she should give her some advice. At the idea Emma silently scoffed—she didn't have her life in any sort of order to be a good person to give advice.

'He enjoys your company, Emma. Even I can see his face lights up when you come into the room.'

'I'm sure that's not true.'

'It is. My father first suggested the marriage be-tween Captain Fitzgerald and me about six months ago. I met him five months ago.' She shook her head. 'I don't know if he feels pushed into the union or if he doesn't like me, but every parcel of time we've spent together in the last five months he couldn't wait to get away.'

'Abigail, I—'

Miss Frant interrupted her with a forceful shake of the head.

'No, it is true. Perhaps he thinks I'm too young and immature. Or too uncultured.'

Emma took a deep breath. Miss Frant was a kind and sweet young woman who felt out of her depth in the world she found herself in. She could continue to offer platitudes and half-truths, or she could put her own feelings and needs aside for a minute and give her some proper advice, as Cecilia had done so many times for her.

'Come and sit with me, Abigail,' Emma said, lead-ing the younger woman over to a bench that in the summer would have a wonderful view of the rose gar-den. Now everything looked bare and was still half covered in a thin layer of snow.

They sat, huddling together, and Emma tried to think how Cecilia would start one of these conversa-tions. She had guided Emma through so many difficult times with her wise words and gentle manner, Emma wished Cecilia could help her with this, but she knew it was something she had to do on her own.

'For a moment put aside reality, forget about your family's expectations and your sense of duty. Forget about what society expects of you. I want you to imagine you have a completely clean piece of paper and on that piece of paper you get to plan your life to your liking.'

Abigail frowned, but nodded her head.

'What would you put on there?'

'I don't know. No one has ever asked me anything like that before.'

'Take a moment and think, really think. If you could design a life of your own choosing, what would it be?'

A minute passed and then another before the young woman finally opened her mouth to answer.

'I want to get married. I would like a large family, lots of children...' she hesitated '...but if it were up to me perhaps not quite yet. I'd like to experience a little more of the world, see some of England, have another Season, dance with different gentlemen.' She was warming to the idea now. 'I would like to swim in the sea in Cornwall and take the waters in Bath.'

Emma nodded in encouragement, seeing a spark in Miss Frant's eyes she hadn't seen before.

'I would like to walk across the moors in Yorkshire and travel through the Scottish Highlands.' She paused and then turned back to Emma. 'I suppose my dreams seem tame and boring to you.'

'Not at all, Abigail. That is the wonder of dreams. Everyone's are unique. Everyone's are personal. It doesn't matter if your dreams are different from mine—in fact, it is better that they are different.' Emma fell silent, wondering how best to phrase the next bit. 'And what of your marriage, the family you want—you said you want lots of children?'

'Yes. At least four or five. I'm an only child and I have always dreamed of a big family.'

'And your husband. If you close your eyes and dream, is it Captain Fitzgerald you see?'

Miss Frant closed her eyes and Emma didn't know if she had gone too far. She wasn't trying to come between her and Guy. Even though she wished things could be different it wasn't her place to try to change things. Guy had to make the decision of what was right for him. No, she actually liked Miss Frant and thought it was a shame she didn't have more friends, more confidants, to help guide her through the difficult years between childhood and adulthood.

'No,' Miss Frant said so quietly it was barely more than a whisper. 'It isn't. That makes me a terrible person, doesn't it?'

'Of course not. So often matches are made by people not having to live with the marriage. This is the rest of your life, Abigail. You deserve to be with someone who is going to make you happy.' Emma looked down at her hands. 'We all do.'

It wasn't going to happen for her, but that didn't mean Miss Frant couldn't make a brave decision and insist on waiting for a love match. Emma knew it wouldn't mean Guy would be miraculously free to marry her—he would likely have to find another rich young debutante with a hefty dowry—but at least someone would be happy.

'He loves you, doesn't he?' Miss Frant was looking at her earnestly now. 'Captain Fitzgerald loves you.'

Emma shook her head, but couldn't bring herself

to deny it. 'We can't be together. That's not why I'm saying this. I wish it were possible, but it is not. I think you deserve to be happy, Abigail. Now you might decide what will make you happy is Captain Fitzgerald—he is a good man, after all, and would make a wonderful husband. Or you might decide he is not the man for you.'

'And you wouldn't mind, whatever I chose?'

'As I said, I cannot be with Captain Fitzgerald and I honestly believe if he is to marry anyone then he would be very lucky to have you as his wife, Abigail.'

Miss Frant sat back on the bench and closed her eyes. Emma wondered if she had gone too far. She knew her opinions were often too liberal for the society she found herself in now.

'I'm sorry if I overstepped,' she said quietly.

'Don't apologise,' Miss Frant said, turning to her, the glimmer of tears in her eyes. 'You don't know how long I have longed for a friend to share these dilemmas with.'

She stood, reaching out and squeezing Emma's hand, then murmuring that she needed to go inside, into the warm, to think.

Emma remained where she was for a few minutes, trying to think of something other than Guy. She knew soon she would have to start making some decisions about her own life, but right now she couldn't face them. The last few weeks had shown her that she wasn't actually averse to the idea of settling down, although the only one she could imagine doing it with was Guy.

'What would you do, Mama?' she whispered into the cold air. Throughout her life, her father and later

Cecilia had given her so much, but there had still always been a hole in her life, as if part of her was missing. Sometimes she longed for motherly advice, for the warm hug and gentle words to guide her on her way.

'You look as though you're about to cry,' Guy said as he came quickly across the garden towards her.

'No.' Emma shook her head. 'I was thinking about my mother.'

'Ah.'

'You haven't proposed yet,' Emma said, changing the direction of the conversation.

'No.'

They sat in silence, side by side for a long time. Their hands were touching as they rested on the bench between them and Emma wondered if they could sit here for ever and ignore the rest of the world and its expectations.

Eventually she started to shiver and knew she would have to move. Standing, she laid a hand on Guy's shoulder for a moment and looked him in the eye. The sadness she saw staring back at her took her breath away, but she knew there was nothing she could do. Guy had an impossible decision to make and, whatever he did, he would end up unhappy.

Chapter Twenty-Four

Guy sat out on the bench in the garden until his fingers were blue and stiff inside his gloves. He knew he was putting off the inevitable, but he couldn't bring himself to track Miss Frant down and do what needed to be done.

'You've been sitting out here a long time,' Miss Frant said as she emerged from the house, walking quickly through the formal gardens.

'I like the view.'

'I can see why. It is a beautiful house and your gardens are so well planned.'

'Mmm... Miss Frant—'

'Abigail,' she interrupted him. 'You really should call me Abigail.'

Guy was feeling mildly nauseated. He was about to do something that would change both their lives for ever and he was not at all sure it was the right thing to do.

'Shall we go inside, find somewhere warm and quiet? I have something I need to discuss with you.'

She nodded, her eyes wide and a nervous expression on her face. Guy wondered if she'd built up a fantasy around their relationship, whether she imagined there was more emotion between them than there actually was.

Guy had to stamp his feet to encourage some of the feeling to return and as he walked he moved stiffly, as if he had aged thirty years in the last thirty minutes.

Inside he ushered Miss Frant into his study, taking the bottle of brandy from the shelves and offering her a glass. She sipped at it delicately, pulling a face as it burned her throat.

'We have a lot to discuss, Miss Frant,' Guy said quietly, his voice grave.

'Yes. We do.'

Before Guy could summon the right words Miss Frant shuffled forward in her chair and began nervously tapping a foot on the floor.

'I know I am young, Captain Fitzgerald, and have not seen nearly as much of the world as you, but I wonder if you would do me the courtesy of speaking honestly.'

Guy wasn't sure where this was going, but inclined his head.

'Why do you wish to marry me?'

It wasn't the question he had expected from the innocent young woman sitting across from him.

She'd asked him to speak honestly so he remained silent for a few moments, deciding on how much to tell her.

'Do you know of the friendship between my father and yours?' he asked.

'Yes. Your father was the only one to make mine

feel welcome when he arrived at a school full of the sons of earls and viscounts and barons.'

'He's always been a good man, a fair man, and from what I know, although your father and mine haven't seen each other all that much over the years, they have corresponded.'

Miss Frant inclined her head. 'So this marriage is to satisfy your father?'

'No. My father is past such desires. His mind…' Guy trailed off. 'A few years ago, while I was in Egypt, my father started to make some bad decisions. At first my mother did not know. Father had always kept control of the money and accounts, there was no need for her to enquire about it.' Guy grimaced—if he had been here he probably would have noticed or at least had access to the accounts. 'We were wealthy, very comfortable, but over the course of a few years he lost everything. I think on some level he knew he was making poor decisions, but the nature of his illness meant he lost some of his insight.'

'Captain Fitzgerald, I'm so sorry.'

'Before his friends knew his mind was failing he borrowed heavily, from good men like your father, and less reputable sources.'

Miss Frant slowly nodded her head as if she was beginning to understand. 'That was when you were called back.'

'My sister wrote to me. I was able to sort out most of the debt, most of the mess through a solicitor, but I knew I had to come home and be where I should have been all these years.'

'Thank you for being so honest with me.'

'This is your future, too.' Guy finished off his glass

of brandy, but didn't pour another. He needed a clear head for what he was about to say. He felt hollow, as if the next few moments would dictate the course of the rest of his life. 'Over the last few months I have settled the rest of the outstanding debts with the money from the sale of my business in Egypt. The only one I am struggling to cover is the sizeable debt to your father.'

Miss Frant took another sip of her drink, bowing her head, but before she did so Guy saw the first hint of tears in her eyes. He felt like a cad, courting her for the last few months without her knowing the reason why.

'He suggested he would forgive the debt if we were to tie our families together.'

'I'm sorry.' Miss Frant looked scandalised.

'Don't apologise. It is a smart move on your father's part. We are penniless but titled, your family are rich but untitled. It is an ideal match in that way.'

'He's forcing you to marry me.'

'No, Abigail. He is giving me the option. There is no force, no cajoling. Your father is a good man. He has been infinitely understanding about my father's situation when so many haven't and he has suggested this union as an alternative, but not insisted on it.'

'I knew there was a connection between our families, but I wasn't aware this was so much of a transaction.'

'It's not a transaction, Abigail. We don't have to marry. I have enough money to pay your father, but if I use it we have nothing. I will have to sell the house and, as you can imagine, my father would struggle to move elsewhere.'

'I wish the debt could be forgotten.'

Guy smiled at her innocence. Now he had to decide.

Right here, right now, he had to decide whether he was going to throw himself into this marriage.

No, the voice in his head screamed. He thought of Emma's full smile, her soft lips, that way she had looked at him as he made love to her.

'We have decisions to make about our future, Abigail.'

She nodded, looking down at her hands for a few moments and then seeming to gather her courage.

'Do you love someone else?'

Guy blinked, taken aback by the question. He didn't answer for almost a minute, toying with the empty glass in his hand, but he knew Miss Frant deserved the truth.

'Yes. I love Emma. I've loved her for years.'

'And she loves you.' It wasn't phrased as a question, but Guy nodded all the same. He believed she did even though she'd never said the words.

Guy felt Miss Frant's eyes on him and suddenly he had a moment of clarity. He couldn't lose Emma. He loved her, she lit up his world. These past ten months everything had been dull and grey until she'd come barrelling back into his life. He wouldn't fail his family, but he *would* find a way to make it all work. To have Emma and ensure his father and sister were provided for.

'Abigail…' he said. She shook her head, holding out a hand to stop him.

'Don't ask me yet.'

Guy studied her and saw the sadness in her eyes. He hated that he was the one who had built her hopes up and now was on the cusp of dashing them.

She stood and walked to the window. 'I know I

should want to be the wife of a future viscount, the wife of a dashing ex-army captain,' she said, reaching out and fiddling with the window frame. 'But I don't want to make you unhappy. And I don't want to be unhappy.'

'You're a very sweet young woman, Abigail. Any man would be lucky to have you as his wife.'

From outside the room there was a sharp inhalation followed by the clattering of feet. *Emma.* Every fibre in his body strained to go to her, to chase after the woman he loved, but he knew he had to make things right with Miss Frant first, she deserved that much. Then he would have a lifetime to show Emma how much he loved her.

'I can't marry you, Abigail,' he said softly. 'I love Emma, I've loved her for a long time, and it wouldn't be fair on anyone if I asked you to be my wife.' He reached out and took her hand. 'I am so sorry I didn't tell you the truth sooner. I felt trapped, pushed towards a destiny that I don't think would have suited either of us, but unsure of how to get out.'

Miss Frant nodded, the hint of tears in her eyes.

'I think you are doing the right thing, Captain Fitzgerald.'

'You are a good woman and I hope one day you feel the same for a man as I do about Emma. Hold out for that, Abigail, you deserve it.'

She nodded and then squeezed his hand.

'I will speak to your father and explain the situation. I wish you the best.'

Miss Frant nodded and left, visibly shaken by everything that had occurred in the last ten minutes, but not seeming overly upset.

Once she had left Guy hurried out of the room, too, eager to clear up any misunderstanding with Emma. The door to her room was shut firmly and he knew instinctively that it was locked.

'Em, it's me. Will you open the door?' He waited, listening, but unable to hear anything. There were no footsteps, no movement at all. 'Em, I really need to talk to you.' Nothing. He knocked again, tried the door handle, but the door stayed firmly closed with no answer on the other side. He couldn't just shout out everything that had occurred through the thick wood, he needed to speak to his family first, to lay out his plans before he let the wider world know.

Chapter Twenty-Five

Emma hadn't planned on eavesdropping, but she had been looking for Cecilia, wanting to throw herself into the older woman's arms and draw some strength and comfort from her. As she'd passed through the hall she had heard Guy's voice, followed by Miss Frant's, and then he had said any man would be lucky to have her as his wife. That sounded very much like a proposal to Emma's ears.

It had felt as though a knife was being driven through her heart, and for a long moment she hadn't been able to breathe. Then suddenly she'd gasped and run, locking herself in her room and burrowing under the covers as she had when she was a little girl afraid of monsters in the dark.

'Em, I really need to talk to you,' Guy called through the door.

She burrowed deeper under the covers and wondered if it was possible to stay hidden in her room for ever.

Her cheeks were wet from tears and she realised that despite what she had said to Guy, and despite what she had told herself, she had secretly hoped he would choose her. Together they would have found a way to make it work, to give Sophia the chance in life she deserved, to keep Guy's father in his family home where he felt safe and secure.

Guy obviously hadn't thought so. He loved her, he'd told her so, but it would seem love wasn't enough. She didn't hate him, didn't even blame him for the decision, but she wished things could be different.

Emma stayed buried under the covers for a long time, trying to work out what she wanted from her life now. It had taken her so long to realise what Guy meant to her, to admit to herself the attraction that was between them. She didn't want anyone else. Guy was the man she loved and he had asked someone else to marry him.

'I'm going to go home,' she murmured into the pillow, the idea taking hold as she uttered the words aloud. She wanted to be back in Egypt, in that wonderful heat. She wanted to sit on the veranda of the house and enjoy a summer breeze. In her fantasy Guy was there, and Cecilia and her father, but even without them it would be better than being here, heartbroken but forced to engage with all the expectations of society.

She sat up, brushing the hair from her face. She would return to London now and thank her aunt for her hospitality, then book a passage on the first boat out of London. It would be wonderful if Cecilia wanted to accompany her, but if she didn't she would hire a companion for the journey and leave anyway. She couldn't be here for the wedding between Miss Frant and Guy, couldn't stay to watch the whole messy scenario play

out. It should be possible to be halfway to Egypt by
the time the wedding occurred.

Emma stood and rang the bell in the corner of her
room. She would ask one of the maids to fetch her
trunk and then she would pack it herself.

'Are we leaving?' Cecilia asked as she followed the
maid into the room a few minutes later.

'Yes. Do you mind?'

'Of course not, my darling. Shall I find Lady Templeton and make our excuses?'

'Would you?'

Cecilia clasped her hand and smiled weakly. 'I am
sorry, Emma. I really thought things would work out
between you and Guy.'

Emma nodded, trying not to let the sadness over-
whelm her. 'I don't think I can speak to anyone.'

'Don't worry. I will sort everything. Pack your
trunk and I will come and get you in a few minutes.'

Emma wanted to cling to Cecilia, to draw strength
from her, but she nodded and allowed her to go. Perhaps it was cowardly to run, to flee without speaking
to Guy, but she couldn't face it. She didn't blame him,
but still she wished he had made a different choice,
wished he had believed they could have everything.

She paced the room, waiting for Cecilia once her
trunk was packed. The door was firmly locked again,
shutting out Guy or his sister or Miss Frant, anyone
who might want to come and talk to her. She couldn't
cope with kind commiserations at the moment.

The soft knock that came fifteen minutes later she
knew was Cecilia's and she almost flung herself into
the older woman's arms as she came back into the room.

'Are you sure you want to go?'

'Yes.'

'You could talk to Guy.'

'I don't want to, Cece. Not right now. I'll write to him once we're back in London.'

'If you're sure…'

'I'm sure.'

Perhaps it was cowardly, but Emma felt she had the right to be cowardly right now.

A footman appeared to take Emma's trunk and Cecilia slipped her arm through Emma's, guiding her out of the room after the footman.

Lady Templeton was downstairs, wringing her hands and looking drawn.

'Do you really have to leave?' Lady Templeton said as they descended the stairs.

'Lady Emma's aunt was most insistent. A family emergency that requires Emma's presence immediately,' Cecilia said calmly. Emma had to stop herself from raising an eyebrow at the easy way her friend lied.

'I'm sure I can find Guy if you wait a few minutes.'

'We really must be going,' Cecilia said as Emma took Lady Templeton's hand and squeezed it, giving her a weak smile. 'I'm sure we will see Captain Fitzgerald in London very soon.'

'You're leaving?' Sophia said, rushing down the stairs. 'What has my stupid brother done?'

'Sophia,' Lady Templeton admonished her.

'Don't go. Stay a little longer, we can work everything out.'

'It was so lovely to meet you, Sophia,' Emma said, seeing the panic in the younger woman's eyes.

'Don't go. Let me find Guy first,' Sophia said.

'I really must rush to my aunt's side. She needs me,' Emma said, the lie tasting bitter on her tongue. 'Say goodbye to Guy for me.' Her voice cracked as she spoke, but she managed to cover it with a little cough. Then she hurried outside with Cecilia and climbed up into the carriage.

Cecilia supervised the loading of their trunks, then settled herself opposite Emma, closing the carriage door behind her. There was no way she could summon a smile and she would be grateful for ever to Cecilia for leaning forward and waving out of the window to their hosts to cover for the fact Emma couldn't.

'Oh, darling,' Cecilia said, shifting seats to come and sit beside her when they were out of view of the house. 'What happened?'

'He started to ask Miss Frant to marry him. I know he had to, but…'

'You hoped he would find another way.'

Emma sniffed and nodded, wondering if she was doing the wrong thing fleeing like this, but also knowing she wouldn't be able to smile calmly and congratulate Guy and Miss Frant when they made their announcement to his family.

Cecilia didn't say anything more, just held Emma's hand and stroked her hair as Emma lay her head on the older woman's shoulder.

'She's gone.' Sophia burst into Guy's bedroom without knocking, a look halfway between despair and anger on her face.

'What? Who has gone?' Guy knew even before Sophia answered him.

'Emma. She's gone.'

'No.'

'Yes. She's left in a carriage. What have you done?'

He stood, striding to the window and looking out in time to see the carriage disappear round a bend in the drive.

'She's gone.' Guy felt an emptiness swell up inside him. It was the same feeling he'd felt when he had learned Will was gone. 'Why has she gone?' He knew she had overheard some of his conversation with Miss Frant, but it wasn't as though she had heard him proposing, just saying any man would be lucky to have the young woman as a wife. In her distressed state she must have misinterpreted what she'd heard.

'Find Mother. I need to talk to you both. Now.'

'Shouldn't you be racing after Emma?'

'Now, Sophia.'

His sister pulled a face, but rushed from the room anyway. Guy started pacing up and down, his eyes flicking to the window and willing the carriage to reappear. Sophia was right, he wanted to be racing after the carriage, declaring his undying love for Emma and begging her to forgive him for being so indecisive, but he had to see to his responsibilities first. He couldn't promise Emma anything until he had worked out what he could give her.

With clenched jaw and balled fists Guy hurried downstairs, feeling the tension in every muscle. He met Sophia ushering his worried-looking mother into his study and followed them in, closing the door firmly behind them.

'What is happening, Guy?' his mother asked, her face flushed with emotion.

'I need to talk to you both.'

'Emma has left.'

'Sophia told me. That's why we're here.' He took a deep breath and then pushed on. 'I told Miss Frant I couldn't marry her.'

Both his mother and sister looked at him with wide eyes, surprise etched on their faces.

'Yes,' Sophia said, throwing her hands up in the air. 'But why has Lady Emma left? Why haven't you proposed to her? Why did she look so upset?'

'Why don't we let Guy speak? I think he has something to ask us.'

Guy nodded, wondering how to put this half-formed plan of his into words.

'I love Emma. I've loved her for a long time and I'm going to marry her.'

'Good,' Lady Templeton said softly.

Guy looked up at her in surprise. He knew Sophia would support his plans, but he hadn't been so sure about his mother. She had the whole family to think about.

'Good?'

'Yes, good. I want Sophia to have the best possible chance at finding the right husband for her, but not at the expense of your contentment. Do you think I value the happiness of one of my children above another?'

'But Father...' He shook his head, he was getting distracted. 'Once I have finished speaking to you I will race after Emma and convince her to become my wife.' The idea filled him with a warmth and happiness he hadn't felt in a long time. 'Of course, that leaves the debt we owe Mr Frant.'

'Don't worry about that, darling. We will find a way.'

'We will,' he said, feeling much more positive than

he had in a long time. He was an intelligent man, used to solving problems and resolving conflicts. If this had been a business matter, he would have relished finding a solution, but where it had involved his family he had been paralysed by guilt and the need to live up to the memory of Will. 'I will speak to Mr Frant, but I wonder whether there might be an option to hand over the house to pay the rest of the debt, but with a clause that Father can reside here until he dies. Mr Frant is kind and reasonable and would not want to see Father more distressed than he needs to be.'

Lady Templeton had tears in her eyes as she nodded. 'That would work well, my darling.'

'Then with Sophia we have a couple of options. The first is Sophia has her debut as planned, but on a much smaller scale. I will use my contacts to reopen my shipping business from here and hopefully in a few years we will be in a better financial position.'

His mother nodded. It wasn't ideal, but they would probably scrape through the next couple of years.

'The second option is a little riskier,' he said, watching for Sophia's reaction. 'Emma and I return to Egypt and start up the shipping business there, where I know it will be successful. Sophia delays her debut by a year or two, until I can send funds to provide her with a dowry. She can choose to stay here with you and Father in Kent or come stay with us in Egypt.'

'Egypt. I choose Egypt,' Sophia said quickly.

'There is no need to rush these decisions,' Lady Templeton said, but Guy could see she was suppressing a smile. 'Yes, Guy, either of these will work, because we will make them. We are a family and together we can all have happiness.'

'What are you waiting for?' Sophia said as they lapsed into silence.

Guy stood and came over and embraced first his mother and then his sister. He felt a great weight lifting off him as he realised for the first time the responsibility for his family's future was not his alone.

Chapter Twenty-Six

Emma sat staring morosely out of the carriage window, not even enjoying the view of the fields still covered with a smattering of snow. Cecilia was quiet beside her, head drooping in rhythm with the movement of the carriage and then jerking up every few seconds as she struggled to stay awake.

She reached into the little fabric bag she used to carry her personal possessions and pulled out the battered copy of her mother's diary. In total her mother had left behind twelve diaries. The first was written in a young hand at the age of twelve and she had kept a journal intermittently for the next fifteen years. Emma had read them all, cover to cover, multiple times, but there were two that were her favourites. One detailed her mother's Season as a debutante, arriving wide-eyed from the countryside to experience the delights and excesses of London for the first time. Emma had pored over the descriptions of the dresses and the hairstyles and the gentlemen. When she closed her eyes she could see the ballrooms her mother had danced through, the moonlit gardens she had run through, giggling with an unsuitable suitor. She loved the passage where her mother wrote about meeting Emma's father for the first time, how her heart had raced and she had known from that first instant that he was going to be someone very important to her.

Emma's other favourite diary was the one that covered the period just before her mother had died. It was filled with memories of happy times, of walks through the estate, of games in the garden. It showed her mother vibrant and energetic, revelling in being a wife and a mother.

This was the diary she pulled out now, opening it to a random page and reading, feeling the tears well in her eyes as she wished for the thousandth time that she could recall one of the events her mother talked about, if she could have one true memory of the woman who had loved her so much.

As she read she leaned against Cecilia a little more, knowing she was lucky to have her in her life.

'Emma.'

At first she thought she'd imagined the shout, calling out her name, but then it was repeated over and over again. She sat up straight, placing the diary down in her lap, and looked out of the window.

She could see nothing at first, just the passing countryside. Even when she turned to look behind the carriage she couldn't see anything. The carriage driver was oblivious, unable to hear over the sound of the horses' hooves up front.

'Emma.'

This time she knew she hadn't imagined it. She stuck her head out of the window again and saw Guy thundering towards them on the back of his horse, gaining on the carriage by the second. For one moment she felt unbridled joy, as she always did when she saw Guy, and then the reality of their situation hit her.

She didn't know why he was chasing her, but she did know only a couple of hours earlier he had been about to propose to another woman. That couldn't be undone. He had chosen Miss Frant, he had chosen his duty, over her. She wasn't angry about it, but she was devastated, and the last person she wanted to see right now was Guy. Maybe in a couple of years, once she had allowed her bruised heart to heal, she might be able to pick up their damaged friendship and try to fix it, but not right now.

Emma slumped back inside the carriage and squeezed her eyes shut.

'Emma, stop.' His voice was getting closer now and Emma knew he would catch up eventually. He was faster on horseback than the carriage was and soon the driver would spot him and slow the horses.

Still she did not thump on the roof of the carriage to alert the driver, but waited for the inevitable.

It was another few minutes before the carriage rolled to a gradual stop at the side of the road and Guy appeared at the door.

'Didn't you see me?'

'I did.'

Emma thought he might show some anger, but instead he smiled.

'I suppose I would have done the same.'

'Good afternoon, Guy,' Cecilia said. 'I think I might go for a little stroll. I feel so cramped after spending time in the carriage.'

Discreetly she slipped out of the door and before

Emma could open her mouth to protest had disappeared out of view.

'What are you doing here, Guy?'

'Can I come in?'

Emma shrugged, watching warily as he climbed up and took the seat opposite hers. Their knees brushed and for a moment Emma could only think about the wonderful night they had spent together and how much she had wanted that to be their reality every night.

'What are you doing here?' she repeated, wanting to get whatever it was Guy had come to say to her over with so she could run back to London and spend the next week locked away in her room feeling sorry for herself.

'I think you may have heard me talking to Miss Frant.'

'Proposing to Miss Frant.'

'No, not proposing. I told her any man would be lucky to have her, but that I couldn't marry her. I told her I was in love with you.'

Emma thought over the snippet of conversation she had overheard. She hadn't actually heard Guy proposing.

'I told Miss Frant I couldn't marry her,' he repeated again.

'Was she devastated?'

Guy shook his head ruefully. 'I love it that the first thing you enquire about is Miss Frant's welfare.'

'What about your family? What about the debt? What about Sophia's dowry? What about Elmwood House?'

'They are surprisingly calm about it. Apparently my mother wants me to be happy.'

'And Sophia?'

'I might have told her she could come and live with us in Egypt.'

'What?'

'I know it was premature. You haven't even said you'll marry me yet, let alone allow me to live in your house in Luxor.'

'What about your father?'

'I am going to talk to Mr Frant, see if he will accept Elmwood House as payment of the debt, but only if he allows my father a lifetime tenancy, however long that will be.'

Emma felt as though her head was spinning and she had to clutch hold of the seat to anchor herself to the carriage.

'I love you, Emma, and when you left I realised I would go through my whole life feeling completely broken, completely devastated if I let you go and married Miss Frant. It wouldn't be fair on anyone.' He shrugged. 'So I started really thinking about the options. I put aside this need to try to be the perfect head of the family and thought about what compromises we could make so that everyone gets to be happy.'

'And your solutions allow that?'

'Yes. And then we would work out the rest. Together. Maybe in England, maybe in Egypt. I honestly don't care as long as I am with you.'

Emma's first instinct was to throw her arms around him, to kiss him and forget about the practicalities. To forget about how much she had been hurting these last few days and abandon herself to the man she loved.

'I love you, Em. I've loved you for a very long time and I'm sorry I didn't tell you earlier.'

'I love you, too, Guy.' Her words were barely more than a whisper and she surprised herself by uttering them.

She watched as he registered her words, saw the relief bloom on his face.

'Can you forgive me?'

'There is nothing to forgive. You were trying to do the best by your family.'

'I was trying to prove something,' he said quietly. 'I was trying to prove I was worthy for the role that should have been Will's and by doing that I lost sight of what is truly important.'

'You are good enough to step into your brother's shoes, your father's shoes. Your family are lucky to have you.'

'And you?'

'Me?'

'Will you have me? Will you marry me, Em?'

She paused, looking up at him.

'Yes.'

He reached for her, pulling her off her seat and into his lap. Emma felt his lips brush against hers and then all rational thought was lost as she kissed the man she loved…the man she had been convinced she would never kiss again.

'Are you sure it will work out with your family?' she asked as Guy pulled away for a second.

'Between us we will find a way.'

Emma felt the rush of warmth as he kissed her again and allowed herself to relax into his body. Already her mind was whirring with thoughts of the possibilities the future held. A wedding, a family, a home here or in Egypt. All with Guy by her side.

'We should tell Cecilia and return to Elmwood House.'

'All in good time. We've got all the time in the world.' He kissed her again and Emma sank back into his arms, allowing herself to be swept away by the happiness she felt.

Epilogue

Letting her hand trail along the surface of the water, Emma leaned back against the edge of the felucca and gave a little contented sigh. The sun was warm on her face and it felt good to be back home in Egypt.

'Those fingers will look tasty to a hungry crocodile,' Guy said, leaning over and giving her a kiss.

Emma knew he was right, but the water was so lovely and cool she let her hand linger for another second before pulling it back up into the boat.

'How long until we get there?' she heard Guy ask the owner of the boat in fluent Egyptian. She loved listening to him speak other languages and on their journey back to Egypt they had stopped at so many countries she now knew he was proficient in French as well as Egyptian, with a passable knowledge of Italian, but his Greek made the locals roar with laughter.

'Another ten minutes. It is around the bend in the river.'

Guy came and sat down next to her and Emma leaned her head on his shoulder, glad of a few minutes of peace before the excitement of the day ahead. It was just after dawn, the coolest part of the day, and she loved how the sun reflected off the sparkling water of the Nile. They had been back in Egypt for three weeks now and Emma finally felt as though she was home.

'Happy anniversary,' Guy said, wrapping an arm around her and pulling her in for a kiss.

'Two years,' she said, shaking her head. She didn't know where the past two years had gone. Initially after they had married they'd planned to return to Egypt much sooner, but Guy's father's physical health had taken a turn for the worse just after their honeymoon and so they had opted to stay and support Guy's mother as she made adjustments to the routines that helped to keep Lord Templeton safe and happy. Emma had enjoyed the opportunity to spend time with Guy's family and knew she would miss the long afternoons sat with Lord Templeton as he reminisced about times past and his occasional rambling stories about her father when they were younger.

'Two wonderful years,' he corrected her. 'When I left Egypt for England nearly four years ago I never imagined I would be back like this, with you in my arms.'

'Me neither. I was so lost when you went. I used to walk along the banks of the Nile for hours at a time and try to imagine where you were in the world and what you were doing.'

'I used to walk along the banks of the Thames thinking the same.'

Emma rested her head on Guy's shoulder and for a moment wondered what her life would have been like if she hadn't realised how she felt about Guy until it was too late. She shuddered at the thought and pushed it from her mind.

'Tell me about the site we're going to today?'

Guy's eyes lit up with excitement. During their extended stay in England he had cultivated his ties with the British Museum and now they recognised him as a foremost expert of Egyptology on-site in Luxor. The museum had supported their return to Egypt to represent England's interests in the archaeological discoveries that were taking place.

'Ahmed thinks it might be a tomb. The entrance was hidden, disguised, but the door is intact so he is hopeful it may have eluded the grave robbers.'

While in England Guy had reached out to start to rebuild his shipping company in Egypt and now it was going from strength to strength, allowing him to focus some of his energy on the things he enjoyed more.

Five minutes later the felucca started heading towards the banks of the river and Emma could see Ahmed waiting for them. He could barely keep still, hopping from one foot to the other in excitement.

'Everything is ready,' he said as Guy jumped from the felucca and turned back to help Emma down. She felt clumsy with her swollen belly and what felt like even more swollen feet, but she wasn't about to let her pregnancy stop her from being here at what could be a moment for the history books. 'We have all the tools. We were waiting for you.'

Ahmed led the way up the bank and away from the river. Even though dawn had only been half an hour earlier it was already beginning to get hot, the sun starting to reflect off the sand and heat up everything it touched.

'It is a mile's walk from here,' Ahmed said, eyeing her uncertainly.

'I can walk a mile.' She was six months pregnant—they had found out they were expecting after they had left England, but Emma was secretly pleased. She had wanted to be home in Luxor for the birth of her first child, it felt right. Cecilia was insisting on making the journey to Egypt to support Emma and would be arriving in a few weeks, excited about the prospect of a baby in the family.

They started to walk, Guy lending her his arm as they picked their way over the rocky terrain. Emma distracted herself by trying to guess where the entrance to the tomb might be, choosing rocky outcrops or hidden valleys, crossing each one off her mental list as they passed it.

'Here,' Ahmed said eventually and gestured for them to start the scramble down a path that looked as though it led nowhere.

Guy went first, helping her along, and after a minute they saw the rest of the men Ahmed had hired to help them with the excavation.

Emma watched as Guy stepped forward, past the line of men, and ran his fingers over the rock that Ahmed was certain hid the entrance to the tomb.

'Would you like to be the first, sir?' he asked, handing Guy a large hammer.

Guy smiled and took his time assessing the rock before swinging the hammer. It took three blows before Guy was satisfied, stepping back to let everyone else see what lay beyond the fractured rock.

Emma couldn't help herself. She stepped forward

and peered inside, having to wait as her eyes adjusted to the darkness beyond from the bright sunlight outside.

'It's a passage,' she said, feeling a ripple of excitement roll through her. 'It's an actual, real passage.'

Guy embraced her, kissing her for a long moment, and Emma felt exhilaration and contentment all rolled into one. *This* was where she was meant to be. Back home in Egypt, with the man she loved by her side, doing what they both loved.

'I love you,' she murmured to her husband.

His smile still made her go weak at the knees. 'I love you, too. Shall we?'

He held out his hand and together they stepped over the pile of rubble and into the passage beyond, not knowing what they would find at the other end.

* * * * *